CONSUMMATA

Other Works by Raoul Plus, S.J.

BAPTISM AND CONFIRMATION
CHRIST IN HIS BRETHREN
THE EUCHARIST
FACING LIFE: FIRST SERIES
FACING LIFE: SECOND SERIES
THE FOLLY OF THE CROSS
GOD WITHIN US
HOW TO PRAY ALWAYS
HOW TO PRAY WELL
THE IDEAL OF REPARATION
IN CHRIST JESUS
LIVING WITH GOD
REPARATION: ITS HISTORY, DOCTRINE
    AND PRACTICE

Burns Oates & Washbourne Ltd.

MARIE-ANTOINETTE, AGED 22

CONSUMMATA

MARIE-ANTOINETTE DE GEUSER

Her Life and Letters

By

RAOUL PLUS, S.J.

English version by

GEORGE BAKER

New York, Cincinnati, Chicago, San Francisco

BENZIGER BROTHERS

PRINTERS TO THE HOLY APOSTOLIC SEE

1931

This translation is made from *Marie-Antoinette de Geuser: Vie de "Consummata,"* by Raoul Plus, S.J., and *"Jusqu'aux Sommets de l'Union Divine: Consummata. Lettres et notes Spirituelles de Marie-Antoinette de Geuser.* Publiées par le P. Plus, S.J." Both published by the Apostolat de la Prière, Toulouse.

Made and Printed in Great Britain

DECLARATION

IN obedience to the decrees of Pope Urban VIII and of other Sovereign Pontiffs, the writer declares that the graces and other supernatural facts related in this volume as witnessing to the Sanctity of Servants of God other than those Canonized or Beatified by Holy Church, rest on human authority alone ; and in regard thereto, as in all things else, the writer submits himself without reserve to the infallible judgement of the Apostolic See, which alone has the power and authority to pronounce as to whom rightly belong the character and title of Saint or Blessed.

CONTENTS

PART I

PART II

CONSUMMATA

TRANSLATOR'S NOTE

EXIGENCIES of space have necessitated a certain condensation in this translation. This condensation has been effected at the expense of the biographer rather than of his biography's subject—as far as possible Marie-Antoinette's letters have been given *in extenso*. The translator is convinced that Father Plus would not have it otherwise.

If, in this translation, Marie-Antoinette lives for the reader, as she has lived for the translator during his translation, then she lives indeed. Her life is surely a challenge to our age. Her diary might well be entitled 'The Diary of a Happy Woman.' English Catholics, acquainted with *The Diary of a Disappointed Man of* W. N. P. Barbellion—Marie-Antoinette's contemporary, whose life in its physical suffering was so like to hers, and in its spiritual content so utterly unlike—will make comparisons that will both sadden and gladden them —and leave them even firmer in the Faith.

Father Plus deserves well of his fellow-men. For he has made known to them a girl, who is not for France only, nor for Europe, but for the world—not for our own time merely, but for all time. She was—Catholic.

G. B.

September 1, 1931.

INTRODUCTION

UPON the appearance of the volume entitled
*Consummata : Unto the heights of the soul's union
with God*, a number of readers asked for further
facts.

Some with the plea that the note-book of a saintly
soul is not the whole of the saint.[1] What was the everyday life of this young girl, whose letters and notes reveal
her so closely united to God ?

Others with the desire for renewed spiritual inspiration. One of these, the Very Reverend Father Abbot
of the Benedictine Monastery of En-Calcat, Tarn, wrote :

' The book haunts me. No other so unites spiritual
depth with sound doctrine, or so joins with these a
mysticism as sincerely simple as it is genuinely
exalted ' ;

and added :

' All that comes from this dear child will be of a
piece. It will do increasing good to the Church.'

The present biography sets out to satisfy these wisely-
inspired requests.

A year after his first letter, Dom Romain, quoted
above, wrote once more to confirm and complete his
judgement upon ' Unto the Heights ' :

' *Consummata* is my constant companion. Of it I
have made a definite study ; or, more precisely, in

[1] Our use of the word ' saint ', of course, in no way presumes
to anticipate the judgement of the Church.

xi

so far as my duties permit me, an act of continuous prayer. The more I read of this life, which breathes of heaven rather than of earth, the more I am confirmed in my first conclusion : in my opinion, *Consummata* is above analysis, above discussion, above interpretation. It needs to be read and meditated on with that simplicity which is its own first characteristic. Only so does it reveal the fullness of truth and spread the sweet savour of Christ.'

The foregoing does indeed concisely indicate the quality of the numerous readers to whom the extracts and the facts collected in the present volume are primarily addressed. No better definition is conceivable of the spirit in which these papers may best be approached. If theologians and spiritual directors seek to discover in them in addition a religious teaching at once sound and, in the finest sense of the word, Christian, it may be confidently said that they will not seek in vain.

PART I

CHAPTER THE FIRST

THE EARLIEST YEARS

1 *The Family Tree*

THE name of her who later was to sign herself 'Consummata' or Marie de la Trinité, was Marie-Antoinette de Geuser.

She was born at Le Hâvre on April 20, 1889, on Holy Saturday, between the *Consummatum est* and the *Alleluia*. Her godfather's involuntary delay compelled a four days' postponement of her baptism. In later life the child was to lament this period during which her body had not yet become the temple of the Holy Ghost.

Two of her maternal uncles were Jesuits, Fathers Anatole and Léonce de Grandmaison. The former was destined to be Consummata's recognised director in the crises of her spiritual life—in the second part of this book he is her correspondent *passim*. The latter, author of a notable work, *Jesus Christ*, at his death was editor of *Etudes* at Paris. In intellectual circles there his influence was considerable.

A paternal uncle, Canon Georges de Geuser, known for his ability as spiritual director and his writings upon matters of the soul, lived at Lille, where he was chaplain of l'Adoration Réparatrice. To the present biographer he made confession of the prayer that a saint might be numbered among his family's forbears and yet another among his family's descendants. ' Nor has my prayer

3

been left ungranted,' he continued, ' since S. Peter
Fourier was of our ancestors, while, as for our de-
scendants, no man could wish a soul more saintly than
Consummata's.'

Marie-Antoinette, visiting Lille from time to time,
loved to pray at length in the Chapel of the Reparation,
where the Blessed Sacrament is perpetually exposed ;
while it shall be related how at one juncture she meditated entering a religious house in the rue d'Ulm.[1]

Among the number of her other uncles and aunts
were a Carmelite—from this fact arose her hesitation
between l'Adoration Réparatrice and the Carmelites
when she had to decide upon her future—a Carthusian
father,[2] a lawyer, and a general—General de Grandmaison, fatally injured at Soissons after a visit to the
trenches during the Great War.

It will be seen that Marie-Antoinette was no Topsy.
She was of good blood and of tried stock. So far only
the remoter branches of her family tree have been under
consideration.

Account shall now be given of her immediate family.
Her father was something of a saint—modest, pos-
sessing rare humility and an incomparable gentleness.
The pattern of his religion, so strict, so simple, so profound ; the inspiration of his teaching, that revealed to
his children his soul's strong foundation of faith—these
were master influences in Antoinette's inner life. The
child inherited from him his aptitude for self-effacing
contemplation—the instinctive aptitude of a spirit
whose devotion was as tireless as it was unobtrusive.

M. de Geuser was to die shortly after his daughter.
The biographer remembers going on one occasion in
his company to the cemetery at Le Hâvre. Thither he

[1] The site of the principal house of l'Adoration Réparatrice
in Paris.

[2] Dom de Geuser, who took vows at the Chartreuse de la
Valbonne, in Gard, and died an exile in Spain.

was wont to go in person to tend the rose tree with its pure white blossoms, which he had planted upon the newly-dug grave. Between them was much emotion, but little speech. The few words exchanged, either then or subsequently, made discovery in him of a remarkable surrender to God ; of a spiritual strength that had come to consummation. The over-lavish use of the word ' saint ' is not fitting ; yet here, seemingly, it, and no other, will suffice.

A State-accredited broker, M. de Geuser was highly respected in his profession, as being exceedingly conscientious and wholly trustworthy in all business matters. By his marriage with Mlle Renée de Grandmaison he had twelve children, including nine sons. Mme de Geuser, woman of the world and talented mistress of the house, was ever eager to help in any cause that she deemed worthy of her aid. To mention here but one of her activities, restricted to one period of her life : very many army chaplains and soldier-priests acknowledge the deep debt which they owe to her tireless charity.

It was then with such a father and such a mother, themselves so richly complementary in qualities so rare, both endowed with hereditary virtues of the first rank, that Marie-Antoinette, thereby an heiress twice over, was to grow in stature, and, in such glorious fashion as is to be related, in the strength of sanctity.

II *A Portrait*

Marie-Antoinette was the first-born of the family. To what can we compare her, this little baby girl ? To one of those shy wild carnations of the Norman cliffs, whose tender and delicate pink blossom is a scarcely distinguishable pale flame amid the ash-coloured leafage ? Or again, to a slender sprig of heather from that Poitou in which she was to spend her holidays and

B

to which she was to give so much of her heart's love—to the heath, that lowly plant somewhat dried of the sun, but strong of stem and with a subtle scent perceivable only when near to the nostrils?

Many delightful photographs of her exist. In one, she is among a pleasure party at Chémouteau, the family holiday seat during the months of August and September. In another, like the queen whose name she bore, she turns haymaker in the rich meadows. In still another, upon a coach excursion into the picturesque retreats of the Vallée du Clain she figures in valiant and skyey exploits among the hundred-year-old chestnut trees, in which the boys have set swings. Again, we have her in family groups, that vary with each new member added to the family.

Hers was golden hair with a brownish tint, fine eyes brown-coloured too—eyes which shyness constantly hides beneath their long lashes. Later, upon this smiling face sickness was to cast its shadow. The lips were still to essay their smiles, but these smiles were sometimes to be, in her own words, ' sourires de sang ' —blood-wrung smiles. Until the last her eyes kept their vivacity. The nearer she drew to death, the more piercing her eyes became, so accustomed had they grown to peer into the invisible.

Between the ages of six and ten years Marie-Antoinette was far from being a tractable child. Rather she was that kind of youngster which spends scant time upon its toilet, cares little for sleep and less for food. Force was necessary to compel her to eat the minimum essential to health. This was to hold good throughout her life.

Whenever possible, she kept herself unseen and unheard. In one particular year her elders had invaded her rustic lodge in the midst of a wood. Generously they conceded to Antoinette and her inseparable cousin, Marthe de Grandmaison, a small space under the staircase. It was cramped and uncomfortable. Yet there she was at ease ; there she was content. Throughout her life she never took up much room. Her nickname was a diminutive—Nénette. For long she was to give the impression of unusual smallness. God, and God alone, was to make her great.

During the ten years beginning from this period she passed as none too attractive of character. Even so, none had ever known her disobedient or angered or contentious, or heard her speak ill of another. Her expression, more intense than candid ; her aversion to company ; the fear she had of falling into wrong-doing, and lastly her physical weakness, gave her a certain awkwardness that made her unprepossessing in the eyes of those about her. Constant care was to render her nature more amenable, and by degrees to make sweetness and serenity hers. Her director spoke to her, at about her eighteenth year, of making a resolution. ' For years,' she replied, ' I have had but this—to make myself lovable.'

Notable instances are known of the energy shown by Marie-Antoinette in this conquest of self. At table she was often reproached with being over-fastidious. In fact, she was never hungry ; her helpings were invariably over-generous. She would cut off mouthful after mouthful, arrange them on her plate, change and interchange their positions, and with these manœuvrings dally until the coming of dessert. Inspired by a more than natural fervour, courageously one day she dipped her spoon in the greasy liquid intended for the poultry-yard, and without flinching swallowed the revolting beverage. Again, she compelled herself—and in a child what merit can dwell in such compulsion—for whole half-hours to remain seated on one spot. When she was asked what she was doing : ' I am waiting for Martha ' (her cousin), was her reply.

Puny, and with small reserves of strength, she might

easily be thought of as a soft and sensitive child. It would be a misleading idea of her. Immediately she attained to years of understanding, ardour and enterprise declared themselves in her daily life. At Chémouteau, an over-baked thorn-stick in her hand, on her head a small red Phrygian bonnet decorated by a sprig of gorse, she dreamed of a desert like S. John the Baptist's ; she led her cousin on madcap escapades, penetrating formidable thickets, climbing tall and hazardous trees, wandering near or far afield, often under a broiling sun.

Chief among her joys was to row a boat upon the pond and navigate it to the far end where leeches were plentiful. There she would plunge her arm among the repugnantly sticky beasts—' for pleasure.'

Despite all efforts to counter it, Marie-Antoinette was long to preserve—thanks to temperament, physical sickness, the divine will, the difficulty, not hard to comprehend, those about her found in understanding her well—a certain almost savage independence, an attitude of shrinking and a relative inadaptability.

Intelligent, in after years astonishingly candid, this child Marie-Antoinette, for the reason that she kept jealously hidden in her heart most of what she saw and felt—her cousin Martha was her sole confidante—at home gave no hint of the riches within her. As little or nothing of her soul's growth was evident, it might have been imagined, quite wrongly, that there was no growth. As a climax, when she had reached the age when serious study should have begun, the physical suffering that was to remain with her till death began to affect her. At nine years old she was seized with a disquietening rheumatism of the joints. This made it necessary for her to be sent to the Sacred Heart at Le Mans, where, it was hoped, the dry climate would do her good. She remained there for fifteen months, doing nothing but weep at the separation.

Very affectionate, yet very inarticulate, at home she was never capable of demonstrating her affection adequately. Far-off from her home folk and above all from her mother, she grieved and suffered. How strange the inability of certain noble spirits to express their deep emotions! Back again at Le Hâvre, she entered the Dominican school. Her studies interested her. But more than her books, the precious friendship of her cousin Martha kept her nature sweet. In 1904—when she was fifteen—appendicitis showed itself. Her sickness was at its worst between August 1904 and May 1905. Two periods in nursing-home or hospital brought only partial cure. By an exceedingly grave operation her life was saved.

Many young girls are creatures of delightful sensibility and restless imagination, for whom dream is reality and reality a thing lost in dream. They are creatures unable to distinguish, so long-focussed are their eyes, where at the horizon earth ends and heaven begins. They are active without defined or even definable purpose. They quest without cease, seek confidences, are rich in unexercised tenderness, are eager for self-surrender but know not where the gift of self shall be made, desire attachment to all things yet have no anchorage, delight greatly to ' think ' and very little to reflect. They are souls in bud, their stems frail and their corollas open to every ideal. They are frenziedly occupied with a hundred delicate and often exceedingly useless trifles. They are silhouettes cast to give diversion. They are sketches left in outline. They are magnetic needles oriented to that future which holds so much allure and often so many risks, the smallest of which is a notorious lack of preparation for the duties of wife and mother.

Marie-Antoinette had none of these traits. When she had put off childhood, almost at a bound she felt the need to be a woman. The circumstances of her life imperiously urged it ; already responsibilities of a maternal kind pressed upon her ; at fourteen years old she had a sister and eight brothers, seven of the boys being at home. Undoubtedly Mme de Geuser's activity and the faithfulness of the domestic staff were reflected in a well-regulated household and in a little world that ran on oiled wheels. Yet it is to be imagined that as Marie-Antoinette grew, her responsibilities grew with her. In her life personal pleasure had little or no place.

'" You know," she wrote to her brother Louis, then in the Jesuit novitiate at Canterbury, " how embroiled I am in the everyday round ; you know that when I have performed my duties to God, to the little ones and to the household, there is no spare time left to me." '

Each hour had its urgent task. The overhaul of the household linen was but one of them. Marie-Antoinette specialised in the darning of socks which the impish troop of boys for ever rioted into holes. She owned a large bag of flowered cretonne, in which there were often piled twelve or fifteen pairs, needing exacting and careful toil. When the meticulousness of her work was admired : ' A stitch in time saves nine ' was all her reply.

Her life had its pleasures notwithstanding. It was a consistently happy household, full of laughter and exuberant vitality. Of this, holidays provide evidence :

' The children, to their great gain, have the run of the entire estate (Chémouteau). This morning from seven o'clock onwards Jean, François and René were busy digging in a dung-heap behind Three Oaks road, in a search for worms with which to fish. It is rainy weather. Bathing is a favourite pastime, though often rain wets the bathers twice over. Gaby and

Hubert have built a box-kite thirteen feet long. It is not quite finished. Probably it will be, either when the winds have ceased to blow, or when four oxen are available to drag it along—so big and heavy is it.' (August 19, 1912.)

Pleasures of childhood these, and pleasures of a communal nature chiefly. Here is no scope, or all but none, for the amusement and diversion of a young girl ; no leisure, no opportunity for indulgence on her part in imaginative day-dreaming. Nor, by reason of her lack of attractive feminine occupation, any possibility for her of the cultivation of those essentially feminine attributes —superficial sensibility, not to be despised despite its superficiality ; instinctive taste in the arts of decoration and personal adornment, and appreciation of the little niceties of life.

Apart from Martha she had no confidante of her own age. In consequence Marie-Antoinette's tenderhearted-ness was rarely demonstrated. The following self-criticism is undoubtedly over-severe :

'It terrifies me to admit how passionate is my nature. If the divine love had not possessed me, what should I have become with a character so prone to excesses ? I might well have been a great criminal.'

In 1917 she made this confession to her brother, Louis :

'I assure you that it is not from inclination that almost all my life I have been my brothers' and sister's keeper. I would have much preferred to have been sister pure and simple with a sister's affection and no duty beyond it.'

Grace makes use of nature. The plan of God is of a piece. Already he was remotely preparing the qualities that he sought to see developed in Marie-Antoinette.

Chief of these were a remarkable altruism, self-mastery attained at an early age, and the early control of caprice. In a noviciate, time is required to mould and discipline character. Though, under God, ultimate failure be rare, a self-willed novice is taught discipline with difficulty. Too often, when the training period is over, the new man will relapse into the Old Adam.

Circumstance implanted in Marie-Antoinette the conviction that she was of small account. Nor did she conceive that in this she differed from most. She believed that all young girls living at home led a life similar to her own. This was far from the truth. Even in large families young girls like Marie-Antoinette were rare.

She was as naturally humble as she was courageously self-sacrificing in everyday life. All her orders were given with diffidence. For this lack of authoritativeness she reproached herself. Her mother was away at Le Mans, when she wrote the following letter to her brother Hubert (December 16, 1919) :

' Here I am mistress of the house. I detest giving the servants orders. I am weak enough to indulge in innumerable " If you pleases," " If it will not bother you too much," and so forth. I tell myself that it is all very ridiculous, yet I can't seem to alter myself. It is very sure that I was not meant to have authority.'

In this she was far from just to herself. During the holidays she managed Chémouteau with great credit, while the boys, despite their many pranks, gave her unquestioning obedience. This letter to her brother Louis, dated August 11, 1914, related to one of these holidays :

' Have I told you that we are alone here except for the tutor ? Everything is as usual. The " *Pulchra Domus* " (a hut made of reeds) has once more been made ship-shape. It and the chestnut-trees are our favourite haunts. The cherry-gluttons have tell-tale stains about their mouths. At four each day excited shouts from the pond prove that the bathers are enjoying themselves. In short, Chémouteau is its old self.'

Later, writing on November 12, 1916, to her brother George, at the time an airman at the Front, she admitted that she was ill :

'Nénette is rather like an old sick horse with the staggers. But as she has strength enough to look after the young rips (the children), the rest scarcely matters.'

Her weakness, she knew, was her own ; her strength was of God.

Sickness increasingly sapped her strength. She worked till she was near breaking-point, yet was obliged to leave much work undone. The fact sheds light upon a later exclamation of hers—' I die daily.' She was constantly on the verge of a collapse. This was not due to any failure in solicitude upon the part of others. When she was sick, they watched at her bedside. If, when she was well, they allowed her to resume her old burdens, none, she least of all, conceived that it could be otherwise.

In such circumstances, to lean on God is the only strength. Marie-Antoinette, made wise by experience, put herself wholly in his hands.

The care-free young girl charms by the lightness of her step and the grace of her bearing. Her lot differs from Marie-Antoinette's, who between the ages of eighteen and twenty-five was charged with the bringing up of eight children, and subsequently the double responsibility that devolved upon her after her mother's serious accident.

Yet it must not be thought that in her earlier years

she was a child grown old before her time, or in her latter a woman prematurely aged, having neither charm nor grace nor mental resilience. The truth was far otherwise.

If her life had been differently shaped, exposed for example to privation, poverty or the exigencies of bread-winning—if it had been deprived of outlet, whether spiritual, artistic or intellectual—conceivably Marie-Antoinette would have suffered such warping. Actually, despite her preoccupations, her life intellectually and spiritually was rich and full. Painting and Latin lessons, social gatherings, an extensive correspondence, opportunities for apostolic activity and the time which she always found for her devotions ; all these had a place in her life.

Family intimacies, tried friendships, the delicate solicitude of her mother, her father's unstinted generosity, various valuable contacts with priests of personality—these gave to her home-life the rich stimulus of real culture and thoughtful piety. Here was no need of those queer and meretricious distractions to which so many comfortable homes are enslaved. If there were a party, Marie-Antoinette, dressed as the occasion demanded, went to it happily. On one such occasion, with the morrow's Communion in mind, she borrowed her brother George's watch, lest she should take food after midnight—a trifling but significant incident.

This letter to a friend, dated August 11, 1913, reveals Marie-Antoinette's delight in travel :

‘ It was nice of you to write to me on your journey, when you must have so little leisure. If you are like myself, you must find travel spiritually inspiring, broadening to the mind, a valuable corrective of wrong perspectives. Having left the trees behind, one begins to see the wood.

' On long journeys the spirit grows tranquil and the thought more profound. In travelling any strenuous effort wearies overmuch, whereas reflection is easy and profitable.'

Apart from visits to relatives in other parts of France, the Chémouteau holiday was the great event of the year. Of these summer school vacations Marie-Antoinette would write vivaciously, revealing the romantic imaginativeness which underlay her sober-seeming exterior. Here is one of her letters, dated July 4, 1913. Characteristically, it affords evidence of the religious feeling which entered into her human joy.

' The idea of Chémouteau revisited brings back old memories and the old need to give thanks to God. Would that Chémouteau could speak ! If those ancient closes could give tongue, what psalms in praise of his love would they raise to the Father ! O Chémouteau, place of laughter and of tears ! '

Six months later to Hubert, then at college in Jersey, she sent two red oak leaves as souvenirs of Chémouteau.

Her joy is exuberant, when July brings the eve of departure. Thus on July 19, 1914, she wrote :

' The great day has come. The trunks, packed long since, stand ready. Parcels of toy-boats, sailor-dolls and dozens of similar treasures are made and unmade. Everywhere you overhear scraps of excited talk. The grown-ups as well as the children share in the general joy. The most ordinary remarks—" Do you know if the date is fixed ? " . . . " Yes, that's for the journey " —these bring back hosts of memories. You remember, Louis, how we too used to be just as excited ? Remembering it, how good to be able to draw from such joys their true moral : human joys are but the shadow ; the substance is in the divine love that for us sacrificed all.'

Marie-Antoinette was restrained in her use of metaphors. Her literary style was as virile as her nature. Vigorous and flexible, it had strength rather than picturesqueness. Her occasional literary figures are invariably exact, logical and illuminating, borrowed from life, and usually from life as lived at Chémouteau. They are homely figures to do with farm-life or swimming or even with impromptu races from one flint-heap to another along the roads about the estate.

The Marie-Antoinette who found such inspiration in her environment was emphatically not one of those ' good ' people, whose acid appearance, vinegary virtue and general aggressiveness are a stumbling-block to others—those good people who neither do their duty faithfully nor live their life joyously. This extract is typical of her (February 16, 1912) :

' This evening George comes to keep Shrovetide, and we are all to make holiday. Great days ! '

To her brother Louis, about to begin his Jersey novitiate with a first probation in the kitchen, on July 16, 1913, she wrote joyously :

' I think of you at your baker's tasks. I too like the kind of work that leaves the mind free to commune with God. I write this, as it were, in a whisper ; for the other day, when I broached this same idea, I was hurt when X made fun of me.'

A further letter, written to her seniors, dealt with the zeal for work shown by her juniors :

' A day or two ago a Latin paper presented a very perplexing problem. When there are but two entrants, since there is no middle place, he who is not first must be last. This is the cause of much tribulation of spirit. To meet this difficulty, in future if no great difference in merit divides the two, the last will be officially " second." The humiliating term " last " will be reserved for the truly bad efforts. The trouble with this particular paper was that " last " and " last but one " were the only placings which could be deservedly awarded. You can draw your own conclusions.'

This pleasing jocularity persisted even in her serious illness that followed the crisis of 1915, still to be related. Thus, writing on February 4, 1917, she administered this whimsical snub to one of her brothers :

' You really should not tell people that I called you an oyster ! I protest that in the term was no ill-nature but only affection and gratitude for all your past kindness.'

Four years earlier, even in a mission held in Saint-Michel Parish, Le Hâvre, fun was to be found. Thus on December 16, 1913, she wrote :

' The children have been very greatly interested to hear references made to " missionaries who have lived with the savages " (" savages," of course, is one of my pet names for the children themselves). I have not disillusioned them. Their mistake was humorous enough, but I think that the moral was not lost upon them, nor the example of those selfless men who sacrifice themselves that souls may be saved, even though the sacrifice takes the unpleasant form of being eaten by cannibalistic gentlemen ! '

This epistolary fragment rings with the very voice of Marie-Antoinette.

Skilful in jesting, she was still more skilful in her ability to pass from the jocular to the edifying. She could speak of the exalted topics of the soul with unaffected naturalness, while at such times her speech had grace and persuasive spontaneity. Usually she contented herself with a single incident, allusion or recollection. Always it was adequate ; always spiritual contact was made. Her hearers, held fascinated, realised that with her piety was not a phylactery ; it was communion with God. Her spiritual life and her life of every day were interpenetrating. The one was the complement of the other ; both had the firm roots of faith. She was no Christianised heathen, heathen at heart beneath a Christian veneer. She was Christian through and through.

To her airman brother George, she wrote thus charmingly :

'What condescension! You the mighty eagle to write to me the crawling worm ! If only for that reason, I shall prize your letter ! Joking apart, dear Georges, take your little sister's heartfelt thanks. You have indeed been " higher than the ceiling ! " Surely to such experiences as yours the soul must make its own response ? When earth dwindles, life shrinks, time stands still and man becomes a midge, the mind must surely turn to that which transcends them all and is alone the soul's true satisfaction. " I am made for the things eternal ; God is the sole reason of my being," said the young saint, Stanislas. . . . My subject is beyond me. I have imitated you too well. I must climb down a little, lest, no aviator, I risk a crash and fall like a stone. (Nov. 15, 1915.)'

This letter is evidence of Marie-Antoinette's charm and of the true womanliness which was hers. There were other sides to her. Her more salient characteristics—consistent self-forgetfulness, self-restraint inspired by a sense of duty, her unique capacity for devotion and her enduring ability to face facts—were definitely masculine.

Nor was it only in these qualities that the masculine streak showed itself amid her feminine nature. Still more notably, she was masculine in her exceptional intellect. Her cultural tastes, like her imaginative quality, were not those of an ordinary young woman. It was as a sick girl that she began her studies. It might have been imagined that bad health with all its handicapping consequences would have permanently stunted her growth intellectually. Indeed, but for her exceptional gifts she would never have retrieved the ground which she lost at the outset. In the end she triumphed. If, during the early mentally-plastic period of her youth, she read and studied little, she reflected much, squeezing wisdom from life itself rather than from the printed page. By subsequent steady application she filled in the gaps, learned Latin, made a study first of philosophy and then of theology. She made this study neither from unworthy motives nor with that butterfly superficiality which flutters unintelligently and profitlessly about this doctrinal subject and that. Her study was impersonal and thorough and instinctive in its recognition of such master-works as Lebreton's *Les Origines du dogme de la Trinité*, Prat's *La Théologie de saint Paul*, and above all S. John, a commentary upon which gospel she planned to make for her own use.

Characteristically mingling grave and gay, in 1917, only a few months before her death, she wrote to her brother Michel, the seminarist, telling him how she had been teased by their Jesuit brother, Louis :

' That scoundrel Louis has been ramming S. John down my throat. His gospel, I admit, enthrals me. No other has written so revealingly of the eternal verities—the Christ, the mystery of the Trinity, the doctrine of predestination, the nature of the divine purpose.'

On January 20, 1917, she writes in the same half-humorous, half-serious strain :

' Talking again of that same tease, believe me he pretends that I make a mere theologian of S. John. On one occasion it was really the limit. I confess with shame that I lost my head and exclaimed : " Ah, Louis is the first, the wisest of men ! " From mother's room—the two rooms communicate—he retorted : " No, you're wrong. In procession I'm last." And I, wrapped up in my over-seriousness, still engrossed in the mystery of the Trinity, answered him : " A little more theology would do you no harm, my lad ! " How he turned the laugh on me. For, of course, he was not talking of theology, but of processional order in church—beadle before choristers, choristers before priest, and so forth. Naturally, I looked—and felt—a perfect fool ! As you can guess, I shall never hear the last of it.'

When she was writing this whimsical stuff, she had reached the peak of her life's mystical communion with God—a fact that is proof beyond cavilling of the superb harmony to which she had attained between the life of every day and the mystical life of her soul. She was one of those rare spirits, who on this gross earth walk as a saint in heaven.

Her fine wit appealed to the fine wit in others. A friend of the family, who chanced to be both a naval man and a philosopher, delighted in their talk together. Of him, on August 23, 1916, Marie-Antoinette wrote to her brother Michel :

' We have had a long and most interesting con-versation. He does not seem to find me even a bit of a bore. For, out in the boat with François this evening, he went so far as to say, it seems, that I was the first woman whom he had met, who wasn't an imbecile. Imagine how flattered I am ! '

Brought up with boys and well used to their talk, Marie-Antoinette was in no way distressed by the language which they used. There was no such sickliness in her soul. Subtle and skilled in psychological intuition, simple yet wise somewhat after the fashion of Joan of Arc (despite the differences between them), ' Consummata ' was a true daughter both of the soil and of her native France. Because God had raised her to his heights, and because upon the heights she communed with him as angels do, she felt no need to scorn the sweetness of this good brown earth.

C

CHAPTER THE SECOND

THE CALL OF CARMEL

ON Whit-Tuesday, June 6, 1911, Marie-Antoinette, then twenty-two, accompanied by her father and another young girl, presented herself at the Carmelite house at Pontoise. Her companion, who was later accepted by the Carmelites, gives this attractive pen-picture of Marie-Antoinette :

'I remember her for the remarkable way in which she combined gentleness with exuberant vitality, and for that almost angelic candour which portraits of her render so faithfully. She talked to me of her little sister, Marie-Madeleine, who, child though she was, according to Marie-Antoinette gave evidence of fitness far greater than her own to undertake the responsibilities of hearth and home.'

It chanced that the Abbot of the Benedictine monastery of En-Calcat (Tarn) was in Pointoise at the time. The Lady-Prioress sent the two girls to him, that he might give them his blessing. Instinctively Dom Romain divined Marie-Antoinette's exceptional spirituality. 'She was born for the religious life' was his verdict to the prioress. It was, in fact, true that even as a child of tender years she had dreamed of giving herself to God.

To one of her girl cousins, herself afterwards a Carmelite, she confided her leanings towards the religious life. Her method was characteristic : 'Take this envelope,' she said, 'and open it in eight years' time'

—this was a year after their joint confirmation. The envelope contained a vow that she would love none other than God.

It was tacitly understood between the two cousins that each had a sense of vocation—that each had heard the voice of the Holy Ghost. Her cousin Martha and Céline, her companion at Pontoise, both took Carmelite vows. Marie-Antoinette, for reasons of health in the first place and for family considerations in the second, had to be content, to use her own felicitous phrase, with ' the Carmel of God's will.'

Let it be consolation to others circumstanced as was Marie-Antoinette, to remember how God ordained that her clear vocational call should be over-ruled by a yet higher vocation and a yet greater sacrifice—denial of the religious life upon which her heart was set and long endurance upon a bed of incurable pain.

1 *Hesitations*

In her eighteenth year Marie-Antoinette was drawn towards l'Adoration Réparatrice at Lille. However, the stricter Carmelite rule attracted her more, while the house of the Order in Le Hâvre, her native place, was naturally first in her thought. Because of the state of her health, at Le Hâvre she was rejected. When, with health restored, she was likely to be accepted, Le Hâvre, like Lille and Le Mans (also considered), had been thrust into the background by Pontoise.

Correspondence between Marie-Antoinette and the Prioress, then mistress of novices, gives interesting glimpses of the Marie-Antoinette of hearth and home. The first of these letters, dated April 1910, stated briefly her sense of vocation, her wish to enter the Order's Pontoise house and the encouragement to follow this course given to her by her confessor and by one of her uncles. A second letter, dated May 8, 1910, expressed her anticipatory joy in becoming the little child of her mother in religion.

Her confessor, M. l'Abbé Lefort, young and of a remarkably receptive mind, as priest and director had great spiritual insight and much skill in dealing with souls. Marie-Antoinette respected him greatly, and, before she died, made him the repository of the wisdom that God had given her in regard to the priestly calling.

From her Jesuit uncle also, Marie-Antoinette received spiritual counsel. Almost every year she joined one of the retreats held by him.

In a third letter to Pontoise she faced the fact that the divine will might over-rule that vocational call, which day by day she heard more clearly.

Her fourth letter was dated July 3. The children were home from school ; another Chémouteau holiday was about to begin. She wrote :

'We go into the country about the 14th. There life is strangely different. The only girl among a dozen boys—brothers and cousins whose ages range from six to twenty-five—unaided, I should falter in my vocation. But making complete surrender to Jesus, strong in his strength I am able to strengthen others. If during the holidays my outer life seems to make greater inroads upon my inner, there is this compensation ; as the only member here of my sex I am the more free to seek God's help at the altar steps. We have, I may mention, a chapel in the house.

'More and more in silence and in solitude no less than in prayer I feel the near presence of Our Lord. More and more I am aware that my will is my will only to make it his.

'Between devotions I have to perform the tasks of the daily round. I am conscious that this is not the work to which I have been called. Yet since it remains

God's will that I shall continue in the world, I know
that thus humbly I am living to his glory. If in my
circumstances I am Martha, in my soul I seek to be
Mary, and to live my life in the love of God. When
he shall will it, I shall take my vows. Till then in
the Sacred Heart of Jesus I find my peace.'

This letter, in the balance that it preserves between
spiritual yearning and everyday duty, was characteristic
of Marie-Antoinette.

Renewed illness and the wishes of her parents interrupted the correspondence, and for a period forbade
Marie-Antoinette to hope for the consummation of her
desire for the cloistered life. In a letter dated May 1911,
Marie-Antoinette gave the facts :

" A year has elapsed since my first letter. I now have
permission, dear Reverend Mother, to write to you
again. I feel that soon I shall come to you at Carmel.
Daily my call grows clearer, the will of God more
plain, and the need to obey the call more irresistible.
My confessor and my uncle are on my side ; my
parents hesitate only because of my indifferent health,
while this last, I think, God himself will remedy.'

Her health did indeed improve. It seemed that the
way was open before her, and that her heart's desire
was about to be granted.

II *Hopes*

On her return from her visit to Pontoise Marie-
Antoinette wrote (on June 9, 1911) :

' I want to express my grateful thanks for the few
hours spent at Carmel on Tuesday. I have no words
with which to tell you what that visit meant to me.
My spirit opened like a flower. I felt that I had come
home ; the divine call came to me still more clearly

and irresistibly ; I realised, as never before, what
supreme joy is hers who follows it.'

On June 10, for the first time the name ' Marie de
la Trinité ' appeared in her letters to Pontoise :

' My dear parents are at last at one with my uncle
and my confessor, and I have their longed-for consent.

' I know that you will not forget me, nor my
yearning to have no other name than the beautiful
name that you and the Reverend Mother have allowed
me to use—" Marie de la Trinité." It is a name so
packed with spiritual riches that, contemplating it, I
am lost in awe."

The name was an inspiration of Marie-Antoinette's
own soul, and a reflection of her favourite spiritual
guides. Of the latter she wrote thus on October 16 :

' Yes, my Mother, I have read *Marie-Aimée de Jésus*,
Elizabeth of the Trinity, and, during last holidays,
Soeur Thérese de l'Enfant-Jésus. The thought of
Marie-Aimée and the abandonment of her devotion to
Our Lord delight me. Soeur Thérese, though not so
greatly as Elizabeth, inspires me also. Her vocation
differs from my own. I believe that I must serve
Jesus in serving others, if that plainly be his will.'

It was at this time of her high hopes of the religious
life at last attained, that her mother fell ill. The sight
of her mother's suffering distressed Marie-Antoinette.
Yet she could not at first believe that her entry into
Carmel would be further delayed. Confessing that her
filial solicitude was a small thing compared with the
divine ardour that at this period possessed her, she
wrote :

' God possesses me entirely. For him I suffer as I
cannot suffer for my mother. I am his host. It is as
if my human self had died within me.

' My suffering for him I hold of no account. I seek to serve him purely ; I dare not care for the consequences. To him I surrender myself utterly. When I am burned in his fire, I thank him for the pain that the burning brings me. Yet Carmel does not fill my thought. Though the days seem long, I am patient. The time will come—till then I curb my desires. It is the conviction given me by God that my obedience to him now will later make his will plain to me. God has always dealt with me so.

' You tell me, Reverend Mother, not to put constraint upon myself. God bids me to satisfy the yearnings of my soul. The two commands are one. I try to obey. At present I believe that God is making a great emptiness of my heart, that, when I am at Carmel, he may possess it completely. It is his wish that the self shall wholly die in me, before my soul shall wholly live in him.'

She then ingenuously explained that previously in her letters, as in her visit to Pontoise, she had concealed her spiritual travail :

' I have been told that most Carmelites have a conscious joy in their sense of vocation. I have feared lest you should have doubts of the genuineness of my own vocation, because I have known not joy but spiritual suffering. My outward joyousness has concealed my inward agony.'

The mistress of novices did not misunderstand. She was aware that though joy is normally the dominant sentiment of saintly souls—as it must be in any intelligent Christian who is conscious of the indwelling living Christ —yet that such joy is not to be measured by human standards, but rather is demonstrated by that austere self-immolation that may seem tragedy in the eyes of men, but whose purging terror and pity is glory in the eyes of God.

Once more on holiday at Chémouteau on August 14, Marie-Antoinette wrote to the mistress of novices :

'I am perpetually in doubt. I cannot, it is clear, come to you until mother is altogether well again, and yet my vocation is strong upon me. Meanwhile, I have my home-folk, and, in serving them, serve God. My life is spent with my brothers—all of them —and with four big cousins, the youngest of whom is about to enter a seminary. Even those who do not definitely know of my call to the religious life, suspect it, and seek me out for walks and talks. The more they seek to draw me into the world, the more I yearn to withdraw myself and to be with him whom I adore. It is my faith that at Carmel I shall be of more use to them than I can be here at home.'

This comment must be made upon the above delightful and revealing letter. It was not merely because of her impending departure that Marie-Antoinette was thus sought out by her fellows, but rather because, steeped in God, she radiated God. Her spirituality did not repel ; it attracted.

By September 17, 1911, her hope of an early departure had grown dim. She wrote from Le Hâvre :

'Certainly mother is not well enough to allow me to leave for a month or two yet. God is indeed good to me. The more I thank him for the suffering of soul I, by his will, am now experiencing, the more suffering he visits upon me. His will is best. Though I am broken with affliction of spirit that I cannot describe, love and gratitude still more indescribable fill my heart that he should so have broken me, so that I can but say to him : "Lord, I am not worthy ! "'

She went on :

'I think that if I do not come to you now, I shall

never come to you. Not a few months of waiting, but my whole future, is in the balance. When I think of it, my heart is torn ; my eyes know tears. For nothing is more grievous than thus to hold back, when the call of God is clear.

' My future is in his hands. His will be done—his adorable will ! I ask no more than that. I know that if I deny my vocation, I deny it for love of him and to his greater glory.'

Marie-Antoinette had foreseen the truth. Temporarily, the prospect of the future tortured her with an anguish that was almost intolerable. She had lost the cloistered life for ever ; she must live for all her days in the hubbub of this hurly-burly world.

She wrote, passing judgement upon herself that was over-harsh :

' I cannot join you, my Mother. I must resign myself to this secular life that daily crushes my soul. It is a life that is empty of God's greatest good, and empty of all that greatest good which I might have realised in myself. I feel that I have failed. Passionately I desired to be commendable in the eyes of the divine Bridegroom. But it is his will—or so it seems to me—that I shall remain poor and insignificant and of no account. To his will I resign myself. With love in my heart I will continue to be his poor little nobody. Marie de la Trinité.'

In fact, her humility was her strength—her strength and her charm. The natural woman and the saint whose sufferings gave her nobility of soul lived and moved among her fellows, by so much the more beloved of them all.

At Pontoise they had speedily discovered how rich and divinely endowed was the personality of Marie de la Trinité. Without hesitation they made offer to her of an exceptional privilege. On October 3, she wrote concerning it :

'To be regarded by you, as your letter tells me, as a novice already, is surpassing joy for me. In heart and soul, if not in body, I am now a Carmelite. I believe that in God's eyes I do in truth belong to the Order.'

To various questions she replied :

'You have charged me to act as nurse to my mother. Let me explain. I can scarcely be called her nurse. I give her not medical treatment, but my companionship and my smiles. Mother gains strength slowly. For the younger ones I have much to do.'

Marie-Antoinette may not have been nurse, though even as to this she under-stated the facts. Actually the management of the home occupied all her day. On November 12, 1911, she wrote contentedly :

'Here at home only Carmel's cloisters are lacking. Peace and joy are the double grille given me by God that I may hide the Carmel in my heart. In it I take sanctuary ; by my smiles I draw the sanctuary's curtain.

' . . . Mother's slow progress continues. My own health is indifferent, but that is of small account.

'For years it has been God's will that I should live in uncertainty. His demands upon me are heavy. Pride, that so strongly besets me, seeks to glorify itself by self-sacrifice. He leads me I know not whither. He destroys utterly both me and my pride. He so destroys me, that only he and his will remain. His desire is my delight. My own desires seem to be dead within me. God knows—and you know too, my Mother—how greatly I have yearned, and do still yearn, for the shadow of the cloister and the garb of

Saint Teresa. Yet I bow myself to circumstance, and, very fearfully lest you shall doubt my vocation, make this confession : if in the end I perceive that I may not be a Carmelite and do the will of God, I will make the sacrifice without repining.'

Forced to remain in the world, Marie-Antoinette was not of the world.

' My eternal vow taken this morning, my vows of poverty and obedience taken previously (under guidance from my director and within the necessary limitations of my home life), together with my cherished scapular : these give me some small part in the life of Carmel.'

A letter dated a few days later completed this series :

' On the 21st I spent the entire day with the little ones, whose confirmation draws near. I had not one moment of real solitude. Yet, though myself I have not approached him, God has done everything and has given me his abundant blessing. A shining cloak seems to wrap me round, making me God's in the midst of my busyness with everyday duties. His surpassing love is folded about me. I have not the comfort of understanding how this may be, yet I know transcendent happiness. Though I suffer much, suffering is my vocation, and I rejoice in it. I lie upon the altar, and the hand of him whom I adore plunges the sword ever deeper into my heart. I burn to know that supreme exaltation of the soul, of which I have dreamed so long—that union with the ineffable unity. Ah, already I live with you *in Christo ;* already I am received into Carmel ; already Carmel and I are one.'

The year 1912 brought no great change. Holidaying at Chémouteau, she rejoiced in the daily communion which, on account of her health, had been forbidden to her at Le Hâvre, and rejoiced too in her awareness of the divine presence in the tiny chapel of her home. She wrote of further sacrifices that her bad health had forced her to make :

‘ On Aug. 25, we had the Forty Hours at Chémou-teau. For this occasion the steward had asked me to prepare one of his little girls, aged eight, for her first private communion. After he had catechised the child, our parish priest gave her into my charge. Mother, fearing that this might overtax my strength, took the little one from my care and into her own charge. I have known and loved this small girl since her cradle days. Yet so to lose the care of her did not grieve me, as I have been grieved in the past on occasions when, for example, mother has forbidden or restricted my visits to the sick or the dying who had been dear to me.’

On September 4, 1912, she wrote thus revealingly of her inner life :

‘ Despite the many human activities thrust upon me by this big household, Jesus calls me close and still closer to his secret Heart. With others I talk much of spiritual matters ; only with him do I hold unbroken communion. My everyday life does not touch my soul ; my soul I have surrendered wholly to him. More and more I am in the world but not of it. Whether or no a particular task is given me to do, I go my way, tranquil of mind. For I am God's and only God's. My life has no meaning apart from him and my love for him.’

Having given details of the lonely death in China of her missionary cousin, Father André de Grandmaison, and asked for prayers to be said for him, she again resigned herself to the divine will, telling of her renewed suffering at the doctor's decision that for some months more for her health's sake she must postpone her entry into Carmel. The same thread of thought ran through a further letter, this time addressed to her Jesuit brother at Canterbury :

'My future is wholly uncertain. Let me share this secret with you alone ; it is death rather than Carmel for which I yearn. For I long to be altogether and for ever his. Yet, if it be his will, I shall be content to work and to suffer upon this earth, so only it be for his greater glory.'

She was not yet to enter into heaven ; she was never to enter Carmel. God was to make her understand that for her the cloister of his choice was ' the Carmel of God's will.'

III ' *The Carmel of God's will* '

In 1913 Marie de la Trinité was twenty-four. Her cousin Thérèse and her young friend Céline had both begun their novitiates. Marie-Antoinette alone remained without the grille, feeling, as she expressed it, ' like a tiny needle set before a mighty magnet.'

She determined at least to recite the Divine Office according to the Carmelite rule. Her seminarist brother taught her her breviary. The gift was made to her of a copy of a Carmelite *Horae Diurnae*, and it was her great joy to unite in the prayer of the Church. From any priest whom she chanced to meet she begged for expositions of the Psalms or for explanations of points of rubric. The following letter dealt with one such pleasant meeting :

'For some days past, Michel, his friend who is staying here, and I have talked together of the Breviary. Michel's friend, a remarkably pious and simple-minded priest whose conversation is delightful, has shown me a fault in myself that I had not before suspected. He tells me that I do not understand the mental outlook of my fellows. Though I had thought that the opposite was true of me, I accept his judgement, and will seek to correct my failing. In a convent where life approaches perfection, it must be hard to realise what joy it is to have imperfection of this kind made plain to one, and what great confidence it inspires in him who has thus made it plain. You, my Mother, I well believe, do realise it.'

From July to December her health grew worse rather than better, and her dream of the religious life more wistfully remote. Slowly she began to realise the probability that, if God willed her to be a Carmelite at all, he willed her to be a Carmelite of a special kind, a Carmelite who should dwell in the world. A letter dated from Le Hâvre on February 8, 1914, for the first time contained the phrase ' the Carmel of God's will.' In its full poignancy it ran : ' O Carmel of God's will ! O sorrowful heaven with its foretaste of infinite joy ! '

By the end of March she had definitely resigned herself to the belief that the continuance of her illness was the will of God.

In June her mother's fall, slight in its first effects, but having, as it proved, grave consequences that neither medical treatment nor Spa waters could wholly cure, robbed Marie-Antoinette of her last hope of entering Carmel. Mme de Geuser became a permanent invalid, while Marie-Antoinette's poor health persisted ; it was as if God wished that mother and daughter, at a crucial period of their lives, should be associated in suffering and sacrifice.

In the rue Faure those were no ordinary rooms, those two with their small connecting dressing-room in which a priest, or a missionary about to begin his mission, or one of the uncles of the family, would sometimes say

Mass. In one of them Mme de Geuser played her part as mistress of the household and pursued her many charitable activities ; in the other her daughter made the spiritual odyssey that carried her to the heights of God—or, as it should rather be said, was in that room transported by God into the ineffable mystery of the glorious Trinity.

Between room and room what touching pilgrimages were constantly made, now of the mother dragging herself to her daughter's bedside, now of the daughter who in the last of her days stumbled from this piece of furniture to that, seeking as far as she was able to conceal the fact of her stumbling, and thus reaching at last her mother's sick bed.

. . . . . .

That was in the future. Invasion and slaughter were about to darken the present.

In July 1914, war came with the swiftness of a tidal-wave. For Marie-Antoinette the outlook was unsettled no longer, but, humanly speaking, bodingly dark. Definitely her duty lay at home. She suffered, but she suffered serenely. There was to be no more uncertainty ; her life was settled.

It was far otherwise with those whom she loved and who were now to leave her for the battlefields.

From this time onward her soul rocked between heaven and—however incongruous it may sound—the Front. With her heaven overshadowed the Front.

CHAPTER THE THIRD

THE BIG SISTER

DURING the war Marie-Antoinette had as many as seven brothers in the army.

Before an account is given of the part which she played in those tragic years, her conception of her duty to her home folks needs indication.

I *The Teacher*

A letter written to Pontoise in 1911, stated very precisely the relation of Marie-Antoinette as philosopher-friend and spiritual guide to her brothers and sisters both young and old :

' Alfred goes to an infant school ; René and Gentille are at home under a governess ; they have a daily lesson lasting an hour, and two hours of prep. I supervise the latter, and it takes a good deal of my time. In addition, I give René a half-hour's Latin lesson each morning. Jean and François are in good hands at S. Joseph's,[1] and want no more from me than an occasional word of encouragement. Louis is studying for his examination. For him I ask your prayers, my Mother, and those of the Community. If he pass, he will begin his novitiate[2] in November.

---

[1] The ecclesiastical college at Le Hâvre, whose headmaster was to become Bishop of Arras—Mgr. Julien.
[2] With the Jesuits, at Canterbury in England.

Georges, still in Paris,[1] likes letters from me that I too seldom contrive to write. Henry is training as at officer here in Le Hâvre, and is at home every evening. Michel has begun a course in philosophy, and has no need of me. So much for my duties. In themselves they are sufficiently trifling, yet they make my days very full.'

In might be thought that a devout young girl like Marie-Antoinette would tend to be essentially impractical. As one of her friends in particular declared with warmth and eloquent emphasis, the reverse was the truth. Further, her knowledge of domestic science frequently amazed older women—mistresses of households and mothers of families—who were best qualified to appreciate it.

Innate virtue of itself does not make a teacher. A teacher needs personality, a sense of vocation and the ability to exercise authority and to exercise it wisely. Saintliness is not necessarily enough, since it may not include these human qualities. Marie-Antoinette was endowed humanly and divinely alike with a teacher's gifts. Her divine endowment was this : she possessed an intelligence that was generous in the best sense of the word ; she possessed too idealism and the spiritual perspective that can correct idealism's excesses, and in addition supreme unselfishness, boundless patience and a passionate love of her fellow-men.

On the human side she was a born teacher, gentle, wise, earnest, strong-minded, quick-witted, virile and authoritative—the type that is most fitted to control harum-scarum young boys.

Her own interrupted studies had happily been completed. By 1909 she was the equal of the most cultured young girls of her day. Latin, knowledge of which she had acquired in that year, enabled her to help her

---

[1] As student at l'Ecole Supérieure d'Electricité.

D

brothers in their work, to read the Bible with facility in that tongue, and to use it fluently in worship.

A letter written in January 1913, detailed her day thus interestingly :

'At 7.30, two days of the week excepted, I have Holy Communion brought me. At 8.15, breakfast over, I do this and that for the children. The hour between nine o'clock and ten I give to my devotions, following this with reading or letter-writing. At about 11.30 I start to sew, and continue till luncheon. Luncheon finished, in fine weather I spend a short time in the garden at work with mother—father, the little ones, and Henry keeping us company. When father and Henry have gone to their work, I supervise the children's lessons. Occasionally I have visitors while so engaged, but they never stay long. At 6.15, on those rare occasions when the children leave me in peace, I read for a brief while. At 6.30 the three youngest read aloud to me what they have previously read silently to themselves. After this I look at the lessons that René has had set him at college. Henry, back from work, often comes for a short talk. When dinner is over and prayers have been said by father, I have mother's and Henry's company while the children are going to bed or are sitting down to their home-lessons. Last of all, I usually hear René his lesson, and end the day with a brief period of recollection.

'In practice the unforeseen often happens. A visitor comes when I am about to go to my prayers, or one of my brothers claims my poor assistance in regard to some difficult point in the paper which he is doing, at the moment when another brother has already come for what help I can give him. In a word, duties often tend to pile themselves one upon another.'

Marie-Antoinette was not merely a marvellous teacher of academic subjects, but the capable Big Sister and acting-mother *par excellence*. She taught the children good habits and good manners alike. Hygiene, personal cleanliness, the care of clothes, attention even to such small matters as finger-nails ; she made all these her charge. If a child were late for his lesson, she corrected or, if necessary, punished him. Childish squabbling or disobedience or insubordination—she dealt with them all.

To encourage good behaviour, at Chémouteau where temptation to behave badly was strongest, she had the original idea of setting up a little shop. For punctuality at meals, for well-washed hands and faces and well-kept clothes, she gave a good mark. For merit in other directions she gave marks also. At the little shop these good marks were accepted as currency ; with them could be bought little trifles of the most various and whimsical description. Though the most considerable of these were worth no more than a few pence, they were very greatly coveted.

As in this letter to Georges she would relate in pleasant and humorous detail her teacher's successes or occasional inevitable failures :

'At home there have been painful happenings of late. Don't be alarmed. They were not very tragical. Just this : Gentille has decided that work is a disagreeable business, and quite calmly has neglected to do any. This was the first blow. Troubles never come singly. For the last three days Marie also has been on strike. This has been the upshot : 1st, no dessert for Marie ; 2nd, my pronouncement with much simulated foaming of the mouth that Gentille is the wickedest of girls ; 3rd (since my pronouncement was as water on a duck's back) the blackest looks and the sternest warnings of which I am capable.

It has all been very ineffective, chiefly because the child is so delightfully ingenuous and so proudly pleased with the two·blue ribbons that she has worn, since her hair has been put into plaits ! The incident is now closed.'

For her pupils' failings she frequently found excuse in her own deficiencies as instructress.

As teacher, she valued most the inculcation of true religion. Her most successful method was to read an informal (though previously prepared) address to her little audience, explaining rather slowly and very lucidly the truth which she wished them to absorb from it and giving them its practical application to their daily lives. Often she would ask her young hearers to tell her in simple language of their yearnings, their successes and their failures.

At Christmas time, in the great glass-roofed hall she set up a Crib. Each of the children had a small toy sheep, distinguished by a ribbon of a particular colour. According to the good or ill behaviour of its owner during the day, the toy-sheep was allowed to come near, or not so near, to the Divine Child.

Sometimes she tried to make her small disciples better than they wanted to be. Her exceedingly virile and vigorous efforts in this direction often caused considerable astonishment in those who watched the teacher at her work.

Her methods were justified by their undoubted effectiveness. She could be summary in her judgements, as witness this letter written by her in June 1914 :

' " You have been a fearful young slacker," I told him after a thorough cross-examination, " and now you find that there's no time to make up for your slackness and to catch up your arrears of work. That's why you're feeling so sick with yourself "—and it was.

The upshot was, as you perhaps can guess, that he went away much relieved in mind.'

It sometimes happened that homework was badly neglected. Then Nénette—' the austere Nénette' as Henry, her eldest brother, was wont to call her—would command : ' No Mass for you to-morrow, my lad ! ' When the morrow arrived, at a quarter to seven precisely, the defaulter of the evening before, a smile of self-satisfaction upon his face, would announce : ' I've done it ; so, please can I go to Mass ? '—' Right you are, old fellow ! '—And still another incident was closed.

In March 1911, Marie-Antoinette was staying in the country with her small sister, aged seven and a half. It was during Lent ; the weather was squally and bitterly cold, snow alternating with rain. Every morning they went to Mass together, she, her cousin and the small Marie-Madeleine, then about to make her first Communion. The cousin, pitying the little girl whose short cloak left her legs bare to the knee, pleaded that she might be excused. But Marie-Antoinette was adamant. Mass was more important than cold legs and knees. So to Mass they all three went.

In after years her young sister showed her devotion to Marie-Antoinette, of whom she told this pleasant story : Marie-Antoinette would often talk to us of the Blessed Trinity, and of how the soul, after baptism, became its holy dwelling-place. When she was giving René and me special preparation for our first Communion, she so drummed into us the mystery of God in Three Persons, that when M. le Curé, beginning his catechism, asked : ' Now upon what am I to question you ? ' to the good priest's almost terrified astonishment René answered unhesitatingly : ' On the mystery of the Blessed Trinity ! '

A teacher's work is subject to innumerable interruptions. Dwelling on the fact in a letter to Pontoise written during lesson time, Marie-Antoinette ends thus humorously :

> ' My only wonder is that sundry exhortations, addressed to the children, do not creep into my letter to you.'

Humour was not rare in her relations with her pupils. One of them confessed to her that he did not find Communion ' as amusing ' as he had found it at the beginning. With grave irony she explained to him that amusement was not the primary purpose of Communion, and that quite good Communions could be made without it.

Another of her charges confided to her his dream of becoming a missionary to the Chinese. His dream was unsympathetically received. For ' he even said a decade of the rosary to get back his lesson-book, since he would not look for it himself.'

The influence that Marie-Antoinette had with her older brothers was as marked as her ascendancy over the youngest of them. Her room was free to them all—a kind of sanctuary in which every form of good-fellowship could be enjoyed. All could foregather there, to joke and talk and tease. In it confidences were exchanged and words of good cheer given. From the time when Marie-Antoinette was forced by ill-health to give up her games of billiards downstairs, family reunions were oftenest held there. It is delightful to think that this girl, who often in her soul's saintliness walked upon the heights with God, was able, naturally and effortlessly, to climb down from the high hill of divine contemplation, and to take her good-humoured and spontaneous part in frolics and friendly talk, in the singing of songs and in the exchange of news and harmless gossip.

The older boys, there is not a shadow of doubt, trusted Nénette completely. With her they could share their most intimate thoughts, confident of her sympathy.

From her they received the kind of Big Sister letters that kept them in the straight path among the temptations of adolescence, and gave them strength in their spiritual pilgrimages. In matters of practical morals she could give, frankly and forthrightly, her ripe and seasonable counsel. Her robust conscience kept the middle path, discounting alike silly scruples and foolish fears. Having herself reached spiritual peace after a period of spiritual travail, she went her tranquil way, serene and sure of soul, a source of strength to those about her.

If Marie-Antoinette put first in her scale of values true religion and its inculcation, she cared also for human personality ; in her brothers she sought to make this richer.

Thus Georges, a great lover of art and of æsthetic beauty, in 1913 spent his holidays at Chémouteau, and there quickly re-discovered in his Big Sister an agreeable companion with artistic sympathies, a skilled assistant in the arrangements for a modest charity fête that he had undertaken to make, and a generous spendthrift of her own scant leisure that his own holiday might be made more enjoyable.

Her piety was no narrow or limited thing. She would walk and talk with God ; she would gaze with dazzled eyes upon his ineffable splendour. A moment after, she could discuss with naturalness and vivacity the æsthetic value of some beautiful production of human art. In a single letter, as in that to Georges dated January 14, 1913, she could strike remarkably different notes :

' You must have had a jolly time at the N.s' house. Between now and Lent may you have many more such jolly times. How does the work go ? You have really started upon the first lecture-course, have you not ? When you see Uncle Léonce, tell him that I am well enough, that I don't worry myself about a

thing, that out of everything—even the mild naughti-
nesses of my small people—I manage to squeeze real
pleasure.

' And what of you, brother mine ? Have your roses
got thorns to them ? Do you know how to gather
them without pricking your fingers ? Certain sacrifices
are not so much spines as the peel that needs to be
pared, before you can get at the fruit of true happiness. Go on seeking that happiness where it is ever
to be found, but do not confuse it with mere pleasure
with all its many snares. I know that in these matters
you are no fool, my Geo. That is why I can write
to you like this. I send you my tender love.'

On October 13, 1911, she gave news of her brother's
novitiate, then about to begin. She made no mention
of what Louis's vocation owed to herself. After his
entry she noted that though there was temporary
separation between them, this was but the symbol of
their divine union in God himself.

On December 28, 1911, at the conclusion of Louis's
' great retreat,' Marie-Antoinette wrote thus to Canterbury :

' *Gloria in excelsis !* It is with the *Gloria* that I want
to greet you on finishing your retreat. For it was this
song that welcomed Jesus to earth, as, dear brother
of mine, eighteen years ago it welcomed you. " Glory
to God in the highest, and on earth peace to men of
good will ! "—in this you have the object of Christ's
life upon earth, and the object also of your own life
in religion. How noble was the inspiration of S.
Ignatius, who wished to make the sons of his Order
not monks merely, not merely men to bear his name
and to obey his rule, but rather men of newer and
nobler mould, in whom Christ, in them re-incarnate,
should be able by apostleship, by prayer and by self-
sacrifice, to pursue his work of redemption. This was

the ideal, was it not, that he had before him, when
he named his sons—Jesuits ?

'You do not need me to tell you, my Louis, how
continually you have been in my thought since the
21st. I live in the Heart of Jesus ; it is my cell in the
world. In the Heart of Jesus you and I have our
rendez-vous.'

In July 1912, she wrote two other letters to Louis,
both from Chémouteau. The first ran :

'I am often alone—except when I start to write to
you, when, as now, I have to put up with a dozen
interruptions—and I rejoice in my solitude; for solitude
and suffering bring me nearer to our adorable Lord.
If you but knew, my brother, how in him I am near
to you ; how from his boundless love I get for myself
the grace which you are to bring into the souls of
men. I believe that we do good on earth in proportion as we achieve union between ourselves and Jesus,
and not in the measure of the good works that we
may do. Therefore I ask of him that you should be
faithful in prayer and apt in contemplation. I ask
that you may quickly know that perfection in unity
which Jesus, before he left this world, desired of the
Father for those whom he loved upon it.

'Seek then to become one with Jesus. Let yourself
be absorbed in his love, so that you may have no life
apart from your life in him. Then shall your labours
be fruitful, as his were fruitful. Then shall it be, not
you but he living in you as if once more made flesh,
who shall labour to the Father's glory. Plead with
him that I too may know this grace ; that I too may
die that he in me may live. May both of us be
annihilated in the love of him who has made of you
a priest and of me a sacrifice. Thus lost in him, let
us ceaselessly express our happiness and our gratitude.'

This was the second letter written on S. Ignatius's day :

'To-day you are rejoicing in the birthday of your father and founder. You know how much I love the Society. You do not know how much I owe it. In the life of Ignatius himself, as in the lives of all those Jesuits whom I have met, it is not saintliness or personal virtue that most impresses me, but rather the subjugation of all human personality and the substitution for it of a human mirror, in which Our Lord is reflected faithfully within the limitations of human imperfection. To know certain saints is to love them. To know certain virtuous men is often to feel for them a human affection. To know S. Ignatius and the Jesuits is, it seems to me, to love God in them, since their human selves they have altogether effaced, that he and only he may possess their souls. They are the psalmist's words made flesh : *Non nobis Domine, non nobis, sed nomini tuo da gloriam.* And there, it seems to me, perfection lies.'

The letter ends with this delightful scrap of intimate home news :

'The young people are to go to see a sick child. With this outing in mind, for the invalid's benefit they are ransacking the house, hunting high and low for any sweets or reasonably unbroken toys that they may be able to discover.'

Such humorous and intimately domestic touches are to be found everywhere in Marie-Antoinette's letters. Often they are sandwiched between, or themselves sandwich, the most exalted topics. They reveal in Marie de la Trinité the lovable human girl who was at home in her home. In this book for considerations of space they are often omitted—a fact that needs to be remembered, lest truth be distorted by this omission, and an aspect of Marie-Antoinette's personality be forgotten, that was as essentially hers as her exalted spirituality.

It was characteristic of her that she never forgot birthday anniversaries. A birthday letter of hers to her brother Georges gave pleasant details of a parish feast held at Michaelmas, too incidental to be set down here.

On the anniversary of Louis's entry into his novitiate (November 11, 1912) she wrote this typical letter :

'I, like you, yearn for holiness. Holiness, it seems to me, is fundamentally a simple thing. We have but to lift our eyes to heaven and to attract to ourselves the gaze of Jesus : in that gaze we shall find all our need. We may climb to him by a Jacob's ladder, whose rungs are the little crosses of our daily life. Of those crosses our great love shall be the great discoverer. Little crosses are the heaviest to bear and the hardest to find, so hidden are they from the eyes of men, though not from the eyes of God. There is no other merit but this : to do the will of God. O my brother, shall we not both desire to look not upon the holiness of the saints, but upon the holiness of Jesus himself ? Upon him alone can we mould our lives without fearing to work ourselves spiritual harm. Can we not achieve this in the easiest fashion ? In a word, by seeking to do his will in the smallest matters and in performing the least of our daily tasks with all the courage and all the ardour with which we should go to martyrdom. For the truth is that holiness does not lie in the doing of great deeds, but in the common task performed with love in the heart.'

When the time of Louis's second ' great retreat '[1] drew near, she wrote :

[1] Jesuit novices perform the *Exercises* of S. Ignatius twice during their period of probation, the first time in their entirety—

'You know better than I that the supreme gift of God is knowledge of his Son; that renunciation is the basis of the spiritual life, and that the self must die before the soul can live in God. For priest as for Carmelite, prayer, meditation, self-sacrifice and absorption in the living God are the only way of life. Some time ago I met with a thought that pleased me greatly. Here it is: "The sole end of priesthood is the contemplation of the divine. No priest is truly a priest, who is not wholly engrossed in God." In this thought, as in that other of S. Gregory Nazianzen, you will find the supreme expression of your ideal. Let me quote this last: "*Qui passionis Dominicae mysteria celebramus, debemus imitari quod agimus. Tunc ergo vere pro nobis hostia erit Deo, cum nosmetipsos hostiam fecerimus.*"'

In June 1913 Marie-Antoinette wrote of that perfection which is the peak of holiness:

'Perfection lies in complete self-surrender to the will of God; in such great love that the soul desires suffering for itself; in joyous acceptance of all that God may send; in the shouldering of the many little crosses to be found on life's road. Not many years ago, to one who loved him, who desired to suffer for the sake of her love, and yet who dared not beg him for that suffering, knowing that in herself she was weak and unworthy, Jesus made answer: "I am asked for very many things; I am asked for suffering even —none ask for complete surrender to my will. Ask only that. For you know not what makes for the glory of God. But I—I know it, and it is this that I offer you."

that is to say, four times a day for thirty-two days they meditate for an hour, with one day a week of intermission; but in their second year, partially only, in that for the greater part of the time they receive instruction from the master of novices, and spend only an hour, morning and evening, in prayer.

' Though words that the Church has not recognised
have small importance, these words that I have given
surely have truth in them—truth that is for all of us,
and that shall glorify God and save the souls of men.'

Other letters were equally rich in good counsel. That
dated April 17, 1913, dealt with the need to be faithful
to grace:

' I believe that we often falter upon our road to
perfection, because we close our eyes for fear that we
shall see something to be done for the Master that we
do not want to do. He who consistently seeks God's
grace—that grace to be discovered in the wordless
words of Jesus, when he meditated in the silence and
the solitude of the wilderness—and who courageously
walks in that path ; though he cannot attain to all
that he would, he, despite the limitations of our weak
human nature, by his own humility and the example
set to others exalts the glory of God.'

On July 28, 1913, she wrote on the subject of the need
to extend the scope of prayer :

' Pray for all of us and for each among us. Pray
for parents, for the old and for the young, that each
may do God's will as best he may. And then, like
true Catholics, let us extend our prayer, till it embrace
all men—till it cover the whole world. Let the love
that we spread around us reach out to every living
soul.'

Only an exceptional spirituality, or an exceptional
knowledge of men and books, could frame such remarkable rules for the soul in search of God. Of Marie-
Antoinette the first was true.

As she never entered a convent, the question does not
arise as to what work she would have been given to do
in the religious life. Undoubtedly she would have made

a remarkable mistress of novices. She could grasp alike tremendous trifle and stupendous whole. Her letter to Canterbury, dated September 18, 1913, illustrated this :

'Be faithful in little things as in big. Be systematic in both. The gain is tremendous, if you do, as I myself have found. Had I not made this discovery, I, who am by nature indolent, would have got nothing done. Had I not worked to time-table, I should have ended in idleness and self-indulgence.'

This was her constant advice to all who came to her as seekers after truth. It was given to her brothers and cousins—as in this letter of July 28, 1912, with its references to her cousin Gabriel Hardouin-Duparc :

'I have talked to Gaby on several occasions. Despite his decision to enter religion, I do not think that he is sufficiently serious-minded. I cannot persuade him to make for himself any definite rule of life, not onerous, since it is holiday time, but precise and firm. He often comes to see me, and we talk of matters of religion. Though he is sincere, such things as tennis and kite-flying distract him too often and too easily.'

She herself well knew the many stumbling-blocks encountered even by the most truly pious of men. Discouragement, spiritual tiredness, lack of confidence, wretchedness of soul : letters written by her to Louis in November 1912, January and September 1913, dealt with these and the best means of avoiding them :
First she bade him confide in herself :

'When you feel at the end of your tether, or grope in the dark discouraged of soul, it is then that you must write to me. For I can understand—would that you knew how well I can understand !'

Again, she urged persistence in face of discouragement :

' Don't be discouraged. The spiritual life oscillates between great strength and great weakness. When weakness is upon you, do not despair. However steep the upward road—however weak your legs to climb it—do not despair ; do not be tempted to cry aloud : " The climb is too much for me." Weak as you may be, climb and go on climbing. Jesus will give you strength, as you need it.

' I know that the struggle against self is long and bitter. It is as if you climbed a long thin rope. Yet, climbing it, do not surrender to your weariness. To climb and to go on climbing : there is no other way. A moment's relaxation and you lose all that you have previously won. When you feel utterly spent, cry to God for help. He will not refuse you his help ; it will be as a knot in the rope that you climb. That knot will be your stay. Rested, with strength regained, you will climb anew.'

Once more, she bade him have faith in his love for God, even when that love seemed to have slipped from him :

' Often love persists in the heart, though we know it not. Although we would desire always to burn with our love for him, when we seem to have lost that love, it is enough if we act as though it were still with us. When our hearts are hot with that love, we would choose to suffer for its sake. When our hearts grow cold, let us act as if it were otherwise.'

In all this Marie-Antoinette, though she knew nothing of the letters of S. Ignatius to his disciples, echoed with curious faithfulness the counsels which those letters contain.

Louis, his novitiate finished, was set to literary studies. His sister's letters of September 18 and December 6, 1913, made reference to these :

'Studies are all very well. But is it not true that the study which matters supremely is the mystical study of the presence of God? If there be no great time for prayer, strength comes of doing all things " with him, for him, and in him." '

A further letter :

'Studies can sometimes cause the soul's ardour to grow cold. If this be a danger, is it not best to make of those studies themselves an offering to God—to do Latin and Greek to the glory of his name, pausing from time to time to know the peace that comes of prayer and the love that dwells in the heart of God? Such prayer is quickly made ; the work to be done gains, not loses, thereby. Indeed that work itself becomes an act of prayer. It is more than that ; it is sacrifice, since such prayer needs effort. Such prayer, such sacrifice, such effort may well swing a soul from the devil's side to God's—is not that thought an inducement to courage? Be of good courage, then. For so may you be the means of saving more souls than even a Jesuit missionary in China.'

II *The Big Sister as Comforter*

1914. Marie-Antoinette was now twenty-five. Her brother Henry, a year younger than herself, mobilised on August 2nd, had joined his unit. Before August was out, he was made prisoner at Montigny, near Virton, in Belgium. Her other brothers were mobilised in their due turns. Georges, who had qualified at l'Ecole Supérieure d'Electricité, was to give up his post at the Eiffel Tower, in which he had done brilliant work, and was later to show no less brilliance as an airman, before, in occupied territory near the village of Misery in the Somme, his fine 'Ariel' machine crashed from a height of 2,000 m. and he was killed.

Louis, the Jesuit, became an artillery bombardier.

At an observation post on the Nieuport sand-hills a shell smashed both his legs, and he was to escape with his life as if by a miracle. Hubert—' her little Thub '—as Marie-Antoinette had named him—from Jesuit novice was to turn second lieutenant, and on July 25, 1918, was to die at Nesles-le-Repons in the Marne during the Château-Thierry offensive. Jean, also a novice, made prisoner on the outskirts of the forest of Saint-Gobain, was to escape, and, almost dying of hunger and exhaustion, to reach Brussels at last, where Fr. Lambo, rector of Saint-Michel college, was for some time to give him shelter and in a measure to build up his shattered strength. Michel, though his health was poor, was to leave his seminary at Rouen for military service. François, called up in the last months of the war, saw hostilities finish before he had the opportunity of avenging his brothers.

August was scarcely over, when Marie de la Trinité wrote :

' Uncle Louis (de Grandmaison) has been wounded before Lunéville[1] on the 21st—wounded in the head, his shoulder shattered and his groin pierced by a shell-splinter. We hope for his quick recovery, and give thanks for his preservation from death. Louis was called up, and joined the artillery about the 25th ; he had to pass though invaded territory before he reached his allotted station. Neither of him nor of any of my brothers or cousins has any news come since the big battles. God's will be done with regard

[1] Actually at Morhange, where he was in command of his regiment, the 153rd of the line, whose depot was Toul. In the beginning of October, returning to the Front as brigadier, he was in command of the 53rd division at Bray-sur-Somme ; was promoted general of division and Army Corps commander on January 20, 1915 ; was sent to Soissons and put in command of a number of divisions ; was mortally wounded less than a month afterwards—on February 18—on Soissons square, dying the following day.

E

to them, even though for his greater glory he means
to take them from us. I know nothing of dismay. I
would only that his poor little nobody could be taken
and the others left. If I, insignificant as I am, could
only by my death secure peace, with what joy would
I on earth yield up my tiny spark of life and love and
in heaven be part of the great consuming fire of his
living Presence ! '

The Germans continued their forced march on Paris.
The Carmelites at Pontoise, following upon certain
sinister rumours as to the fate of other religious com-
munities in the path of the invader, decided to ask
asylum of the Order's house at Avignon. On October
1, 1914, to her usual correspondent, now for the above
reason a refugee at Avignon, Marie-Antoinette gave
news of her uncle, and continued :

' Henry has been made prisoner. Pray for him,
please, that he may be patient and that his captivity
may mean for him an accession of grace. Because he
could face them squarely, he faced death and suffering
joyously. But how will he endure prison ? May he
keep his faith ! If he were exchanged for a German
prisoner of war, we should, of course, rejoice. But
God's will be done ; for he knows best.
' My cousin Emmanuel de Geuser also has been
wounded and made prisoner.'

After giving further details of the fate in battle of
men of her family, and mentioning that her mother
remained a complete invalid, Marie-Antoinette finished
her letter with words that honoured both the men at the
Front and those they had left in la rue Faure :

' My Reverend Mother, you exaggerate my merit.
As to Louis, so only he be faithful, I have no grief for
him. So with all my brothers, uncles, cousins, though
I love them greatly, I shed no tears for them. For I

love them less for themselves than for their souls. I
would rather know them killed, than know them to
have escaped death by some petty betrayal that
should dishonour God. Of my own soul I do not
speak. I no longer seek to explore it, but only to live
in the love of God. It is this that is the link between
you and me.
                                        ' Marie de la Trinité.'

On November 3, 1914, first detailing the bereave-
ments and sufferings of her own family, and com-
miserating with the Reverend Mother's similar sorrows,
she wrote :

    ' All these sorrows accord with the will of God and
    serve his greater glory. They are sent to bless us—
    even those of us who bear them with no great bravery
    and from whom the Master probably asks less. . . .
    For all that may come to pass, let us be grateful now
    and always. Suffering is the gift of God ; surrender
    of self the greatest of joys.'

During 1915, Marie-Antoinette's health grew gravely
worse, and her life itself was in danger. During the
four years which preceded her death, she lived a kind
of death in life. It bewildered the doctors that, although
her body was broken, her soul had such strength that
she was able to pursue her spiritual activities—particularly with her pen—with rich benefit to a far wider
circle than that of her actual correspondents.

Writing on December 2, 1914, to Hubert, then
taking his philosophy course at the college of Notre
Dame de Bon Secours, she showed her moral courage
by telling him frankly that the military heroism with
which he longed to prove himself possessed, was not so
great a quality as heroism in the struggle for moral
perfection :

    ' Many are brave under fire who were cowards at
    their college work. To fight the Germans is an easier

task than to do a Latin paper. He who is master of his own soul is greater than he who merely makes himself master of an enemy town. Often those who have been heroes in war fall back into cowardly slavery to their old sins. To face death bravely on the battlefield is easier than to live life bravely in face of temptation. Do not mistake me. Love France as you have always loved her. But remember that there is no beauty of bravery like that of the soul.

'All are patriots willing to die for their country. Few indeed are willing to die for God. Give yourself to God and the religious life, as during the holidays you told me that you were longing to do. That is a finer thing—since fewer men are capable of it—than your present wish to give your life for France. For you surrender to God is the ideal. He will reveal to you what form that surrender shall take. In my view, any novice of the Society of Jesus who, desiring to go as missionary to China, falls killed by a Prussian bullet, is stealing from heaven the joy it has in one martyr more. He who gives himself to God, gains all. He who gives himself to glory, gains only glory.'

From time to time Marie-Antoinette wrote meditations upon the War. Their thread ran through various letters written by her during 1916. Thus on September 26, 1916, the eve of Hubert's departure to the Front, she wrote :

'Now above all be faithful. Is yours to be a short or a long life ? That matters nothing. It matters everything that your life shall be lived only in Jesus. Be filled with him ; to him be faithful.'

She wrote these other remarkable words :

'If the day comes when you must fire at the bodies of German soldiers, remember that those bodies are the receptacles of souls as immortal as your own. Let your prayers save those souls for God, into whose eternity you may be responsible for sending them.'

In 1916, a tragic year for the de Geuser family, in the second week of April Marie-Antoinette wrote to Hubert of Louis's terrible wound :

' Father has gone in the hope of seeing Louis ; though his legs have been shattered, there is some hope of saving him. . . . As for you, Hubert, seek after holiness—holiness—holiness.'

Again :

' For Louis the great deprivation is not that of his legs but of his priestly calling. Would that this great suffering, borne with love in the heart, might prove for all priests and all brothers the path to the highest holiness ! May God will also that this martyred life live long to his lasting glory ! '

On October 22, Marie-Antoinette wrote to Avignon :

' My Reverend Mother, I ask your prayers and those of the community for my dear Georges, who on Sept. 17 died gloriously in unequal fight with the enemy, one of whose machines he shot down. An airman comrade saw from a distance his last fight, and has given us an account of it. Engaging single-handed three enemy aeroplanes, he accounted for one of them, and then himself began to fall in a spiral. At a height of 2,000 m. the wings broke from his machine, falling more slowly to earth. Nothing, of course, could save him then. The spiral fall makes it probable that he was badly wounded in the air, or, expert flyer that he was, he would have vol-planed. I cannot think that he was killed outright in the air ; for then it is likely that, like the German, he would have fallen in a nose-dive. What happened during his last moments ? I must believe that mercy brimmed his cup, and that a great accession of grace then over-brimmed it.

' I have for long been sure that Georges ran the race of holiness. It is my faith that he for whom a thousand years are as yesterday enabled Georges to finish the course in a few brief summers. My dear young brother died, not unprepared. Grace had lifted his soul towards God. My beloved parents grieve much, but their courage is greater than their grief. Help me, I beg you, to thank him who in his mercy gives them such support.'

To Hubert, also exposed to the risks of war, she wrote on December 28 :

' Since you have taken up your new station, you have been much in my thoughts. I realise that you may be standing on eternity's brink. But we will not shrink, you and I ; we will do nothing that might take from the beauty which eternity holds in store. We will lift our thoughts and our hearts above these things of earth. We will strive with all our mind and with all our strength that, to the Father's greater glory, Christ may be king of the souls of men.'

She went on with the fearlessness and frankness that were characteristic of her :

' It was a thing that I loved in Georges that, faithful in his patriotism, he consciously subordinated that patriotism to a holier cause. Neither in his letters nor in his speech was there to be found one word of patriotism as men normally know it. He desired to be commendable in God's eyes—and this was all of his desire. I have heard him say so in as many words. Some, doubtless, would have been shocked by this seeming lack of patriotism. For me I praise it as an approach to perfection. The exclusion of profane and merely human sentiment must surely assist this approach. In concentrating solely upon his ideal as a Christian, he assured, and more than assured, the realisation of his ideal as a Frenchman.

'Let us devote ourselves, therefore, to the eternal cause of him and his glory so dear to our hearts. No other cause, however worthy in itself, is worthy of our soul's devotion. Dedicated only to God, we shall best defend our country, while our dedicated lives shall in their power for good know neither national frontiers nor the limitations of human time.'

During the hard winter of 1916-17 Marie-Antoinette wrote further to Hubert, who, fearing that his sister's end was near, had thanked her for her devotion, and begged her forgiveness for his faults and failings of past days :

'Forgive you ? Those tiny troubles of the past are all forgotten. For any little help that I may have been able to give you, God has repaid me a thousand times over in the high vocation that he has sent you. When you obeyed the voice of Jesus and joined his Society, you gave me happiness beyond my hopes. It is you who have given me far more than I have given you.'

In his turn Jean, the sixth son, went into the field. Of him on October 21, 1917, his sister wrote :

'He is not very happy, it seems. But soon the Master will make his young disciple understand that he is not forgotten. So his Big Sister has no fear for him. For she knows that her small-boy brother is safe in the arms of the Mother of God, and watched over by the all-embracing providence of God himself. . . .
'Of this there is no doubt, the will of God supersedes all things else—even the Body and the Blood of Jesus.'

In 1918 Hubert was granted four days' leave. At this time his sister was sinking fast, and her death was feared with each new day. On May 25, returned from this leave, he received a last short note from Marie Antoinette :

'Your brief spell at home in this pleasant spring-time was a great delight to me. Oh, Hubert, you are all that I dreamed you to be—truly religious and a true soldier of Jesus. In you I have great confidence and great joy.'

Hubert, in fact, was to be the first to die, his sister dying shortly after him. They were ready to die. Before her death Marie-Antoinette wrote thus to Louis of her life and its handicaps :

'You tell me that I live in my brothers' lives as well as live my own. The thought is a great comfort to me. My own life is too poor and weak to hold the flaming fire of my love for God and his glory that burns in my soul. May it be that in you and in many others also, my hopes of holiness may know realisation. I am like an engine that has power enough to drive a dozen cars, and that is built into some old crock of a motor whose running days are over. It is always working under pressure ; imagine how it shakes me to bits. This only gives me patience : when that old crock, which is my body, at last worn out, shall fall to pieces, my soul's engine shall make function many fine cars—those cars that are the souls of others—and these by their performance shall glorify his name.'

CHAPTER THE FOURTH

THE EXTERNAL RADIANT WOMAN

1 *Her Friends and her Good Works*

AS her health became worse, Marie-Antoinette, forced to keep within doors and in the end to her room, had to give up, one by one, all her outside activities—her catechisms, her visits with her mother to the poor, her socials for young girls, and the rest.

Of the happy period of those earlier activities a friend has kept this record :

'At the time when I knew her, Nénette was seventeen. We would take tea with her ; her smiling good humour was invariable, and knew no distinction of persons. Young as she was, her serenity and self-mastery were exceptional, and won the hearts of all.'

In the winter of 1904-5 Marie-Antoinette learned to dance, but the social diversion of dancing had small appeal to her. She cared infinitely more for the higher art of pure devotion.

In 1906 Mme de Saint-Quentin began to organise church social activities in the Raffineries quarter of Le Hâvre, where a temporary church and church hall had already been established on the site of a burnt-out factory. Into this work for the poor children of the district Marie-Antoinette threw herself with characteristic wholeheartedness, seeking by games and singing to divert and in a measure discipline 'the poor little

61

hooligans,' as with whimsical tenderness she was wont to describe them.

At Chémouteau too she delighted in devoting herself to the small girls of the neighbouring farms and hamlets. These she would take to the family chapel, now for an exhortation from her brothers' tutor, now for a talk given by herself on religious subjects. Further, she taught them to sew.

Of her own needlework she had made something more than a fine art. As quite a young girl she took part in sewing classes held for poor women, while at the Dominican school she had learnt to embroider with exquisite skill. An example of her work was an alb, intended for one of her brothers on his consecration, upon which she spent two years, leaving it still unfinished at her death. It was only after long search that in a particular convent an embroideress was discovered, capable of completing worthily the miracle of her exquisite handiwork.

She would permit no other to concern herself with the church linen at Chémouteau, often being content to devote long months to some ornament that had been designed by her uncle André.

The assistance which she gave in earlier days to the catechist was as skilful as it was regular. She had a genius for dealing with young girls whose good intentions were equalled only by their casual attendances. She was solicitous for their souls ; for their caprices she had only sternness and disapproval. When physical weakness made it impossible for her to continue this work that she loved, she gave it up, accepting with detachment of soul rather than with resignation the necessity for the sacrifice, and having faith that the sacrifice itself was of more worth than her old solicitude for souls.

She delighted too in visiting the sick. At first these visits were made in company of the local Sister of S.

Vincent de Paul ; later alone.   It was always her wish
that the worst cases might be allotted to her ; this that
she might prepare them to die as Christians should.
' My charges all die beneath my hands, but only that I
may help them to enter heaven,' was her whimsical
remark.   The words which she found to prepare them
for the Sacraments often seemed inspired.   She endeavoured to awake them to eternal truths and to
induce them to have no other thought than for their
souls.   She tidied the room of each, made ready a little
altar and did all things else that might make easier the
soul's approach to God and his love.   One touching
instance is known of a young mother, whose reluctance
to die and to leave husband and child Marie-Antoinette's
inspired consolation turned to resignation and the
blessed peace of a good and holy death.

The last work which she undertook was in connection
with the establishment of closed retreats for girls of good
family.   The first of these, conducted, as were all the
others, by her uncle, Father Anatole de Grandmaison,
took place at Saints-Anges in Rouen, in April 1907 ;
the second in outer Paris, in June 1909 ; another, held
in the spring of 1910, at Le Hâvre, her home town, in
the old Dominican monastery.   Into this work she
put all her enthusiasm, dealing with details of organi-
sation, watching over the Retreat's daily conduct,
drawing up its rule, and assuring herself that the rule was
kept faithfully yet with no foolish slavery to its mere letter.

As acting-directress, she gave counsel and encouragement, and, above all, to others a shining example in the
matter of recollection and the discipline of silence.   Yet
in the one daily break, as often at meals, her heart's
gaiety would frequently provoke the most exuberant
laughter.

It was her wish that these retreats, interrupted by the
war, should be resumed after it.   But this did not prove
possible.

Marie-Antoinette was a model friend. She welcomed all who came to see her with her radiant smile, and made them feel that in their visit the obligation was on her side, instead of, as the fact was, a generous giving of the best of herself to her visitor. She was never bored ; for her all men and all matters had their interest. Mention to her this person or that good work, and the powerful aid of her prayers was assured to him or to it. Her judgement was as excellent as her great good sense ; upon the former he who needed advice in a difficulty could depend ; upon the latter any who were about to make a decision could implicitly rely. Her thought was lofty ; her speech worthy of her thought. Yet neither in thought nor in speech was she stiff or frigidly austere—in this differing from those novices who grasp the letter rather than the spirit of the saying that ' speech is given to men that by their words they may do good in the world.'

She was not of those who because of their many activities find no time for friendship or even for letters to friends. She never forgot an anniversary, whether of a birthday or of some more sorrowful occasion ; though she herself might be weary or sick, she never failed to scribble a letter, long or short, that might bring to a sad heart comfort, or to a shaken heart new courage, or to a friend's heart the simple assurance of her own enduring affection.

Her confessor put into her charge many of those who came to him for spiritual help. Her ' children,' as she called them, had implicit trust in her. Her soul's serenity drew them to her, and led them willingly to make her sharer of their secrets. To many she revealed their vocation. None took her unawares ; none were sent by her empty-handed away.

Family joys and family tribulations found her readily sympathetic. She sympathised as readily with the delight which young people knew in setting up house together. Because she was the friend of God, she was the friend of all the world. If one, preoccupied in other affairs, neglected her in her sick-room, for him she had no reproach. If another wholly gave up his visits to her, for him she found prompt excuse.

Social contacts as such she neither sought nor shunned : all whom she met, whether at home or abroad, she endeavoured to love for their souls' sake.

In seeming God wished to narrow the field of Marie-Antoinette's apostle-like work for him. In truth he was seeking to extend it—to constrain her pen to write those letters that death could not steal from the world, as it stole Marie-Antoinette herself and the influence of her oral precepts. These letters will assuredly prove her enduring memorial. Those who received these letters talked of them and begged others to read them. In these letters was revealed a soul that radiated light, a mind that was rich in good counsel, a heart that won the love of all. These written pages burn with divine fire. Virtue emanates from them, as once it emanated from the garment of Jesus, touched by the woman who had the issue of blood.

To her brothers and to her intimate friends she wrote much, drawing on her contacts with the divine. When she wrote, she wrote with the ecstasy of divine communion upon her. Her letters were prayers, when prayer proper would have overtaxed her afflicted body. In them she wrote of heaven, or of earth as heaven beholds it. Almost all her correspondents were Carmelites. In five houses of the Order she had relatives or friends, while both circumstance and inclination made Carmel her life's greatest inspiration.

Ardent with her love for God, desirous only of bringing herself and her loved ones into closer communion with him, she found in her gift for writing a potent means of achieving her high purpose. For words as words she cared nothing. Yet in ecstatic contemplation of the infinite she found such inspiration that she became a writer of distinction and—immeasurably more important than that—an interpreter of the soul as faithful, as vital and as lucid, as any we have known.

Her letters need no commentary. They reveal Marie-Antoinette. They are Marie-Antoinette. They contain all her irresistible personality. They may be left to speak for themselves.

Thus on June 11, 1912, she wrote to her cousin Thérèse, Carmelite at Le Hâvre :

'Here is one of my seedling thoughts. This morning in reading the Acts, I was struck by these words of the Holy Ghost : " Separate me Saul and Barnabas, for the work whereunto I have taken them." Surely here the Lord of love has a word for us all. For so it must be with us ; though our souls live to the one end, our bodies know separation. Yet the separation is only apparent, since in him—in his love and for his glory—now and always we can be one.'

When war came in August 1914, her habit ' of living spiritually above the battle ' gave Marie de la Trinité a remarkable ability of showing that boundless charity which for most at this time, by reason of our human limitations, became exceedingly difficult. She wrote :

'Of the war, that subject which preoccupies all French hearts, I do not speak. Certainly we should pray for our France and her soldiers, and then, like true Catholics, we should make our prayer universal, since to spread the love of God over the whole world will bring heaven's blessing upon our own country.'

Again, to Thérèse on October 29, 1914, she sought to express in words this same universal charity that she felt dwelling within her :

'We cannot limit the Infinite. In these days of

blood let us preach the blood of Jesus to all men, even to " our brothers on the far side of the Rhine." '

In a further letter, dated August 8, 1914, she recalled her baby sister Thérèse, dead in infancy :

' I share the sorrow of your bereavement, and remember my own of six years ago, when my little sister Thérèse died. To know the loss of a tiny child is to know poignant sorrow. Yet in that sorrow is sweetness—a sweetness that none have known, who have not shed tears by an empty cradle. For it is joy to think of the happiness in heaven of the soul of a little one that has never opposed the will of God.'

This is one of the many instances of Marie de la Trinité's true sensibility.

Father Alexandre Constant,[1] an army chaplain, before setting out for the Front had stayed for some time at Le Hâvre, and had often brought Communion to Marie-Antoinette. To him on January 19, 1916, she wrote, giving her grateful thanks for his services and visits to her. She continued :

' I pray God that he may so use both you and me that " though still on earth we may be citizens of heaven." Forgive the frank way in which I write to you. Though I have not the boldness of my small sister Gentille, who calls you her big brother, it is to you as a big brother that I presume to write. Let me say with all respect that I am conscious of our unity in God, and I would have your prayers that my love for God and my gratitude may increase with each new day.'

Not for its own soldier sons only, but for a crowd of others at the Front—army chaplains in particular, and

---

[1] A Jesuit of the Toulouse province ; before the war, professor at Maduré ; killed before Douaumont on October 25, 1916.

not least the present biographer whose gratitude no words can adequately express—the household in la rue Faure was a kind of base-camp of the soul, whence came sweetness and strength and the succour of prayer, and those more material expressions of all three—letters and parcels.

To the fighting soldier, as in this letter to Father Constant, Marie de la Trinité could write with a curious felicity :

' *Deo proximus, proximo devotus, sibi mortuus*— Father, how fortunate are you in your priest's ideal. How happy is the life that you live in Jesus. There are times when, wistful always of this ideal, I am irresistibly attracted to it. I, a woman who may not be a priest, cannot attain it. Yet my faith is strong that my great yearning will not be wholly in vain, but will be realised in those who are, or who are to be, consecrated priests. When, Father, I think of your ministry in the Argonne, I feel that in you my yearning has been already realised, and I give thanks to our beloved Master.'

Priests alone may follow the priestly calling. Yet women and girls may possess the priest-like soul to the end that they, like Our Lady, may have intimate understanding of Jesus Christ, the divine Mediator, and of the great gift made to all Christians in the sacerdotal experience that was theirs at baptism. Marie de la Trinité was pre-eminently of the number of these sacerdotal souls.

It would seem that God made use of this quality in Marie de la Trinité, since he charged her with the spiritual care of several priests—with one above all. Such a charge, as those know well who possess some experience of the mysterious world of the spirit and some acquaintance with its remarkable missions, is one of the highest and most formidable of all responsibilities.

As Marie de la Trinité drew nearer to unity with God, as in the case of all true mystics the bright flame of her apostolic soul grew proportionately brighter. Those whose spirituality is small imagine that a soul, absorbed in God, in its absorption grows limited and egocentric. It is true that for such a soul God alone exists. Yet more and more clearly the God-absorbed soul perceives all that is implicit in the will of God, and, chief of all, the salvation of men. To contemplate Christ is to contemplate all that Christ means—or should mean—for souls at large.

On June 17, 1916, the eve of the feast of the Sacred Heart, Marie-Antoinette wrote to her Carmelite cousin Thérèse :

' To repose upon the breast of Love himself, as we shall do on to-morrow's feast—there is no higher thing than that. To slake the thirst at the waters of life is to know ecstasy. How wistful we are of all that may increase, and still more increase, our life in him ! For others as for ourselves we would break down all barriers, we would remove all obstacles, that the waters of life may sweep through all the souls of men.'

Marie-Antoinette, unlike certain others, felt no call to specialise her spiritual activities. To Marie-Suzanne, Carmelite sister at Le Mans, on July 5, 1916, she confessed :

' Others may give themselves to the task of saving as many individual souls as they may, or of delivering those who suffer in purgatory, or of converting sinners on earth, or to any other worthy cause. For myself I feel no call to any of these, but only to give myself in love. The two things are one, you will say. True, and yet—for me the best is to contemplate only him, and to leave him to use me, thus surrendered to his will, to his own ends.'

F

On March 7, 1917, she re-stated her conception of her apostolic work in somewhat similar terms, ending her letter thus :

' In a life whose true Catholic influence reaches boundlessly out to serve his glory, we poor little nobodies realise our spiritual destinies. For their realisation we have only to dwell in Jesus, and he in us. How simple it is ! '

Her postscript ran :

' Forgive this lengthy scrawl. It is my sick woman's failing not to be able to condense what I have to say, or to get it clear in my head beforehand. Too often, in sentence after sentence, I let my pen run away with my soul.'

This confession makes it clear that the authentic soul of Marie-Antoinette is to be met with in her letters. She was constantly interrupted. The doctor came, or a friend, or a boisterous brother ; it all mattered nothing. Her thought remained consecutive and her prose rhythmic. She had literature in her bones, born artist that she was. Yet of Marie-Antoinette's merits this last was the least. The ebullient power which is sensed beneath the lyrical surface of her words was fed from no merely human spring.

To her cousin Thérèse on June 7, 1917, Marie-Antoinette wrote of the ecstatic joy of death :

' The thought of death has strong appeal, in especial for us who are Carmelites. If we yearn to be one with him, it is less that we may know joy in him than that he may joy in us. Our urge towards holiness is the urge to reach more nearly to perfection—and thus to do him honour—and to lead others to live such lives as too may honour him. We are—and shall be till this world end—his apostles. There may be little visible bravery in the service performed by us in

our lives, while those lives themselves may be short.
The first is not demanded of us ; in the last we have
no say.

' As we love him intensely and do his will, so we
lay up for ourselves incorruptible treasure in heaven.
We dare not be spendthrifts of time ; for in eternity
our acts in time shall reverberate.'

If any correspondent told Marie de la Trinité of
spiritual gain acquired through herself—as did her
friend Thérèse to whom she sent the following letter,
dated March 9, 1915—she gave thanks to God with a
simplicity and a forgetfulness of self, that revealed how
detached she was from ordinary human vanity :

' If indeed our great God of love have used so sorry
a tool as I, I accept the fact, and am by it assured
that his all-powerful love will again make use of me
on your behalf. If this in any way astonish you,
remember that I have often told you of my belief
that the adorable Master delights in using the most
wretched of tools to further his purpose, in order that
the glory shall be given where the glory is due, and
not to the tool of which he has made use. Feel
yourself free with me, whether silence or speech be
your need. I am his poor little nobody, no more
than that and no less ; with what concerns myself I
have no concern.'

If her correspondent misunderstood her thought, or if
she herself failed to make it wholly plain, as in this
letter of February 7, 1918, in simple, humble words she
wrote her excuses :

' It is rather I who should say to you : " Recollect
my great ignorance." I am, and have been, a sick
woman. My studies have suffered in consequence.
Prayer has made me a little less ignorant of the divine
than I am of the human. Even so, I am, in every

sense of the words, like a thrusting, untrained plant.
If I have seemed over-clever, it is only because I
have expressed myself badly. My literary skill is
small ; often I fail to be lucid. My impulsive and
stubborn disposition for ever seeks to get the upper
hand, or at least to make me stiff and disagreeable in
what I do. Help me then, dear Marie-Agnès, to
become gentle and lovable ; for that is what I most
would be.

'Forgive me for having used ill-chosen expressions
that may have hindered you in your God-ward
march—I beg it of you who have always helped me
upon my own road to God.'

II   *Aspects of her Apostolic Mission*

Marie de la Trinité's mission was frankly apostolic.
She herself was aware of this, and wrote explicitly of it,
as in this letter, dated March 9, 1915, to a friend who,
living in the world, spent her life in good works :

'I thank God, dear Thérèse, that he makes use of
you for good works in the world. Nor do I fear that
such works hinder your union with him ; to do what
pleases him cannot bring separation from him, pro-
vided only that you do not surrender yourself to
these works, but only to him for whom you do them.
For plainly his will—and the performance of it—
cannot divide us from him, since it embraces all
things. We should seek to resemble the magnetic
needle of a compass that swings back to the North
each time that it has been shaken from it. When our
human weakness has shaken us from our true spiritual
orientation, let us swing back to our souls' North, the
adorable Lord, restoring to him that joy born of
contemplation which we have stolen from him. Thus
may we make our own failings serve us. . . . I have

tried to tell you in these simple words in what trifles I find my strength.'

There is no real antagonism between the contemplative life of the soul and the life which is given to good works. This Marie de la Trinité knew well, as is proved by her letter to Le Mans, dated June 30, 1917 :

' I see action and contemplation as spiritually complementary—I would divide my life between them. I do not conceive holiness as once I conceived it—as a kind of scales in which contemplation is unequally balanced by action. Now, as I conceive, contemplation is to action as the root is to the plant ; the first is the indwelling life which can find perfect manifestation only in the second. True holiness lies surely in the combination of the two. Action serves God's greater glory ; contemplation brings him greater delight.'

In another passage she related this generalisation to her particular case :

' We Carmelites are vowed to contemplation ; in what kind of action shall we discover our contemplation's complement ? In eternity, most surely— adoration ; in time, as surely, apostleship for God's glory. On earth the broken arcs of action and imperfect contemplation ; in heaven the perfect round of adoration and the contemplative life at its highest. In this temporal life we should seek first to quicken our roots that the sap may surge through the plant, and then whatever may glorify God for ever— whatever may aid the apostolic work to be done by us between our death and the world's end.'

Marie-Antoinette shared with S. Thérèse de l'Enfant-Jésus the desire to give to God glory and adoration by dwelling in this life ' in Christ.' And the means ? Humility—this before all, annihilation in herself of all

that was not Christ, mastery of the flesh, suppression of
the self, authentication by her soul of the *Jam non ego*
of S. Paul.

Writing to her brother Louis on September 23, 1917,
she completed her thought :

'I love S. John for the lucidity with which he
writes of the Blessed Trinity. Latterly, however, I
have neglected him for S. Paul. None has written
more stimulatingly than he upon the mystery of the
redemption. He pushes my soul's horizons into the
infinite.

'To rise above ourselves to him who is very God,
we need to close the eyes of the mind. For mere
reason cannot bear to look upon the shining face of
divine truth. Through these only may we gaze upon
it seeingly : faith and hope and love and that unity
of unities which embraces every sacred mystery.

'There is no nobler thing than this Catholic truth
that finds essential harmony between the whole and
the least of its parts. If I were a man, I would not
write merely a *Commentary on S. John*, but a work that,
dealing with both theory and practice, should present
to men the Trinity as the hidden heart whose love,
like the blood in the body, is pumped from the
centre into those sacred mysteries, linked each to
each, that lie about it. I tell you this in confidence.

'My task is simpler. To live in Jesus, and to toil
to the best of my poor capacity at the great work
which his death began and in which he claims our
co-operation.'

In this and similar letters Louis found, like treasure
in a field, spiritual counsel too rich to be reserved to
the two of them. He begged his sister to allow others
to share in it. She answered :

'Your idea is good. It would be a great joy to me

to share with others what has so abundantly been given to myself. Not material things only, but things of the spirit, should be held in common for the common good and to the Father's greater glory.

'Yet—you talk to me of "setting down such matters in writing." That makes me hesitate. I would do it very willingly, if, as a sign, God would give me the opportunity so to write. At present the difficulties are many. Here is the chief : there is little about which I can write, since, as you know, I see all things very simply ; while if I am to interpret what I see, that interpretation cannot come of thought. For I am sick, and one of sickness's many small betrayals is that it makes a traitor of my intelligence.

'This only I could do ; whenever the urge came, to allow my soul directly to guide my pen, and to permit perception to trickle through my intelligence rather as the sun's light trickles through a prism, through whose medium only can that light's true colours be distinguished

'Plainly such reliance on providence for immediate inspiration in regard to a variety of subjects must result in kaleidoscopic effects. I shall need to control that kaleidoscope. However, if it be the Master's will, you and I shall discuss all this at length. I will write to you frankly and in entire simplicity, confident that you will understand. You, on your part, will give my crude thoughts shape, till their unripeness ripen, and their ripeness become refreshment to the souls of men. Nor will you fail to tell me where, as it seems to you, I have missed the truth or have put it into wrong perspective—the last a great weakness of mine.'

Marie-Antoinette on several occasions reverted to this idea. In secrecy she was to sow. The seeds sown by her, become ripe grain, others were later to reap. As she herself realised, she would not live to see the harvest. Thus, on November 3, 1914, she wrote to Avignon :

'To publish abroad the miraculous sweetness of my life in him would be great joy to me. Yet now and, it may be, for always it is his wish, I feel, that his humble Marie de la Trinité, as once his beloved Mother, shall treasure all these things in her heart.'

She repeated this thought in a slightly varied form in a later letter, also to Avignon, dated November 12, 1917. To Louis on November 24, 1917, she wrote at length and with finality upon her conception of the apostolic rôle :

'On earth only the broken lights of truth can be seen by us, but the glory of grace shines as bright as the sun at noon. Just so are we limited in our apostolic work, but unlimited in our soul's apostleship —the apostleship of the inner life.

'Apostleship ! That is our true vocation, yours and mine. In that we are increasingly one ; one in our response to the Master's call ; one in our mystical life that transcends all others, whether in principle or in practice, whether in action or in contemplation.

'Though some think otherwise, I must believe that there is no conflict between the contemplative and the apostolic life. The one is the root, the other is the spreading plant. The ripest souls are those that are equally rich in faith and in works, though, as I realise, it is not God's will that all souls shall be thus ripe. Nor do I forget that S. Paul (1 Cor. xii, 28) in his hierarchy of members of the church names " first, apostles."

'For me there is no division between God and his works ; if I know and love God, I know and love his works. In his infinite diversity there is unity ; in the contemplation of the divine the soul, made one with God, attains to full and true apostleship. It perceives the parts equally with the whole ; it perceives the unity and harmony that exists between them ; it perceives the relation of the divine mysteries one with another.

' Unity with God, whose coveted attainment is the quintessence of S. John's teaching, widens the soul's horizons, and, as S. Paul indicates, extends the range of its vision. The mystery of the Trinity, of the Incarnation and of the Redemption are in this unity seen to be related one with another. The glory of Christ is the glory of the Father ; they are two and yet they are one. For the life of love, which Christ's life is, is the life of God, projected through Christ into souls sanctified by grace.

' The supernatural world in which all things are re-established in Christ, is the world in which the apostolic soul must dwell. It is in this world that I approach to that unity with God, to that life in Christ, to that love for the Father and to that zeal for his glory, which sweeps me towards the Blessed Trinity itself, towards the supreme sacrifice made by Christ for men—the sacrifice made perfect by grace given of the Holy Ghost.

' Man's salvation is the gift of God.[1] Those whom God chooses for apostolic work, God makes use of to confer his blessing upon saved souls ; they serve Christ, in that through them, and to the glory of God, he makes perfect his work in the Holy Ghost.

' These I conceive to be the fundamentals of the soul's apostleship. It can have no higher vocation.

' In its unity with God, the soul spends all its strength that " all may be one."[2] In this unity too the God-absorbed soul is swept into his transcendental

[1] Eph. ii, 5-8.   [2] John xvii, 22-23.

glory, coming at last to that peace in which " God is all in all."[1]

' I like to think that each soul has its share in the Father's glory, and that through the grace of the Holy Ghost it may come to a realisation of the vocation which God has willed for it. The humblest soul is like the most insignificant stone in a Gothic building ; without it the perfect praise of the Father would be incomplete. The thought that so high a destiny is reserved to the lowliest of living souls inspires to new ardour and to new serenity.

' The apostolic soul does not lose sight of the teaching of S. Peter,[2] or of the truth of predestination, or of the fact of the prescience of God, or of the existence of " the elect," chosen by God in his prescience.

' To preach the gospel is the outward manifestation of apostleship. So splendid a mission demands holiness as splendid, and that " light of life,"[3] which alone can enable the evangelist to preach the gospel in its subtle and luminous entirety to the satisfaction of the need in men's souls.

' If with the aid of grace the undistorted truth is to be put within the reach of all ; if good and evil alike are to be discriminatingly understood ; if the austerity of uncompromising truth is to be reconciled with the infinite pity of love—the self must die, the soul must be one with God and so the servant of our fellow-men.

' We can but abide in him, in whom truth and love alike abide.[4] In that is true apostleship ; in that is the soul's attainment to perfection. Such perfection can be attained only in " him who is able to do all things more abundantly than we desire or understand, according to the power that worketh in us."[5]

---

[1] 1 Cor. xv, 28.   [2] 1 Peter i, 1-2.   [3] John viii, 12.
    [4] John xv, 4.   [5] Eph. iii, 20.

'Now, we can but dwell in the " life that is hid with Christ in God."[1]   In the Blessed Sacrament we come to Jesus ; we adore the Father ; we are confirmed in our apostleship.   Let us be the shadows of him, whose substance is the glory of God and the salvation of souls.   Let our lives and our conversation be in heaven,[2] descending to earth only as the needs of our fellows demand it.'

[1] Col. iii, 3.   [2] *Vide* Philip iii, 20.

CHAPTER THE FIFTH

A SOUL AFLAME

NOT books or studies or the counsels of others, but the Holy Ghost informed the spiritual life of Marie de la Trinité. Among the living her confessor, her uncle, her mother, the Carmelite prioress were her guides. Of books she herself wrote (on February 28, 1916):

'My crucifix and my *Pieta* (after Michelangelo's *Pieta*) are the books I use.'

Of the Bible, the Psalms and the Prophets, S. Paul and S. John were most frequently chosen by her for the meditation which she loved. Less than thirty when she died, she knew more of the teaching of S. Paul and S. John than do many priests at the end of their careers. She had the gift of making vividly personal the numerous scriptural and liturgical quotations and allusions to be found in her letters. In this they have a considerable resemblance to those of S. Bernard.

S. John of the Cross too stood high in her estimation. On October 13, 1911, she wrote:

'In the little Carmel of my soul S. John of the Cross is a shining figure. His *Ascent of Mount Carmel* especially inspires me. Few books have found such response in me as this. In it I seem to follow S. John from sacrifice to sacrifice, till at last I am absorbed in God. To die that we may live in God: this is his teaching, simple and sound and full of comfort.'

S. Francis de Sales was well known to her ; Marie-
Aimée de Jésus, the Carmelite of l'Avenue de Saxe, she
admired for her great love of contemplation ; Gemma
Galgani had less appeal for her, because of the streak
of strangeness that ran through her spiritual life. She
preferred Elizabeth of the Trinity to that other Carmelite, Thérèse de l'Enfant Jésus, because—in her own
delightful words :

> ' Elizabeth and I understand each other so well,
> and because by her I have been taught so much.'

1   *Her Fundamentals*

God in us.

For Marie-Antoinette the Blessed Trinity was the
mystery of mysteries. She returned to it again and again
in her letters, and wrote of it with an eloquence and a
lucidity, an ardour and an audacity, remarkable even
in her :

> ' Oh, to know the gift of God ! Oh, to know Jesus,
> the only Son of the Father, who came into the world
> that we too might become sons of God, partakers in
> his divinity ! Let us not limit the gift of God. Let us
> by our belief accept his promises in their fullness.
> Let us have faith in the indwelling Holy Ghost and in
> the grace of God, which is his life in us, and in which
> we live in him, till in his love we are made con-
> summate. It is that love which enables us to give
> instant and whole-hearted obedience to our vocation.'

Marie de la Trinité delighted also in meditating upon
the mystery of man's primal innocence, his fall and his
redemption through Christ. To a friend on December
20th, 1916, she wrote :

> ' Jesus is the very stuff of our souls. To draw near
> to him is the soul's supreme satisfaction ; " in him
> dwelleth all the fulness of the Godhead corporally ; "

in him we are made free of all the things more excellent.

'There is but one thing lovelier than this communion with him—the " gift of God," which is the sharing of our souls, bought by the blood of Christ, in the nature of God himself. For by this gift, through Christ and in Christ we become the Father's sons, the Father's heirs. Men do not realise, as they should, the nature of the " gift of God," or they would love him more, who so greatly has loved them.

'We who know the gift of God must be faithful ; we must by grace make our lives more like to God's, till he himself possess them wholly, and we are wholly one with him.'

In June 1914, she wrote to Le Mans :

'On this earth we are to live *in coelis*. Only in silence can the soul touch the peak of ecstasy. *Silentium tibi laus :* there you have it. The urge to " blaze abroad his miracles " is hard to withstand. But how can we worthily publish them, we poor little nobodies, who can do no greater thing than this : in our gratitude and our love to lose ourselves in him ? '

Three years later—as is proved by a letter, dated June 30, 1917, also to Le Mans—this remained the core of her faith.

As S. John Eudes said with audacious truth, a Christian soul living in grace is ' part of Jesus Christ himself.' This unity of Christians in Christ Marie de la Trinité, in her life as in her writing, revealed to men as few have done. The conclusion of her letter to Marie-Marthe, dated November 22, 1917, was characteristic :

'Even we, poor little nobodies that we are, are able to add to the glory of God and to the beatitude of men. For Christ has chosen us to be his co-workers in redemption.'

To her cousin Thérèse on December 20, 1916, she had previously written of those true ' co-redeemers,' in whose number she was undoubtedly to be included. She concluded :

' In God's eyes not our deeds count, nor the greatness of them ; but the love in which we do them, and the greatness of that.'

From her ceaseless meditation Marie de la Trinité drew strength for her soul and the ability to share in the communion of Saints. For its spiritual biography the letter written to Le Mans on March 7, 1917, has especial interest :

' Jesus cried to the Father : " *Rogo ut omnes unum, sicut tu, Pater, in me, et ego in te, ut ipsi in nobis unum sint. Ego in eis, et tu in me, ut sint consummati in unum.*" In these words is all my vocation.

' How good to know this absorption in God's unity. How good to be a little *consummata* in the unique *unum*. I know no higher ideal than this.'

The Eucharist.

In Christ, the Second Person of the Blessed Trinity, Consummata did not forget Christ, the divine Man. Thus, on August 31, 1913, she wrote from Chémouteau :

' After Benediction this evening we all walked in procession ; the men went first, and Georges was leader. Singing the *Magnificat* we marched till we reached the end of the avenue. Here the big new rood had been set up in place of the old, which had become battered and weather-beaten. I watched all our little world file by—my parents, brothers, sisters, cousins, uncles, and the neighbouring farmers, their wives and their children.

' It made my heart grow tender, this spectacle of the one household—one in its faith, one in its charity ;

one in its love for Jesus, the head of the house ; one in the affection that master bore to man, and man bore to master.'

At Corpus Christi in the following year she wrote :

'In the Blessed Sacrament I take ever increasing delight. By it I am brought near to God in Three Persons, and made to understand that truly *nostra conversatio in coelis est.*'

On October 15, 1915, she wrote to Thérèse at length of her great joy in communion, that 'sacrament of his love.' She used these striking phrases :

'How good it is to be love's prey. Willingly to allow the eagle of God to work his will with the poor little things that we are.'

As her health grew worse and her confinement to the house more rigorous, her wistful joy in the Blessed Sacrament, which she could too seldom receive, grew in intensity. In a letter to Marie-Marthe, dated June 18, 1917, she related the Blessed Sacrament to the religious life of Carmel and of the Society of Jesus. For, she said, the hidden Jesus of the Eucharist is as the novice, whom the grille or the cloister hides.

On September 7, 1917, she wrote to Avignon, telling of the visit of a priest to la rue Faure, and of her great joy in the Mass which he had been empowered to celebrate there :

'A few days ago my uncle came. Father had arranged the little room between mother's and mine as a chapel, so that each of us could see the altar. We had Mass on Aug. 29 and 30. The mingled holiness and homeliness of the setting gave those of us who were there a very precious memory. Apart from the priest's there were ten communions in all ; while our little server, René, seemed deeply moved by the holy task which had been entrusted to him.

' I can find no words to tell you of my own emotion. It was so long since I had heard Mass—need I say more than that ? I do not think that I have ever before perceived such beauty in the sacrifice of Calvary, thus re-enacted upon our altars. In my own home to look upon the very blood of Christ ! Would that I could go up and down the world, making all men sharers in his grace ! '

Her great hunger and thirst for the Body and Blood of Jesus Christ are in part explained by the wistful attraction that the priesthood had for her. To her brother Michel on June 24, 1916, she wrote :

' Your account of the ordination interested us greatly. It has aroused that old vocational urge, long latent in me. Laugh at me if you like, but I still yearn less for Carmel than for the priestly calling itself.

' Though it seem fantastic, and though it be unrealisable, in me this attraction is so strong and urgent, that I must believe it to be of God. For God does not purposelessly implant such yearnings in our souls. My vocation shall be realised in others, if not in myself. I shall sow the seed ; in their vocations the ripe corn shall be harvested. But this is strange stuff that I am writing to you. Forgive me.'

Our Lady of Sorrows.

A letter, dated October 3, 1911, and written after a visit to Lourdes, confessed that she felt Our Lady of Sorrows to be in a special sense her guardian :

' The Mother of Sorrows has shared with me the secret of her martyrdom. She has made me understand that only if I am one with her in the travail of her love, can I be one with her in the treasure of her purity. She, who is alike the Queen of Martyrs and the Queen of Virgins, allows me to share in her Son's redemptive work.'

G

For Marie de la Trinité Our Lady was pre-eminently she who, ' blessed among women,' gave her Son's blood and her heart's tears for the salvation of men ; who was the Virgin of Sorrows not at Calvary alone, but throughout her life, prescient as she was of the cross in whose shadow her life was lived.

In her letter to Pontoise of March 9, 1913, alluding to S. Francis of Assisi, Marie-Antoinette wrote :

' I would have the holy Stigmata printed not upon my body, but upon my soul. For so should I more nearly resemble the Queen of Virgins, who is the true, the unique, Marie de la Trinité.'

In October she elaborated this thought :

' I would be as poor as S. Francis of Assisi, as pure as S. Aloysius, as much a martyr as S. Stephen. I would mortify myself as did the famous penitents ; I would be as great an apostle as S. Francis Xavier ; as great a lover as were SS. Teresa and John of the Cross. I would be more even than this. . . . Yet all my yearnings are satisfied in God himself and in my union with him and with his beloved Mother. In all things I seek to make her way of life my own. One with her, I can give to God all that I envy in the saints—and so have no more need to envy them.'

Again, in May 1914 :

' In the Blessed Virgin what holy simplicity ! To contemplate her and to imitate her, how easy ! To talk of her or to explain how she may be imitated, how difficult !

' As she, I would seek to make my own only the " things above " ; I would live only " the life that is hid with Christ in God." '

Finally there is this note, written to Thérèse on February 9, 1917 :

' She lives in our midst for ever—*Maria abscondita in Deo cum Christo*. If we will, we may share her life in heaven. In her sublime hands how ridiculous do our pitiful good works appear ! '

II *Aids to Holiness*

A passion for prayer, a love of silence : these were her aids in devotion. A joyous spirit and a confident soul : these were her spiritual endowment.

The Life of Prayer.

From her earliest years Marie-Antoinette had a natural inclination to seek God in prayer. In so devout a family everything—Mass and communion daily, opportunities for meditation, religious readings—fostered her inclination. When she was in charge of the children at church, without suspecting it she would protract her thanksgiving. The children, their patience failing to match her fervour, would tug at her arm. Since she had flown away over the church roof—' gone higher than the ceiling,' to use the expression of her brother Georges—she must be brought down to earth.

At home duties pressed upon her, as once they had pressed upon Martha. Yet amid her Martha-tasks, choosing the best part she moved as Mary. Untroubled by her many duties, she was careful only to keep her spirit above the battle. This helped, not hindered, her ; for the nearer a man is to God, the better he does his daily work.

During sickness she used her enforced leisure for the purpose of prayer. Sitting or lying upon the couch in her room, she surrendered herself to God. Of this she wrote rejoicingly to Pontoise on November 10, 1912 :

' This solitude in the midst of the world gives me a foretaste of eternal happiness. Though I cannot see him, I can feel his gaze upon me. A great peace wraps me round. I am become love's prisoner. I ask no more of life.'

She rejoiced even in the insomnia from which she constantly suffered. Thus to Thérèse on December 20, 1916, she wrote :

> ' To think that there are healthy folk who find the days too long, and sick folk to whom their sleepless nights seem endless. Spent near to him, time is too short ; while how good to reflect that " the kingdom of heaven is at hand." '

To Pontoise on March 9, 1913, she had previously written :

> ' How precious is solitude ! It is sacramental. Given by God to the soul, it gives the soul to God. Would that my faith were stronger, that not intermittently but ceaselessly I might be absorbed in union with him. Alas ! too often I falter and fail and lose him from sight. Then, with faith by his blessed will renewed, I find him again, and dwell in the peace that passeth understanding.'

Prayer breaks down the barriers between the soul and God. On October 17, 1915, Marie de la Trinité told Thérèse of all that prayer meant in her life. She concluded thus modestly :

> ' Would that I could find words that in their splendour should match the splendour of prayer ! But I cannot. Dazzled by that splendour, I can only adore in silence.'

' Adore.' This one word contains all of Marie-Antoinette. In prayer she neither asked for forgiveness of sins, nor begged God for gifts. For her to pray was to praise, to glorify, to adore. She expressed it thus (to Pontoise, on November 11, 1911) :

> ' To be his little host of praise ; in that I find my vocation and my true happiness.'

Six years later, on June 10, 1917, she wrote to Martha :

' The dumb beasts praise him. They praise him by being true to the nature which he has given them. Of us, to whom more has been given, more is demanded. It is for us to praise him with mind and heart and soul and strength.'

' To be his host of praise ' : by this Marie de la Trinité understood a gradual transubstantiation, as it might be termed, of man's living soul, until it became one with the living Christ. In her by the direct intervention of God this transubstantiation[1] approached to a completeness that is rare indeed. On November 11, 1911, she wrote explicitly to Pontoise on this subject :

' The divine Priest has, I believe, consecrated me as a host of praise. As he hallows the Host at Mass, so he has transformed my soul into the soul of Christ. On earth the Host is the true sanctuary of the Blessed Trinity. So I, his little host of praise, with the self dead within me—dead and dissolved and become a nothingness within me—make of my life a sanctuary by living it only that I may contemplate him.

' Marie-Antoinette, as once she was, has vanished as completely as vanish the wheaten grains in the consecrated Host. The Blessed Trinity, as I conceive, has no more concern with my pitiable self than it has with the material bread upon the altar.

' In this call to be a host of praise I find satisfaction for all my soul's needs. Altogether absorbed into the divine unity—become possessed of all the merits of my adored Christ—I love him even unto

[1] This term is plainly used in a strictly limited and wholly approximate sense. Upon the altar the material bread becomes the veritable body of Our Saviour. In the soul there is no change of spiritual substance, but only such loss of its own entirety and such absorption in God that the very stuff of the soul is seemingly transformed.

death, and chant his loving kindness in a *sanctus* and an *alleluia* without cease.'

Again to Pontoise in 1912 :

' Each time that I repeat the words " host of praise," it is as if I were exalted from earth to heaven. Thus I am able, even on earth, to be with God in Three Persons. The presence of others does not distract me from my conversations with the Father, with the Son (whose bride I am), and with the Blessed Virgin, my beloved Mother ; for they are conducted in silence.'

Once more, to Thérèse on November 2, 1916 :

' Because I love him, to praise him is not enough. Because I love him, I must give him thanks for the privilege of loving him.'

Marie-Antoinette was not of those who give thanks, primarily if not solely, for benefits that they have received. She gave thanks for the divine splendour of such mysteries as that of the Blessed Trinity and for her God-given right to share in them.

Thanksgiving for communion with God through Jesus, the divine Mediator, leads on to that unity between Christ and those who are members of Christ.

Thanksgiving in another of its aspects was treated with rare precision and impressive logic in the following letter of Marie de la Trinité :

' When we give thanks and thereby glorify him, we attain to our own highest happiness. Seemingly this detracts from the merit of our canticle of love. For as our heart's desire is for his greater glory, when we are wistful for any other thing, we apparently turn from our " unique necessity." In truth, as we quickly perceive, by this is our gratitude made perfect in humility—made rich in the " increase " given to those who " seek only the kingdom of God," and to whom all things are added. Nor does this enrichment turn our gratitude from its true end, since the glory

that the Father has of his children and the blessedness
that he makes theirs are one and the same.'

Her serene trust.

Marie de la Trinité was as serene in her trust as she
was large in her soul. In her surrender to God there
were no reserves. She wrote :

'If sinners and the indifferent and discouraged
would but abandon themselves to the powerful love of
God, what serenity would be theirs ! If they could
but see that God is all in all, how at a stroke they
would break the chains that shackle them to earth,
and be made free of their heritage in the infinite ! '

Or again :

'Joy is but half. What matters if, when we drink,
the taste in our mouth be bitter, since it is Jesus himself
who proffers the golden cup ? '

In her self-criticism she was thoroughly likeable :

'I once knew a girl—I had the very best reason for
knowing her who at the smallest slip in her climb
towards perfection gave way to a despairing belief
that all was lost. How stupid she was ! Because of
this particular stupidity one of her uncles used to call
her " Miss Neck-or-Nothing."

'Did such teasing influence her ? I do not know.
I only know that a day came when this girl had no
other wish than to give all to him and to accept all
at his hands. From that day this particular stupidity
left her. With all her desires turned towards God, she
perceived none but God, and was at peace. Even
so, had she examined her subsequent life, she might
well have been dismayed. Yet what would her dismay
have profited her, since he is concerned less with
achievement than with endeavour ? He asks no more
than that we shall love him with all our soul during
all our days.'

To Pontoise on April 1, 1913, she wrote of the soul's escape to God :

' My suffering is not my own concern, but his. My concern is to be wholly occupied in him. When either melancholy or pain troubles my soul, at once I flee to him as to a sanctuary. It is surely true that to know unchanging peace we must walk this earth, asking for no support from it, putting out into it no roots ; content to lean on God alone. Find all your need in him ; have no need that lies outside him : surely here is the secret of happiness.

' Often I have been unsettled of soul. Life has seemed a vanity and the earth a void. Then I would reflect : he is there, my Father, my God, my guide, my Jesus, infinite love himself. At once my path would be made plain before me : it was to do his will, helped by his omnipotent power, made strong in his infinite love. Straightway life seemed no longer a vanity, nor the earth a void. For my concern is with God, who fills all the earth with his living love.'

Marie de la Trinité was not of those who, making spiritual mountains out of spiritual molehills, imagine that some small fault is sufficient to make God turn his back upon them :

' My insignificance does not divide me from God. " The lowly shall be exalted : " he has made this true of me also. Compared with the infinite majesty of God, between a great and a little soul what distinction exists ? In the infinite loving-kindness of the Father the sins of Mary Magdalen disappear equally with the mere human weakness of Martha, the sins of the prodigal son equally with the lesser failings of his brother.' (Pontoise, Dec. 26, 1912.)

Nor was she of those others, who, spending themselves to do what good they may, yet live in agonised dread of

purgatory and of hell itself. In fact this whimsical
exclamation was reported of her : " Purgatory—hell :
they are the baby brother among my soul's fears ! "
It was a significant saying. For her God was loving-
kindness before all things. With what might happen to
her after death she did not concern herself. God's will
would be done. Meanwhile she would seek to do
what should please him. Her soul and its fate she
was content to leave wholly in his hands. To Marie-
Marthe, on November 22, 1917, she wrote with happy
picturesqueness :

'Do you know what floating is ? It is the resource
of those who cannot swim and yet who would not
sink. To float successfully all you need to do is to lie
straight and still upon the surface of the water. The
one essential is that you shall not be afraid. So with
the soul. When hope is gone, hope on. It is the
easiest thing in the world. Trust blindly, abandon
yourself in utter fearlessness to the Father ; his arms
shall hold you up.'

Weakened by illness, temperamentally a lover of
solitude, Marie de la Trinité might easily have become
unhealthily introspective. But there was no sickliness
in the soul housed in her sick body. While she avoided
introspection, instructed by her uncle (and director) she
found in self-examination one of the bases of piety. Yet
she kept her sense of spiritual perspective ; she knew
the danger that the sixpence of the self, held too close
to the eye of the soul, might blot out the sun which is
God. Thus, two years before her death she wrote :

'Self-knowledge without doubt is an aid to holiness.
Equally without doubt self-knowledge seldom comes
of self-dissection. Contemplation of him who is our
ideal is an immeasurably better method. For by
using it we become acquainted with the differences

which divide us from our ideal. The more we know Christ, the more we are aware that he is all and that we are nothing.

'We have no need to look behind us for wisdom. He is before us; wisdom and the opportunities to practise it await us at his side. Nor have we need to calculate how long may be the cords that bind us to the nothingness of evil, or how best they may be broken. We have but to make the leap of love that shall carry us to the Father, in order to break those cords and to gain the all which is Christ Jesus.'

March 13, 1917, the date of this letter, needs to be noted. The letter was written when Marie de la Trinité had attained to that unity with God, which her soul coveted.

CHAPTER THE SIXTH

THE SAINT MADE MANIFEST

WHEN it seems that a man, or above all a girl, is being led in the extraordinary ways, an opinion should be formed only after great caution has been exercised. What, then, are the signs of the true saint?

First, there are these human qualities—uprightness, sincerity, generosity, sanity of mind, freedom from passion, inclination towards the high and the holy allied to a desire to be no more privileged of God than other men, true humility, the possession of a sensitive conscience. Secondly, that mystical ability which has been possessed by all the great contemplatives without exception—the ability to synthesise all these qualities into a harmonious whole that manifests the divine wisdom, and argues (in him or her who possesses this ability) the attainment of a degree of spiritual perfection that is above the common.

In Consummata all these signs were in evidence.

1 *Simplicity, Candour, Humility*

On November 21, 1908, Marie-Antoinette wrote:

'During Benediction I experienced an inexpressible sense of unity with God. I know neither how I was exalted, nor how long my exaltation lasted, nor what I felt during this exaltation, nor whether my body shared in it. I only know that, coming out of it, I

cried impulsively : " Withhold such blessedness from
me, O God, if to withhold it will not take from your
glory. Give me rather suffering, and no other thing
but that."

' I have never before known such illumination of
soul. It was a promise of the ultimate, unutterable
union with God himself. (Yet it was not that
union.) May he whom I adore grant to me the right
to suffer for his sake, and reserve to others such
surpassing joy ! My sole desire is to be one with
Jesus Crucified. I would come to him by the road
that all men tread.'

The last sentence could scarcely be more explicit, or
more eloquent in its testimony that she possessed one of
the qualities specified.

Her deepest experiences she kept hidden from all
except her directors—and much more occasionally a
tried friend who needed her spiritual help, or who was
worthy of her apostolic confidences. When the first
extracts from her notebooks and letters were published,
her brothers, the youngest among them in especial, were
amazed. To them she was the Big Sister, whose soul
was noble (they knew), but whose soul's strength (they
thought) was drawn far more from earth than from
heaven. Her reticence did her honour. It was only in
1915, when she came near to death, that certain words
and expressions escaped her, hinting at that ' secret of
the King,' in which she shared.

It is notable that, at times when her mystical life was
most exalted, the good counsel which she gave to others
concerned itself with practical prayer and the daily life
of men. Thus to her brother Louis, on June 19, 1912,
she wrote :

' On the day of your name-saint (S. Aloysius) I
would have you be in the Society of Jesus what
Thérèse de l'Enfant-Jésus is to Carmel ; that is, I

would have you reveal in the daily round the heroic qualities revealed by the great saints.'

Again to Louis (in August 1912) who had asked her for advice in regard to prayer :

' How should you meditate ? Myself, I use but one of all the methods advocated by S. Ignatius and the other saints. First, I read the Gospel (or other) text upon which I mean to meditate ; second, I think of the context ; third, I ask God for his special grace in regard to it ; fourth, I think deeply of all that the text involves, and finish by a talk or an intimate discussion with Our Lord.

' My first, second and third, if I may say so, are but the bones of meditation. My fourth is the living blood. Confronted with Jesus, I put to myself such questions as : Can my way of life be reconciled with the teaching of this text ? If not, what can reconcile them ; in what does my life fail ? Thus I seek to strengthen my love and my courage, that they may either accomplish or accept what sacrifice may now or later be demanded of them.'

Again :

' We meditate solely that we may come to God. Methods of meditation are but devices adopted that we may without too great dallying arrive at our goal. When suddenly the soul knows transfiguration, then methods have served their purpose, and need to be discarded. When his grace is upon us, we must obey its dictates. So shall we find God.

' I have sometimes blundered by constraining myself to meditate upon a subject prepared in advance. It is not with meditation as it is with life : the verse which attracts us at the moment is the verse upon which we should ponder. In meditation preparation by us is, as it were, dictation to him. In my own case he would have me know that not upon me but upon him all things depend. To do his will we need to be docile as well as whole-hearted, even though the way by which we are led be both narrow and steep.

'At the moment when, in the words of a saint, "meditation becomes mortification," we need most to be fervent and faithful. For the greater the difficulties which we overcome upon our road to perfection, the more rapid is our advance upon it. Since S. Ignatius has prescribed it before me, you do not need me to do more than indicate to you his wise and practical counsel to be followed when meditation seems laborious ; in that case (he bade) make your meditation not five minutes shorter but five minutes longer.'

This passage illustrated happily the spiritual sanity of Marie de la Trinité. On the one hand she did not scorn to learn the use of tools, before she began to work with them. On the other, she knew when to discard a particular tool for one more delicate. She knew when life should be done with leading-strings, just as she knew that the Holy Ghost must not be expected always to keep to the trodden paths of men.

She was aware that to herself prayer was not given for the delight which it brings to the soul, or for the peace which comes of resting tranquilly in God, but for the purpose of preparing her to face with loving generosity the necessary sacrifices involved in the daily round. Thus :

'Normally I seek but the one end : in meditation to strengthen my love and with new courage to win through love still closer to him. As strength is given to me, the ideal before me grows still more lofty and luminous. Love and self-denial are surely alternate rungs in the ladder which leads to God. For at each act of self-denial our love is increased, and with each

new degree of love made ours, we are given the strength
to deny ourselves further.'

The date of the above letter—August 29, 1912—gives
it a special value. At this time, as during the previous
seven weeks, she had attained to the highest peaks of
the mystical life. Her notes on things of the spirit, her
letters to the uncle who was her director, brimmed over
with joyousness. Such restraint shown at such a juncture
revealed a remarkable discretion, itself an evidence that
Marie de la Trinité's mysticism was authentic.

In what she said and what she did, she asked for
guidance. For in her was neither vanity, nor pride, nor
that egoism that tends to heresy.

Even in those periods of her greatest spiritual exaltation she begged for guidance, convinced that she could
not safely guide herself. She never wrote for the sake
of writing. Her note was sober, her statement precise.
When she had said what, as she believed, she had been
called upon to say, she made an end. It was she who
held the pen ; it was a greater than she who directed it.

Her humility was consistent. Thus the letter last
quoted finished :

' Remember, Louis, that I have never passed
through a novitiate. In consequence all that I say
to you is wholly tentative, except in so far as it is not
I who write, but another and infinitely wiser than I.
Before you accept them, these ideas, set down in
simplicity by me, must in each case have your own
soul's approval.'

Truly humble, she did more than merely distrust her
own judgement. In the good which she sought to do,
it grieved her to see (in her own phrase) ' Grace come
to others a little soiled through contact with herself.'
It distressed her to think that there were some who
' did not know what evil inclinations she had.'   Her

consistent aim was ' to do as the others did,' and so to move undistinguished among them. She sought to be ' more imitable than admirable ' ; and again ' out of humble-mindedness to give up my preference for simplicity, and to pretend to a little more vanity than I possess, if this make for the pleasure of others ' ; or, lastly, ' to accept the humiliation of being esteemed far too highly ; to accept praise as if it gave me pleasure. God knows how truly wretched I am made by such praise and over-esteem. Yet to hide my wretchedness is the better part.'[1]

How did she consider that she looked to God ? Continually she refers to herself as ' his poor little nobody.' The phrase expresses precisely her sincere conviction. In her unpublished notes this passage occurs :

' In Dec. 1907, wishing supremely to glorify God, and unable because of my unworthiness to gratify my wish, I begged Jesus himself to make me holier. If he give me my wish, as I ardently hope that he will, his will be the merit no less than the glory, which my greater worthiness shall serve.

' His answer was long in coming, but oh, the joy when it came ! A year later he made it known to me that he wished me to be holier and that, if I yet wished it, I had only to follow him and he would make the rest his care. As in my pitiable self there is no possibility of holiness, he will destroy this self utterly, that he may substitute himself for me. Thus will my great God of love have of his poor little nobody all the glory that is his through Jesus, while in that glory I shall have no part at all. Of me there is nothing left, but only Jesus. And it is he that is my holiness.'

[1] Written during the 1907 retreat which was completed in 1909.

In August 1913, she concluded a letter to Pontoise thus :

'You bid your little novice tell you her faults. Well then, despite her efforts to control her evil inclinations, she is too often far from lovable, while frequently words escape her in which is neither sweetness nor grace. The infinite charity of Christ is in her soul, but temperamentally she appears to be afraid for it to be seen there. The " pitcher of clay " will need to be broken beyond repair, before discovery is made of the divine treasure within it. I care for the welfare of men's souls, and I am afraid to let them see that I care.'

She had written previously :

' Pride is the biggest barrier between me and that union with God for which I yearn. Just now I am trying to steep myself in humility and to realise that the old self will need to be utterly destroyed within me.'

She continued :

' Recently a girl friend and I were working together. I sketched ; she painted. Knowing that she could sketch better than I, I suggested that she should try her hand at sketching also. She would not be persuaded, since (she said) she was not sure that she could sketch well, while she undertook nothing at which she was not certain to succeed.

' What an exposure of my own inferiority ! For in nothing that I undertake am I sure that I shall succeed. So if I acted on these lines, I should do nothing. When I feel it in my bones that what I need to do I shall do badly, I put into it all the love and the courage that I have in me. I do it, I am convinced, worse than badly. In the end all I can do is to thank God for the sense of humiliation that he has sent me ! '

H

A memory of Chémouteau would visit her :

' In our part of the country the woods are cut
yearly. The tall sturdy oaks bring in some small
profit. Their purchaser makes use of them now for
building purposes, now for making furniture. In the
copses is brushwood—commercially it has no value—
that is tied in bundles and the farm hands use as
firewood to keep them warm in winter-time. In
God's eyes the Church is assuredly like a wood of tall
trees. Of those more lofty souls, whom merit signal-
ises, God makes use in the great edifice of his glory.
As for those insignificant souls that are of little value
and less use, in order that they may not be wasted,
God burns them in his love. It is their lot to be
wholly consumed that others may be warmed by the
fire of love with which they burn, and which God
shall spread till it cover the whole earth. Among
these meaner souls your little novice is surely to be
numbered.

' This evening I seem to be writing you a story-book
rather than a letter ! I have stayed so long in my
room, that mother will think that I have flitted to
Carmel ! '

To her brother Louis, on July 19, 1914, she wrote
of the great value of secret sacrifice :

' Would that you shared in the secrets of that love
which lies at the heart of sacrifice—above all of
sacrifice that is made in secret. To some God sends
great sorrows at which all men marvel. I do not
speak of these, but of those little sacrificial acts that
bring God's peace to the soul. Trifles like these :
silence kept when one word would justify us in others'
eyes or would win us their (perhaps too high) esteem ;
small services rendered to others who will never
know of them ; good done or pleasure given and our
own identity as doer or giver concealed ; small

kindnesses performed as though the obligation and the pleasure were wholly ours ; in a word, all those little things that Jesus alone sees and that men often misunderstand.'

After the death of her airman brother Georges, seeking to honour his memory, unwittingly she revealed herself :

' When I was very ill indeed, he came to me and with a touching simplicity asked me this question : " Little sister, when one is about to die, what deeds, remembered then, bring contentment ? " I answered him : " When one is about to die, my Georges, it is the memory of trifling things, performed for none but God and with none but God for witness, that bring one pleasure." And from that time forward he sought most zealously to hide from us all everything that might do him credit in our eyes.

' Now he is dead. And comfort comes to us in haphazard ways. Strangers bring it, or the recollection of a chance word of his own.' (October 29, 1916.)

A pleasant cross-section of sister and brother alike !

II *Faithfulness—Renunciation*

Direct communion with God alone can explain the wisdom of soul which Consummata possessed, as the great contemplative saints possessed it before her.

Fidelity in every day tasks—renunciation in the spiritual life ; these are the authentic signs of that saintliness which is born of prayer.

In that they have lived their daily lives in accordance with the bidding of their diviner impulses, all true mystics have been ascetics. The more straitly a mystic walks in the paths in which God has set his feet, the more completely he practises renunciation, extolling it and making it his life. S. Francis of Assisi, the greatest contemplative of the Middle Ages, declared : ' Self-conquest and willingness to suffer shame glad-heartedly for Christ's sake and for the sake of the love of God are of all the gifts of the Holy Ghost which Christ has made to his friends the most precious.' Three centuries later S. John of the Cross echoed this : ' However high be your endeavours, unless you renounce and subjugate your own will—unless you forget yourself and all that concerns yourself—not one step will you advance upon the road to perfection.' And lastly, S. Ignatius : ' Self-conquest is a greater achievement than the raising of a man from the dead.'

To Thérèse, her cousin, on February 9, 1917, Marie-Antoinette generalised upon this subject with character-istic skill :

' Each of us is like a poor wretch whose miserable home the divine artist intends to transfigure and make glorious. Let but the cottage door be flung wide—the Master be permitted to set to work—and straight-way the hovel is transformed into a palace. Whose but God's is the achievement ? The poor cottager, thus made rich, is aware that his riches are a free gift, and not the reward of his own effort ; for he has had no share in the work, no share at all.

' One compulsion only is laid upon him. It is a bagatelle, and yet it is a bagatelle of immense impor-tance. He must open the door. That is, he must open his heart to the grace of God, and welcome all his behests. He must open the door—open it wide ; open it without delay. So should we too allow him to set to work ; be willing to see our old house de-stroyed before our eyes, and his will made paramount in all things. In this there is no merit for us—only the duty of fidelity.

' God's part and man's differ. Each is wholly

responsible for his own. Unless we fail him, God never fails us. In that which makes us holy, our part is as essential as it is negligible.'

' Whose but God's is the achievement ? '—there spoke Marie de la Trinité's profound humility. ' Our part is as essential '—and there her complete fidelity. From her earliest years she cultivated both the one and the other. The graver temptations did not assail her. The lesser trials of the daily round she turned to triumphs of non-resistance to God's will :

' I do what God demands of me. Because I do no more, and because of the joy and the grace which are my reward, I blame myself as a faint-heart.' (To Pontoise, June 16, 1910.)

' I have begun the *Canticle* of S. John of the Cross. The book inspires me. No one makes plainer the need to conquer self, if union with Jesus, the Beloved, is to be attained. Just now especially, I realise that he demands all of me ; ceaselessly I seek to kill the self, which as ceaselessly revives in me. Despite my efforts frail human nature persists, constantly crying out against the suffering which it is called upon to bear. At such times, weak and wretched, I throw myself into the Father's arms, and am comforted by his fatherly care, and made once more confident by his loving-kindness.' (Written in July 1912.)

Many can be faithful through brief hours of insight ; fewer keep their fidelity through long hours of gloom, when spiritual cowardice finds them lax or leaves them vulnerable. Marie de la Trinité was not of these. Her letters are separate notes in one great harmony, with this for theme ; she would give herself freely, and yet more freely, to her God.

' To his little host of praise Jesus gives suffering ever more abundantly. My gratitude grows daily, as daily

I appreciate more how admirably he is teaching me all the little secrets of renunciation's better part. How simple are those secrets. To forsake all that is not of God ; to lean only upon God himself.

'The flesh in its frailty is often protestant. But the soul, made rich and full in God alone, has of him a hundredfold increase. The bitter turns to the sweet. The hard rind of sacrifice is but the covering of the rare fruit which is God.' (To Pontoise, July 11, 1913.)

Some suppose that noble souls live above the battle : that God has made them what they are without cost to themselves : that in them is no natural frailty, but only the supernatural promise which shall later turn to the ripeness of achieved perfection. The comforting truth is otherwise.

As has been admitted already, as a child Marie-Antoinette was far from amenable. As she grew older, she made courageous attempts to improve herself. In this she was not immediately successful. She had her faults—and God made use of them.

Thus she had an almost fanatical liking for orderliness. If anything in her room were untidy or out of place, she was distressed, and would frequently make complaints. By servants she was deemed exacting : though they had much respect for her, they had also a little fear. It needed great and persistent effort on her part to discipline this fanaticism, so that its fundamental good was kept but its incidental evil—its too great rigidity—was shed.

Again, during illness she could be stubborn towards her doctors and nurses. If she thought fit, she would refuse outright to follow a particular course of treatment. This was no very grave fault. She had, it was true, made God's will her law. But God's will and doctors' prescriptions are not necessarily synonymous. This particularly applies in so difficult a case as Marie-

Antoinette's, when, perplexed, doctors hesitate, give conflicting opinions or impossible advice. They were thorns in the flesh of this girl, who loved wisdom and had to struggle to suffer fools gladly. Nor was it her flesh only that suffered. She suffered in spirit, troubled by conviction of her flesh's frailty.

Then there was the food difficulty. They wanted her to eat more. This was unfortunate. For often she had an almost invincible dislike of eating anything. In her serious illness of 1915, crusts dipped in water were frequently all the food that she ate ; for these alone (she declared) did not nauseate her.

Those who have known similar states of mind, whether in themselves or in others, will understand the indecision, the mental struggles and the spiritual agonies, in which they may involve any who seek greater purity or a nearer approach to perfection.

If her human weakness brought some small spiritual set-back, her resolution did not fail her. For she was neither fool nor coward.

'If through lack of fidelity we lose ground, by humility we can regain it. For God, who is our Father, out of his mercy wills it so. We have but to avail ourselves of his mercy.' (To Marie-Marthe, July 1917.)

Marie-Antoinette was not content with spiritual renunciation. For the sake of complete self-conquest and despite her health's delicacy, she mortified her body. Thus, her youngest sister related, not without humour, the discovery which she chanced to make : ' In the year of my first Communion I was sleeping in Nénette's room. At night, when she thought me asleep, I watched her whip herself with no light hand. I did not understand that this was penitential scourging, until, telling one of my young brothers in the strictest confidence of what I had seen, he explained that the saints were wont to mortify themselves in this manner. Astonished and admiring, he listened that night outside the bedroom door. From that time on, our respect for Nénette grew deeper ; for we began to understand that she was not as most folk are.'

Their big sister never suspected their discovery, or she would have ceased the practice. She was not deluded into thinking that such physical austerities were other than a means to an end, or that they exempted her from more useful, if less picturesque, obligations. Nevertheless, the incident has its interest, and its narration value.

For her things of the spirit mattered infinitely more. In turn she surrendered human affection, personal inclination and, by piling renunciation on renunciation, even her highest vocational call. To prolonged prayer she always preferred the continuous adjustment of her will to the careful fulfilling of her duty. She made no grudging surrender of spiritual delight :

' I have,' she wrote, ' so often given up my soul's joys, that I no longer look to have more of them.'

As ungrudgingly she made sacrifice of her proper pride, and of her own desires in regard to those things for which she prayed or denied herself. Finally, these resolutions made by her for her two retreats of 1907-8 are well worth study :

—Never to be influenced by first impressions.
—Never to relax in a task till the last minute assigned to it has been used in its performance.
—Never to fail to use my time to the best advantage and in the service only of God, and to spend all my courage and all my love in so using it.
—Never to shrink from a sacrifice, but always to seek it out.
—Never to procrastinate.

—Never to allow myself a purposeless pleasure.

—Never to day-dream ; always to repress my earthly inclinations.

—Never to cease my efforts to become joyous, tranquil, gentle, lovable. In this to put all my mind and all my strength.

These resolutions were the badges of a brave, of a more than brave, of a heroic spirit. This girl knew her weaknesses. She fought and conquered them. She won to blessedness by surrendering her will wholly to God's. Thus on April 17, 1913, she wrote :

' Intimate union with God demands a complete denial of self, a life lived only in him and to his glory, a ceaseless self-adjustment to his holy will and as ceaseless a refusal to consult our own, if it conflict with his. To make his will ours ; to confound our will in his : this should surely be our ideal, however difficult of attainment it may prove.'

Marie de la Trinité burned most of her outlines for meditations. This upon the will of God has, however, been preserved :

The Will of God

1st preliminary : To place myself in the presence of God ;

2nd preliminary : To pray to God that his adorable will be in all things fulfilled.

1st point. *The Importance of God's Will.*

' My life has but one end—to give God all the glory which he asks of me—and but one means of achieving this end : to do God's will in all things.

' The will of God serves alike his glory and my own and others' greatest good. My great need to realise the importance of God's will : in it is the whole secret of the highest holiness, which he most manifests, who most faithfully performs the will of God.

'That soul is ripest and most perfect which most fully performs God's will.

'God's most holy will is that of Jesus who, on coming into the world, cried : *Pater, ecce venio ut faciam voluntatem tuam.* In those words he declared all his mission.'

2nd point.   *The Obstacles to God's Will.*

'Two things prevent my performance of God's will. Either I fail to recognise it, or, recognising it, I have not the courage to do it.

'To remove these two obstacles I will meditate. Meditation is not an intellectual exercise, but an exercise in love, designed to increase love. I will perform this exercise in love. Love will light my path, even as it gives me strength to pursue it.

'To know what may be God's will, I will seek tranquillity of soul. Unless a lake be perfectly tranquil, it cannot faithfully reflect the sky. A clear mirror is not enough ; the eyes that look into it must be as clear with health. I will seek then to make my intention wholly pure and to see all things from the perspective of God's glory. Made acquainted with God's will, I will strengthen my love by those meditations most calculated to give me the courage to do his will.

'God at no time withholds either guidance or strength. (The blind are usually those who do not wish to see, lest they shall perceive some sacrifice that God asks of them, and that they are unwilling to make.) If I seek sincerely that which he asks of me, he will make it known to me. As I do what he demands of me, he will demand yet more ; he will disclose an ideal yet loftier than the old. So, as S. Paul held, advancing from enlightenment to enlightenment, I shall be re-made " in his own image." '

3rd point. *The Happiness involved in doing God's Will.*

' Thus the Father's will shall become my soul's sustenance. By faith and love brought into close union with him, on earth I shall find heaven. When I am tempted or forlorn, I shall be able to say, as Jesus said : " He has not left me alone ; for I do always that which pleases him." Or, with S. Paul, that we have been born in Jesus Christ to perform those good works, which God has prepared beforehand for our performance. These " good works " are no other than his holy will. I will never forget that I have " a good work " to do—a good work " prepared beforehand " by the supreme wisdom and infinite love of the Father. I will reflect that though, omnipotent as he is, he could have given me many other things to do, out of them all he has made choice of that which best will serve his glory and my own and others' greatest good.

' I will be as glad and as grateful to do his will in the smallest matters, as I am to accept the supreme gift of his love. With God's will made my will at last, at last I shall understand Isaias : " You shall be known as she in whom my will is done ; in you the Lord shall be well pleased ; in you the Lord shall take joy." '

There is evidence that Marie de la Trinité did in her life realise this idea. Thus : ' It has been said that God's will is the A B C of the Christian life. Is it not also perfection's last word ? ' was once her question ; while on March 30, 1914, she made this further confession :

' Increasingly obsessed by the divine will, increasingly I fail to see the difference between suffering and joy. For me nothing has importance save the Father's will.'

To do the duty of to-day and every day is our surest road to blessedness. To her Jesuit brother she wrote :

'Since it is God's will that you shall study, for you study is not merely hallowed, but hallowed as no other thing may be. We should, it seems to me, never think that in another situation, or in other circumstances, we should have more opportunity to practise virtue and to make spiritual progress. God is our infinitely wise Father. For us there can be no more blessed, no more glorious, choice than his.'

This letter concluded with the thought expressed in the third point of the outline of meditation already set down here.

The complete surrender to God, which Consummata urged, in no way stunts the soul's activities. It is true that we must have no will save to do his will, and as true that, when we do his will, we must do it with all our heart and with all our strength. She stressed this repeatedly :

'My life may seem to you enviable for its peacefulness. On that account you need not envy it. Whatever the particular vocation, in following it no talent can be left unused. The vocation most faithfully followed must use every talent to the Father's advantage and for his greater glory. To obey such a call to holiness requires effort : the self must die before the soul can know union with God. However many the means, there is but one end.' (April 17, 1913.)

Marie de la Trinité was to become a notable mystic ; she was to receive from God his highest favours—the gift of infused contemplation, the ecstasy of intimate union with himself. Yet throughout, her energy in action was remarkable. Effort, action, self-conquest : these were the recurrent beads on her life's thread.

Though renunciation does not of itself lead to obtaining mystical graces, yet, if God be pleased to confer them, renunciation enables the mystic to make full use of God's gift.

Mystic as she was, Marie de la Trinité exalted the workings of God's grace :

' Do you know that saying of S. Ignatius, Act as if all depended upon yourself ; leave the consequences of action, as if all depended upon God alone. These may not be the exact words, but is not the thought expressed a valuable rule for conduct ? Is it not the call to a complete surrender of self ? Truly God cannot work his will with us, unless we put all our energies at the disposal of his will.' (To Marie-Marthe, April 23, 1917.)

She continued :

' In action inspired by love we need to spend all our powers to do his will. For since we love him, our one desire is that " all that is in us shall glorify his holy name." In our communion with him acts of love best manifest the grace which he has given us.

' So, Marthe, your name is surely in perfect tune with your vocation. It is for you to be active in all that makes for your sanctification. Jesus and Mary will abundantly add to your blessings.

' Will you not seek to be Marie-Marthe de Jésus ?

' Mary and Martha—the two complementary names make one perfect symbol, the symbol of works wedded to the contemplative life—of the soul surrendered to God's grace. To Mary Martha will give energy ; to Martha Mary will bring peace. There surely is holiness at its highest ; an undying fire of love, a beauty of unshaken peace.

' Do but meditate upon this name, and to what far-off and splendid heights will not your meditations sweep you ? Through grace to serve his greater glory, by love and actions performed in love to come to perfection through the grace of Jesus! To be Mary and to be Martha both! To be " Marie-Marthe de Jésus ! " '

This ideal that Marie de la Trinité held up to her Carmelite cousin was her own ideal. She did not passively take; she actively gave. She spent herself for God, that he might work his will with her. There could be no better guarantee of the quality of her contemplation. For true contemplation has its springs in the high peaks of sacrifice and the strong, courageous devotion of the soul to the furtherance of God's purposes.

The Great War was to give Marie de la Trinité a supreme opportunity to reveal her faithfulness to God and her complete submission to his will, not only in the small heroisms of everyday life but in that pure heroism demanded of the times :

> ' There could be no better time than this for sacrifice of self. These are days of universal slaughter. In what better days could we seek to become a host of praise, a holocaust of God ? ' (To her cousin, October 29, 1914.)

Again :

> ' You ask about my health. I may recover ; I may die. The disease very slowly gains ground. In my utter uncertainty I abandon myself blindly to the arms of the Father. And there could be no better thing than that. Give thanks on my account.' (To her friend, February 28, 1915.)

As she grew in pure spirituality, she remembered always that to love is to have the will to love and not necessarily to have the experience of loving :

> ' Do not fear, little sister, that you may fail to do all that he wishes you to do. Because you long to do

all, you *will* do all. In the small matters of life God is
no busybody. With him it is our heart's intention that
counts. Once our souls are aware of his will, he will
win their consent to it.'

Event followed event. News came of the death of her
much loved airman brother Georges. She did not
give way to her heart's grief. Her calm was so complete,
her resignation was so remarkable, that those less dis-
ciplined in their emotions might well feel outraged by
her lack of demonstrativeness. First stressing the need
' in love to submit to God's good pleasure in all things,'
she wrote to Thérèse :

' How good to love him, putting no bounds to our
love and without reservation to surrender ourselves to
his adorable will. In time all our desires will, thus
simply, know satisfaction.'

Thus poignantly she continued :

' Little sister, I have something to ask of you. Of
your goodness and your charity pray for my intention.
Georges is dead. I loved him very much. He died
in an air duel on September 17. His enemies out-
numbered him. One of them he shot down.'

Finally, her heart's human affection exquisitely
interpenetrating her soul's love of God, she concluded :

' Yes, I loved him very much, this young brother of
mine. Yet how good for me is God's will ! He takes
from me what my heart loved tenderly, that my love
may leap to embrace his will, nor know the smallest
bitterness at the sacrifice demanded of it.'

Here is sorrow not recollected, but sustained, in
tranquillity. There could be no better revelation of
Marie de la Trinité's vigorous virtue than that in these
lines with their pitifulness and their restraint.

Her spirit's amazing generosity was further illustrated in her note of October 22, 1916, to her cousins Thérèse and Marthe :

'Hubert has visited the headquarters of the "fighter" air-squadrons. There he heard regrets expressed that on the 17th Georges did not refuse to take out a plane other than his own—a special machine of the latest type. It is usual, it seems, for "cracks" like Georges to refuse to fly ordinary planes. On the day of his death Georges's own machine was still under repair ; it had been damaged by shell-fire. When called upon he flew the ordinary Nieuport ; this cost him his life. They regretted that he had not waited for his own machine, when (they said) he might have been alive to-day. For us, we do not regret it. He died, because he obeyed. His obedience is the best consolation that we have.'

S. Ignatius recognised three degrees of fidelity ;[1] fidelity to God's will in great things, in which unfaithfulness would be mortal sin ; fidelity in small things ; fidelity to an aspect of God's will, as a particular soul perceives it. Georges's fidelity came into the second of these categories—if into that. 'Better to know him dead,' declared Marie de la Trinité, 'than to think of him as disobedient to the will or the desire of God !'

When her brother Louis, Jesuit and artillery bombardier, had both legs crushed at his observation post at Nieuport, she wrote (on April 8, 1916) to the Reverend Mother at Pontoise :

'When this reaches you, I beg your prayers and those of the community for our Louis, who has been grievously wounded.

'Let us adore the will of our great God of love, now and for ever worthy of our praise. When our

[1] 'Humility' in the *Exercises*. But the meaning is clear.

dearest hopes lie broken beneath his feet—hopes that
we cherished only for his glory—then above all is he
to be adored. For not to us, but to him, is best known
what most shall glorify him. May our heavenly
Father achieve his blessed purpose in my beloved
brother, before he takes him to himself ! May he
spare him to us, if that be his will, and if it serve his
greater glory !

'May his will know perfect realisation in all things !
May honour be paid to him now and for ever !

'Marie de la Trinité.'

'It is for us to sing *Alleluia*, since even now my
beloved young brother may be singing it in heaven.
He and I have been very near and very dear to one
another. The day will come, when we shall meet,
never again to part. I look forward to that day.'

In the history of the Saints is there to be found a
nobler serenity than this ?

Again to Pontoise, on April 12, 1916 :

'A brief note to thank you and to give you news of
my poor young brother.

'They have amputated both legs to the thighs. He
is exceedingly plucky, they tell us, and there is still
some small hope that his life may be saved. What joy
for us—what indulgence on God's part—if it be his
will that this martyred life shall be spared for his
glory's sake ! His martyrdom will be less a martyrdom
of suffering than a martyrdom of love ; for the cross
is altogether dear to his heart. For him there is no
sacrifice but this : the loss of his priestly calling.
May this, his greatest sorrow, prove the inspiration
of many noble vocations ! '

And in conclusion :

'I exult in your handiwork, O God ! How mighty

I

are the works of your hands ! How sublime your mind's conceptions !

'There, my Mother, you have the breath of your little Marie de la Trinité's life. The will of her God so absorbs her, that in her all desire is dead, save the desire to see his will performed. On Louis, I confess, I had set my greatest hopes for God's glory. Yet I longed to see Louis a priest, only because that seemed to me most to make for his glory. His will be done ! For so his glory will best be served. I do not suffer, though my dearest hopes lie broken beneath his feet. And yet not broken ; for they will have a fulfilment that as yet we cannot conceive. *Per tuas semitas, duc nos quo tendimus ad lucem quam inhabitas.* By your paths, O God of wisdom and of love ; for they alone are holy, as they alone lead whither we would go ; of your own glory be yours all the glory and all the love which you desire ! '

On September 8, 1910, Marie de la Trinité had made the vow of self-surrender to God. With her the vow was more than a vow. It was to be written across the pages of her life ; while on those pages some of the letters were to be letters of blood.

'I have vowed to do God's will in all things. The vow makes me not bond but free. For God's grace comes of it. In it there is only gain. Or if there be loss, it is because we do not sufficiently believe in the working within us of God's grace.' (To Marie-Marthe, July 1, 1917.)

Again (to her aunt, also a Carmelite of Le Mans):

'How good to realise that God's will alone is desirable ! That the more we are crucified by it, the more is his glory served ! How in that simple thought dwells the peace that passes understanding ! '

CHAPTER THE SEVENTH

GRACES IN PRAYER

G OD initiates; the soul responds to his love's initial call. Even so the soul retains its independence; for its response, whether eager or reluctant, depends upon itself.

Marie de la Trinité gave herself heart and soul to the work of her sanctification through God. The mystical gifts which God heaped upon her were so much the more potent because of her exceptional asceticism. It was the considered opinion of one of no mean authority—he was instructor at his Institute of ' Fathers of the third year '—that ' the degree of mystical union to which she had attained could not easily have been surpassed on earth.'

1 *First Contacts with God*

These are not conjectural. Under the title, ' God's Mercies,' Consummata set down the principal divine favours received by her from the time of her first Communion till 1912, that is to say, from her eleventh to her twenty-third year.

'June 14, 1900; my first Communion. I was as if lost. Marthe (her cousin) tugged at my dress. For I no longer knew what answers I was making.'

Probably this was not the first occasion on which she had known such rapt absorption. Thus this letter to Pontoise related specifically to an earlier period :

' I cannot remember a time when I did not yearn to give myself wholly to God and to suffer for his love. As I grew older and my yearning for Jesus stronger, it was my regret that I could not follow him by surrendering myself to him utterly.' (June 16, 1910.)

To resume : ' Feb. 2-7, 1902 : *Take up my cross. The will of God.*'

At this time she was only thirteen years old. Yet these two phrases were more than the simple pieties set down as reminders by a young girl, already earnest of mind and serious of disposition. Later, immediately before she died, one of her young brothers at her request burned many of her papers. But this particular note, with others, she then gave to her mother, remarking that she alone knew, guided by certain pencil indications, the varying richness of spiritual experience which these notes recorded.

When she first made known that, as she believed, she had a vocation for the religious life, she was definitely discouraged. This was when she was about fourteen and a half years old—in 1903-4—and the upshot was the decision that she would follow the ordinary way. Disconsolate as she was, she revealed that good sense which she retained even at the time of her greatest mystical exaltations. For she wrote : ' Before all, I must correct my faults, so that at least I may become a good Christian.'

It was characteristic of her that, knowing it to be unwise to trust entirely to her own understanding, when this seemed to direct her to renounce all and to give herself wholly to God, she felt the need to find a director : ' No longer able to seek the Master in his own place, it became necessary for me to find someone to whom I could open my heart.'

Individual and independent as was Marie-Antoinette, when it was a matter of her own physical health or of

her doctors' treatment in illness, in matters that concerned her soul she was submissive and obedient in all
things to her spiritual directors.

'November 13, 1904 : *God's Call*.'
Her decision to live an ordinary life in the world was
challenged by God himself. Her critical illness followed, and in December 1915, when she appeared to
be dying, her operation for appendicitis. Though she
believed that she was about to die, she was entirely
without fear. 'I had grown so accustomed to the
thought of death that seven months later, when all
danger was past, I was like a ship without an anchor.'
Like a ship without an anchor. Till she died, this
was to be true of Consummata. It was with her as with
young Ernest Psichari, of whom it was said : 'He was
always an inch too tall.' There are spiritual giants who
in our pigmy world seem for ever out of place. They
suffer much. Great happiness may be theirs, but that
happiness itself is suffering. For not upon such happiness are their hearts set. For them S. Paul's *conversatio in coelis* is the only rule of life. Earth's gross air
oppresses them. Their suffocating souls gasp for air.
They leave this earth for heaven's ethereal heights.
Restored to health, her definite conversion, as she
called it, took place during the summer holidays of
1906. She wrote : 'At Lourdes on August 19, the
Blessed Sacrament was revealed to me.' Again :
'September 21, my conversion ; my heart knew a
great inrush of love.' Finally, on October 31 : 'Jesus
—my vocation from him.'
The word 'conversion' was not used by her in its
usual sense. For her it meant not religious faint-
heartedness become suddenly religious fervour, but an
invasion of her soul by the supernatural life. This took
place at Chémouteau in the small private chapel of the
house. There Our Lord demanded her heart of her,

calling her to aid him by living a life of reparation. At the time she saw in this a direct call to the Carmelite life. Actually Christ had willed that she should, in the phrase of S. John of the Cross, ' Cross the threshold ' which opens on the ' secret cells.'

From 1907, when she was eighteen, dates that Rule of life which is set down in Part II of this book. Though at a later date she improved and completed this, she made no modification in its essentials. *Courage, Charity, Union with God*, these were to be her unchanged and unchanging watchwords, even as they were the sum of her soul's life.

The year 1908 brought her great spiritual riches. Our Lord, it seemed, was resolved to reward his generous child. Since she gave her infinitesimal all to him, he would give her a share in his infinite whole. Once again Jacob was about to wrestle with the angel. It was, as always, to be a paradoxical conflict, strange with a customary strangeness, unfamiliar with a familiar unfamiliarity, rich in blessing and the blessing in which it was rich a crucifixion. This conflict, its strategy of love and its glorious issue, needs to be related.

Marie de la Trinité's mystical life owed little to her home life. In some households there is an indefinable atmosphere that, either consciously or unconsciously, stimulates those who live in it in their search for God to follow the way of mysticism. This was not true of Marie de la Trinité.

Mme de Geuser was too clear-sighted not to have some guess at the contacts with God which her daughter sought to hide from her, but which on occasion were too plain to be hidden. Yet she refused to believe the evidence before her. For, devout as she was, she distrusted all that was not ordinary in devotion. To a girl who disobeyed her doctors' orders, would God grant his gift of infused contemplation ? Her mother thus expressed her feeling : ' I have been much perplexed because the child's character is so complex, and now this new strangeness makes me afraid.'

Maternal solicitude found a further cause for anxiety. Her daughter ate so little, that it seemed to Mme de Geuser that her physical health must necessarily suffer. There were periods in particular, when to Marie de la Trinité food was little less an abomination. This attitude, her mother considered, might well originate either in whim or in ill-advised austerity. In the end her mother was convinced. The persistence of divine manifestations wore down her doubts. 'Belatedly, I believed,' Mme de Geuser was to write.

It was all to the good that in her home circle Consummata was checked rather than encouraged ; that despite the great intimacy and understanding between her mother and herself in most matters, in the beginning they were not wholly at one in this greatest matter of all. For such facts themselves carry the conviction that God manifested himself supernaturally in the person of Marie de la Trinité, that the authenticity of these manifestations is beyond challenge, and that there was no question of innocent excitation on the part of others.

II   *Passive Purifications*

God makes use of suffering as a test for the soul, which seeks to give up all for him. Such a soul must be capable of limitless love. Suffering confers that capacity.

Physical suffering came early to Marie de la Trinité. In her latter days illness made her a recluse. Photographs taken by her young brothers show her lying upon her couch or in her bed, her face pale and wasted, her eyes bright with illness. Yet her yearning for God was a far greater strain upon her than her bodily sufferings. These, mysterious as they were—baffling to her doctors, perplexing to those about her—were but

an outward symbol of the spiritual fire which inwardly
consumed her :

'To suffer so little on account of my physical
sickness makes me somewhat ashamed. I welcome
this sickness as God's gift to me. My beloved Jesus
shows such loving-kindness to his poor little nobody,
that he makes this gift of grace more and more generous. In his mighty love all my suffering is swallowed
up. When physical weakness is most upon me, I am
most aware that it is altogether he, and in no wise
I, who works such wonders in my soul.

'Ah, with what joy would I praise his pitifulness !
Yet I perceive that he does not wish this of me ; he
wishes that I shall have no concern but for him
alone. Dominating all his mercies, dominating all
my suffering, dominating all things—is God. " God
is ! " That is everything. I would dwell in him,
who is my God, my all. Lost to all things else, as
did my Mother, Our Lady, I would " keep all these
words and ponder them in my heart." I would die,
that I might live in Jesus Christ, in whom is all
suffering and all love ! ' (To Avignon, December
27, 1914.)

Before this year, 1914, Marie de la Trinité, to whom
anguish born of the war and of events about to be
related was to give a serene and unearthly detachment,
had undergone austerities of spiritual purification :

'As for the sufferings and the struggles of which
you have made guess,' she wrote to Pontoise on June
16, 1910, 'I will not dwell upon them now. It
would take too long, and, it may be, serve no very
useful purpose. Further, my Mother, you know, as
I must believe, what can only be known by experience :
God's manner of dealing with the soul, which he has
chosen to be his living host. Nor are you ignorant of

the sorrow known to that soul, which holds back
when God wishes to draw it into the living light of his
wisdom. You have asked the question. Because you
have asked it, I have answered you thus frankly. I
know that you will give glory to our adorable God for
the strength to endure all things that he has so
generously given to the weakest and most wretched of
his creatures.'

The Prioress wished to know more :

'God is good indeed to make me suffer—and
surrender—so much ; for thus is his glory served.
When I am so broken of body that I can no longer
talk with him, I think that the broken fragments of
his little host, whom he destroys, by their brokenness
yet praise him—praise him in a canticle of love and of
thanksgiving. It is true that I seldom talk with him ;
for it is but seldom that he withdraws the sword,
which he has plunged into my lonely and suffering
heart.' (July 1917).

In December she spoke of ' a gulf of suffering,' which
she needed to cross, before she had made her own the
purification which God desired. She confessed :

'My sufferings could not easily be surpassed. Lest
they be perceived, I dare not open my heart.'[1]

In the intimacy of prayer she had glimpsed God.
She had seen the shadow of his glory. She had stood
upon the brink of the infinite. She had, at one time
or another time, felt so near to him, that, it seemed to
her in her simplicity, she had but to put out her hand
to touch him. Then without warning the glimpse had
been lost ; the shadow of glory had vanished ; the
infinite had become the finite ; she had been given the
torturing understanding that between the infinite,

[1] In her letters to her uncle of about this date (which are to
be found in Part II of this book) she wrote in similar words.

which was he, and the nothingness, which was she, there was no contact to be made. With that understanding there had come to her such sorrow as few can comprehend, since few are capable of such boundlessness of love,

From creatures man can expect nothing. That is recognised. And from God? God, to whom man's aspiration is directed, is equally beyond man's reach :

'These words of S. John of the Cross have brought me happiness. For they are true indeed : "Finding support where there is no support, I give myself to be destroyed by love." It is as if my soul were wrapped about by a vast black cloak, concealing it from all eyes. Upon the side where God is, the cloak hangs open. On the side turned towards earth there is but the cloak's blackness. The fact gives me great joy.

'This darkness given of God is my delight. In it I have sense of security ; in it I am beyond the reach of my fellows and of the powers of evil ; in it I am alone with God. I may not see him now. But in days to come, upon his little nobody, who lives now in the darkness of his absence, he will shine like the sun in glory.

'Unfortunately I too seldom know this cloak-draped nakedness of spirit. The cloak is repeatedly torn from me. At once the powers of evil fall upon me, thus left defenceless, and seek to devour me. Throughout Advent I have been so assailed. The struggle has been full of pain. I have suffered indescribably. Illness, sorrow, anguish, temptation, death : these were sweet and gentle compared with the travail that my soul has known !' (To Pontoise, December 29, 1911.)

A month later her anguish had grown in intensity :

'His little host continues in her torment. God's gift to me is something that transcends suffering. My soul is in dissolution ; the self is dead within me,'

In the midst of her agony she ' naturally had recourse to the Psalms and the *Magnificat*.' There is rich insignificance in that word ' naturally.' She continued :

' Though this desolation is upon me, there are times when I know great happiness. There are hours in which God's sword is plunged so deep into my soul, that I seem no longer to suffer. For God, it may well be, then takes possession of me, dead at last to self, dissolved at last in him. I perceive that he destroys me utterly. This certainty that he makes a living sacrifice of his little nobody fills me with joy. On earth there could be no greater happiness than to die for him. When, therefore, he makes plain to my eyes the destruction which he has wrought in my soul, I am happy indeed. Such happiness comes rarely. Usually he strikes, nor allows me to know that I am stricken ; he destroys, nor permits me sight of my destruction.

' He reveals to me the profound mystery of his own sacrifice, and his desire that I shall have share in it. In this mystery of love Jesus the Redeemer who was slain for me as for all other men, and I, who am slain for him—make a single sacrifice. So would I be to all eternity, enslaved—destroyed—annihilated—by love.

' To be one with Jesus in his Redeemer's work : it is my dream and my one desire. If I yearn to climb out of the abyss in which I am plunged, it is not that I may know joy, but that I may love Jesus and suffer with him. I ask nothing but to yield myself to God's sword, that I may be re-created in the image of Jesus the Redeemer. (*Signed*) Your little host of praise, who in the midst of her exceeding wretchedness, is exceedingly happy.'

Uninitiated, we with difficulty understand how such spiritual travail could co-exist with the perfect peace which dwelt in her soul's depths. For us Calvary is

Calvary ; Thabor, Thabor. Can any hill be at the one time both Calvary and Thabor ? The seemingly impossible is indeed possible. The mystic, Marie de la Trinité, at this particular stage in her God-ward climb, had such insight that she could behold the two as one.[1]

On March 8, 1912, Marie-Antoinette marvelled at the manner in which in a life of outward happiness God contrived to make joy his sword's sheath. Her own soul's night persisted :

' Even Jesus seems no longer to recognise his little host. The Father has stopped short in the work which would by the loving hands of the Holy Ghost have raised me up. I am utterly delivered into the power of death. *Factus sum sicut homo sine adjutorio.*' (November 10, 1912.)

There followed this characteristic addition :

' Nevertheless I am happy and at peace. I have surrendered myself unreservedly to him who is my guide. I feel that the Father is watching over me. By sacrifice—he alone knows by what great sacrifice —I am able to win through suffering to that path of living light, which stretches from his feet—that path by which we must journey, if we are to know joy or to show endurance upon this earth.'

In January 1913 :

' When I look upon my little Redeemer in his crib, it is this lesson that I seem to learn : he desires for me that I should be one with him in his condition of weakness and of helplessness. I seem to understand that great works in the world are not for me ; that of me, his little nobody, he demands that all shall be

[1] On this subject reference should be made to the classical *Life of S. Teresa*, written by herself, ch. 20. It was, however, Christ himself at Gethsemani, who furnished the incomparable example of this ' intricate and exquisitely poignant martyrdom.' See the excellent commentary of J. Huby, *Évangile selon saint Marc*, Paris, 1924, pp. 340 *et seq.*

performed in the secrecy of my soul ; that lastly my
way will now and always be the way of love—and
love's instrument that suffering of which only God
has knowledge.'

She believed that suffering helped supremely to make
union with God possible. Accordingly she cherished it.
Suffering is known only upon earth. Because this is so,
she could bring herself to write : ' There is no suffering
in heaven ; in all else heaven is rich.'
She continued with this admission :

' In heaven we shall need it no longer ; for we
shall have known all the suffering that he wishes us
to know. For us still upon this earth, that is not yet
the case. It is our privilege to go from suffering to
humiliation, from humiliation to suffering. For so
are we one with the Crucified, and with his Mother,
the queen of martyrs' (To Pontoise, May 18, 1913.)

On December 13, in a letter that was a blundering
search after the secrets of unity with God, she wrote :

' I scarcely know what I write, my Mother. This
only I know : my soul is filled with such great and
such rich suffering, that my understanding gropes in
bewilderment before it. And of this only I am sure :
to know that I do his holy will is ecstasy ! I love him,
and I am destroyed by my love ! To that love there
are no bounds.'

Marie de la Trinité wrote yet again of God's way with
her in her ceaseless search for union with him :

' In spite of all, God's work in my soul goes on. I
bless him for it. I see that his plan is of one piece. I
understand that by his plan I am led directly to him ;
all obstacles, all seeming contradictions, notwithstanding.
' From the Assumption to Pentecost I have made a
retreat. I have made it alone with God. He will

have none other to share that solitude. In it he spoke to me in the Scriptures' words : *Ego ero merces tua magna nimis !* This solitude with him is a disproportionate reward for me. Our earthly affairs are as feathers in God's balances. The self in me that suffers agony has no worth at all. I set aside its worthlessness ; I can do no other, since he who rules the world —he who is infinite love—is there in my soul, making it a closed monastic cell. In that cell with what joy do I entertain my divine guest ; in what rapture am I lost in the vast love of him, who visits it unseen ! This grace brings with it no sense of strain ; it is as if for the first time by faith I am able to see all things in their true perspective ; to understand that God is all ; to perceive that, wholly possessed by him, through him I am possessed of all ; to recognise that I no longer share his solitude, since that solitude has become absolute, the I that was I having become a nothingness.

'Alas ! my faith often falters and fails, and I no longer see all things in their true perspective. The featherweight affairs of earth rob me of vision and of understanding. I am no longer aware of God immanent, or of his living love for me. If it were otherwise, earth would be heaven. As it is, when my faith is strongest, it is like a beacon set upon a hill. By its light all things are made plain.'

God in Three Persons dwells in every sinless soul. By such a soul the divine presence is perceived vividly or not so vividly. God living in us : that is the state of grace. Ourselves in communion with God who dwells in us : that is the state of divine intimacy. Ourselves in a measure aware experimentally of God who dwells in us : that is the mystical state.

Marie de la Trinité was to profit exceptionally by this direct and intimate contact with God immanent.

Detachment from self brought her increasingly into the divine intimacy :

' He no longer makes it his purpose to isolate me from self and from the world. He seeks instead to draw me to him. To follow him I no longer need to slay the self, but rather increasingly to resurrect my soul in him. I have reached the second stage. Emerged from the once-submerging self, I need make no effort but to dwell in him. I have not, as once I had, to shut myself from earth ; I have to open myself to heaven. I need less to free myself from the wheel of life than to fix my eyes upon the Lord of life —less to forget myself than to remember him and none but him.

' To arrive at union is no more my need, but to make closer the union to which I have arrived—not to be transformed but rather to be transfigured. By ceaseless contemplation of God shall this be secured. *Nos vero omnes, revelata facie, speculantes in eamdem imaginem, transformemur a claritate in claritatem, tanquam a Domini Spiritu.*[1] These words of S. Paul express my thought better than I can express it. (To Pontoise, September 4, 1912.)

At the age of twenty-three—she died at twenty-nine— it is plain that Marie de la Trinité had travelled far along the road to mystical union with God :

' How can I describe my happiness to you, my Mother ? God hides himself upon his holy hill ; Mary dwells apart ; every citizen of heaven is seem- ingly asleep. Yet God utterly possesses me. Cease- lessly and consciously I give him to himself, and add to his own glory. Ceaselessly also I am conscious of my union with him. How may I tell of it ?—It is rather as if I were the possessor of an encasketed jewel,

[1] 2 Cor. iii, 18.

which, still in its casket. I gave to a friend, and myself
had no pleasure of it. Happiness given solely to
another, the giver claiming no share in it, far ex-
ceeds that which comes of pleasure personally experienced.

' There is no greater happiness than this of mine—
the ability to love him worthily and to make him an
infinitely precious gift. Does that sound presumptuous
madness? Yet (I think) it is the truth. For in this
union with God, when I love him, I can but love him
with his own love—when I give him myself, it is
himself that I give him. Confronted by these secrets
of love and of unity, aware of the mighty work that
he has wrought in his little nobody for his glory's
sake, I can remember only my own pitifulness and
the need to express my boundless gratitude. (To
Pontoise, February 13, 1913.)

This ability to love God with the very love of God is
in a measure the privilege of every soul that lives in
grace. Only the aid of the Holy Ghost enables men to
love God ; for the Holy Ghost is but the love that
emanates from the Father and the Son. To be aware
of this by faith ; to be made conscious of it by a measure
of direct experience : this is reserved to the few. Marie
de la Trinité added :

' His love for us confounds us—do you not agree,
my Mother ? We would spend our lives in humility
before it. Yet even this humility is not the greatest
of our needs : indeed it is swallowed up in needs
still greater. Chief of these is the need to love with
so strong and pure a love, that we are plunged deep
and still deeper into God ; while there is born in us
a trust so audacious that no tittle of doubt remains.
The tiny child has such knowledge of the might and
the infinite love of his Father, that he feels no necessity
to make known his needs. So it is with me. The

right which he gives me to draw upon his love is as limitless as that love itself.

'Next to this is my soul's impulse to hide myself in him—to be dead to all but him. Altogether absorbed in him, I am no more I but he.

'This is his way for me. It is a way that leads over abysses of suffering and of love, such as are known only to him. Walking this way, I find sustenance for my soul in the Psalms—such Psalms as the 29th, 44th, 61st, 102nd, 144th, 145th, 97th—all the *alleluias*, *Laudates* and *Cantates*.

'Normally, however, the Master plays upon his little instrument the tunes which please him best. This does not mean that for me there is no more suffering. It does mean that I know peace. Say rather, that while suffering is in me, I am not in suffering.'

A term had been reached in her mystical life. From this time on her mystical experiences were to become more frequent. More and more often he whom Marie de la Trinité called her ' adored love ' was to carry away his ' poor little nobody ' into the mystery of his triune life, and to give her to drink at the source of love itself :

'Surely no other thing is needful, but only love. In love all things are made perfect. Judas himself, had he lost himself in love, like the other apostles would have been a saint. I delight to come before Our Lord as another Mary Magdalen, oppressed by a sense of my own pitifulness ; aware of my complete insignificance, of my utter unworthiness ; *minima*, yet second to none in my trust and my love. When I come to him so, he leads me into unity with him.

'It is then that I understand why Mary kept all things hidden in her heart. For to think of " these things " is to profane them. To tell of this state of

K

ecstasy is in a measure to make it less marvellous. To tell of it is to need to climb down from the heights. Mary walked always upon them, descending from them never, and thus lived for ever in consummate union with God. So would I too live, though I know that I may not live in such perfection of unity. Once descended from the heights, I cannot describe them. For words are but shadows and the understanding a traitor. The glory of those heights for ever breaks through language and escapes.' (To Pontoise, April 1913.)

Here Marie de la Trinité spoke for all the great mystics. As our poor human beauty will make the artist stammer his despair of expressing it, so before the supreme beauty of God's divinity the mystic's speech is but a stuttering, while soon the stuttering—and it is better so—becomes a silence :

' To live only in him, as though for me eternity had begun already : this only is left to me. All the little nothings of this earth—health, whether good or bad, insignificant happenings, petty plans—all are lost in love's unity.

' Elizabeth de la Trinité declared that, till this world end, she would go soaring " like a little rocket " towards the throne of the Three in One. But for me I cannot soar ; I cannot even stir from where I am. For I have come to rest in the living love of the Threefold God. I have no words with which to set down or explain this ultimate truth, my Mother. I can but be content to live it.

' He leads me by the one way. He humbles, not exalts me. He plunges me into the depths of my own pitifulness ; he does not raise me to the heights of his perfection. Beneath my lowest depths, he is. Plunging headlong, I am dashed into the only true holiness, that holiness which is his. Because she is indeed *minima*, he permits his little nobody to live in unity with him ; he heaps her with his divine favours.' (To Pontoise, June 23, 1913.)

False mystics are made known by their pride ; true mystics by their unsurpassed humility : they are come so near to God, that they dare not lift their eyes to behold his face :

'Earth has no words that may tell the secrets of the soul. *Nostra conversatio in coelis est :* I have latterly dwelt much upon the wisdom in that. Yet its wisdom is a hidden wisdom ; it cannot be expressed—*me decet silentium*. It is not, as you know, my Mother, a wisdom of this life, but of the other. Between this life and that there hangs but faith's thin curtain. At times it seems that the curtain is about to be rent. What beauty and what truth are ours ! How remote and removed are earth and all earthly things ! How there is none but he !' (To Pontoise, March 30, 1914.)

Further :

'To be silent—to feel lost in him—there is no better thing than this. In silence is the last word, the one word that says all.'

Again :

'There are times when the vision leaves us and only faith remains. Such times are hard to bear. For to have seen his holy hill, and then no longer to see it, is to know loss unknown to them who have not beheld it. There is then but one thing left to us : to remain in unity with him.'

When she knew such unity in its completeness, she knew ecstasy :

'When our great God of love bears away his little

nobody, that she may know unity with him, that unity is so complete and so profound, that neither thought can plumb nor words utter it. I cannot understand it : I can but be lost in it. Than this there can be no thing more simple, as there is no thing more unutterable.' (To Pontoise, July 1913.)

As these direct contacts with God became more frequent, they became also more continuous :

' It is as if all else were fled and forgotten : alone with him I rest in peace, peace filling my soul. He is my God, my all ; his relation to me, my relation to him, cannot be set down in words, so intimate it is. In our love we are one spirit. For me I seek only to dwell in him.' (To Pontoise, September 22, 1913.)

Resuming :

' Would that I could tell you more of this high mystery ! But I cannot, lost as I am in him. To tell of these things I should need to climb down from the heights. And that I cannot do.'

When she had ' climbed down,' she found that still she could not utter these things that she had in her soul. It was not that God forbade her ; it was that all words were too poor and too unworthy. Words can speak truth ; words can also lie. It was this that prohibited her ; it was also more than this. For it is man's miserable lot that, bond-slave as he is to his mere humanity, he has but worthless words with which to capture God the uncapturable :

' There is surely no more sorrowful thing than this : to know joy and happiness and grateful love, and to be altogether unable to express them. What words can be adequate ? Those of the Psalms please me well : *Silentium tibi laus*. Only that union's silence can speak the full truth of union with God. Only by that silence can thanks be meetly given.' (To Pontoise, December 13, 1913.)

After a period of absorption in God :

' About three weeks ago the eagle of God let drop his little prey of love. Yet for me there exists none but he. When he dropped me, I was like a child lost in the dark. I knew well that of my own strength I could not win back to him. I watched him, therefore, with love in my eyes and the expectancy that he would return and again seek out his poor little nobody. But this he did not do. He showed me a great pit yawning at my feet. It was the pit of my worthlessness. He made me understand that the heights were not for me, but the depths of that pit. He bade me plunge headlong into it. I did as he bade me. At the pit's bottom I found myself once more in unity with him. For in my downward plunge I lost the self and found once more my God. And now it is plain to me that in the depths, as in the heights, he is ; and that to find him, all that is necessary is to lose the self. There is but one thing to add : when it is in the depths that he is found, the soul knows greater surety ; for it can fall no further.

' These things I cannot express.' (To Pontoise, July 3, 1914.)

She could express them. Few of the mystics have expressed them better. It was her great gift, this ability to set down in lucid language her divine experiences :

' I am going to answer your questions, my reverend Mother. I have first begged God, through the intercession of the Blessed Virgin, to enable me to set forth the truth as best I may.

' The eagle of God swoops upon his little prey, each time that she turns expectant to him. Often when she is busied with trivial daily affairs, without warning he stands suddenly before her. Straightway, as a great lodestone a tiny needle, he draws her into contact with himself. If she be engrossed in some exterior matter—a conversation, it may be—she possibly resists him. Yet in her resistance she is conscious only of his sweet magnetic power. Once more at leisure she is borne willy-nilly to him, waiting for her there.

' In this union—or so I think—there is freedom, either complete or all but complete. For this absorption in him is brief, a matter of seconds only. As frequent as it is brief, in effect it leaves me in a state of continuous union with God. This union fills my life : in it suffering can no longer find a place. For when suffering assails my soul, I seek sanctuary there where suffering cannot come. Latterly, this absorption has been more lasting and more continuous, constantly renewed as it has been. It is an absorption that at no time debars me from action.

' Yet it is not of this absorption that I wished to write, but of the way in which the eagle of God bears off his little prey. Of this experience I had knowledge before, but not personal knowledge. Let me describe it. Closer to him than breathing, I felt the earth recede. As the earth receded, I was made free. Earthly things fell away from me. I felt no longer the need, which I feel when I am fallen low—that need of silence and solitude, if I am to be no more bound to those things that are not God.

' Sometimes for several days together I am plunged so deep in wretchedness, that I have no more consciousness of union apart from the deep peace and abiding happiness in my soul. At these times the eagle of God comes seldom to bear away his little prey. He leaves her day after day in the depths of the pit, that there she may know suffering. From time to time he visits her, not to bear her away but to strike at and pierce her afresh. It is at these times that, though I am conscious of union, I am not assured of it ; while sufferings that I do not understand engulf my soul.

'When I speak of " the pit," I do not refer to exterior things ; nor by " sufferings " do I mean the consciousness of my pitiful insignificance in contrast with God blessed in Three Persons. Suffering, as I understand the word, is that state in which the soul no longer feels itself " glutted of God," but knows itself to be an exile. Where once it was one in essence with him who is all, and one in union with not merely the true, the beautiful, the wise and the loving, but with very truth, very beauty, very wisdom and very love : it has lost this unity in which it has known its true home and its true happiness.'

She concluded :

'I realise that without God's special grace you will not be able to understand me, so badly have I expressed myself. But these things are inexpressible. Words are so inadequate, that constantly one statement seems to contradict another. Yet thank you for your questions. They have helped me to clarify my thought. There is so much that I have to say to you, that often I do not know where to begin. At these times I beg God to be my guide and myself write down the things which he directs me to write, convinced that, insignificant as these may seem, they are those which he desires to have written.' (From Chémouteau, July 25, 1915.)

III *On the Brink of Eternity*

Marie de la Trinité was not made for earth, nor had she any dread of leaving it. All things drew her heavenward :

'Yes, my Mother, death is indeed desirable. It is the fixed goal. It is attainment, glory at its greatest, love at its highest, a gift of the soul to him. How lovely is the thought of death! How certain it is that God will take us at the supremely fitting moment! What joy to think of that life everlasting, in which we shall know all those things of earth " more excellent " made eternal, unchanged and unchanging!' (To Pontoise, May 18, 1913—the feast of the Blessed Trinity.)

In March and April she reached eternity's ante-chamber. She grew increasingly weak. Sudden fever attacked her. It was believed that she was about to die. She believed it herself. She asked for Extreme Unction. With a glad heart she made her sacrifice. Then in pro-found peace she waited for God's hour to strike.

On one particular day it seemed as if the end had come. Injections of caffein no longer renewed her failing strength. The death agony, it seemed, was upon her. Suddenly the worst of her sickness sloughed from her. In its place these phenomena manifested themselves : her arms stretched crosswise out ; her eyes, lost in ecstasy, seemed to gaze upon some vision not of this earth ; her face shone with an unearthly light.

At the bidding of her confessor and the priest who had been summoned, Mme de Geuser tried to bend her arms and to force them back to their normal position. It was impossible. The rigidity of her muscles was not to be overcome.

At intervals her doctor would seek to bring back his patient to a consciousness of her outward circumstance, and would offer her nourishment. His task was no easy one. The good man was troubled by these hap-penings that he had difficulty in understanding. ' Come ! ' he said to her on one occasion, ' cease playing at your little Saint Teresa : it exhausts you too much.'

With but small and intermittent success he would resume his gentle efforts to bring her back to what he called realities.

Her parents were disturbed and made anxious by the prolongation of this state. They decided that for the time none should enter the sick-room. Consequently neither servants nor friends saw her in this remarkable condition. However, a nun and several monks, her confessor, her director (he was her uncle : he had come from Paris) were witnesses of the facts. None doubted that here was a case of supernatural intervention by the Spirit of the Lord.

When she had come out of this strange state, Marie de la Trinité, with the precision that was characteristic of her, gave her parents messages for her uncle, her director, her brothers and cousins, and the two doctors —messages that were to be greatly treasured. She joked good-humouredly upon the subject of the philistine view of her ecstasies taken by one of her two doctors. According to him (she laughed) they had three stages : ' In the first she was not quite all there ; in the second she began to recover ; in the third she was herself again.'

At these periods of divine seizure fragmentary phrases escaped her lips. These fragments of phrases glittered with heaven ; burned with love :

' Death is no more a passing. It is the peace of God. It is his love. I have crossed the threshold. I have reached the sanctuary of his love. I shall die, as I would have wished to die. I shall die, knowing that his will is the ultimate truth.

' There is no more simple thing. It needs but this : to have no care but for him. In a brief space in us he performs his great work—the Blessed Virgin listens to us, and gives her grace, when we beg her for it.

' Let me not hinder but help you. You too shall

know the union which I know. Do not be troubled.
God's love is almighty. Let your gaze be fixed only
upon his love !

'God has done all. I used to feel that holiness was
not for me. I begged him to make me holy, not for
my sake but for his, not for my glory but for his own.

'Believe in his all-powerful love. It is incredible
in what short space he has performed what mighty
work in me. Eight years ago in September—it was
the 21st, that unforgettable day—I came to love him.
Yet I did not then know love in its fullness. Even
then how lovely was his will ! But now what fullness
has been added to that loveliness of old ! My spirit
no more knows vexation—when God departed from
me this morning, he left me his peace. Be his will
done, if he wish to prolong my life, whether for few
or for many days ! Be his will done no less, if he wish
me to stay no more upon this earth ! This has been
my heart's cry to him.'

At that point she appeared to remember where she
was : ' Oh, I have let slip my secret ; I have told all,'
she cried. She stirred in her bed, making a slight
movement towards her mother. ' Mother,' she said,
' once to-night I thought that death had come. It was
not so, but I am content. When death is near, one
comes to understand as never before the adorable will
of God.'

She continued as if in reverie :

' By his will I suffer still. Would that I could
persuade every living soul to seek only heaven ! . . .
Once—I was coming away from Vespers, I remember
—I heard his voice distinctly : he told me that from
me he required nothing less than all. O love whom I
adore ! O Father who art in heaven ! . . .

She ceased. She began to talk as if to God :

'Take all I have ; take all I am. Make my love so great that I may die of love. Take all—take all, that your will be done. You know that I love you. In heaven as on earth you, God, shall be my one desire—you, O God, and none but you, who are my desire and my delight. How sweet and how adorable in all things is your will, O my God !

'. . . On earth let all things be given to God ; in heaven all souls be given to him ! Now and for ever let us give him to himself ! Let us give him to all on earth, to all in purgatory ! *Non nobis Domine :* let none attribute merit to me, but to him and to him alone. Let *non nobis* ring through all the world ! To all fathers and mothers and brothers make this gift of God ! On earth tongue may not tell it, nor lips be shaped to utter it. . . .'

She paused. She turned to her father and mother :

'Father—mother—in God I shall say good-bye to you ; for love of God I would see you no more on earth ; I would see nothing any more on earth—for love of God, for love of God.'

A little later she spoke thus remarkably :

'Seek me only in church. In church you shall always find me. Because of the Blessed Sacrament, which I have always so much loved, you will find me there. It is there that you shall have my help.'

Now she uttered a thought of her own, and now a request concerning others. One such had to do with her airman brother, Georges :

'Tell Georges to keep constant watch over heaven's wall.'

And then of priests in general :

'O Christ my spouse ! You know that it is God in me, and God alone, who has performed all things in his little creature. He has done all ; he is all.

' To all priests give this message from me : I love them because they are priests of Jesus Christ. Like a sower I will spread love abroad. I will sow in men's souls those vocations that are of God. All living souls I will give to God. My beloved brothers, my parents, all priests—I beg them all only to love ; for love is all and all should be love. It is God who has wrought all things in his little nobody. It is for his love that I die, for nothing but his love. Oh, love is all—all.'

For all priests of the Society of Jesus, whom she had met, she left this message of remembrance :

' I would like all priests whom I have known, to say a thanksgiving Mass when I am dead to the Blessed Trinity, for all that it is and for all that it does.'

Shortly afterwards in one short sentence she uttered all her soul :

' When I die, may all of me be consumed in a great fire of love ; may there be nothing left of me but a trail of shining truth ! '

The apostolate idea, the thought of the world's salvation, continued to haunt her :

' What love I have for the souls of men ! Would that I could be the means of saving them all ! '

She counted the gifts which God had made to her :

' There is nothing that he has not done. In all things he has been faithful, Christ my spouse. At all times he has been my guide. The clue by which he has led me is the performance of his will. That is the secret ; there is no secret but that. And in its performance he does all ; I in my insignificance nothing.'

At intervals she murmured to herself this date or that, each associated by her with some important happening in her spiritual life :

' November 13 and 14, 1908—February 19, 1909—September 21 : how love rushed into my heart ! October 31 : it was then that I resolved to be faithful. . . . Of how many things have I failed to take note !

' November 13 : God's great work in consecrated souls, that work which drives them to reparation and thanksgiving. The maximum of glory that is his from such souls consecrated to the great work of the Father's glory—of such souls whose strength is in the prayer : " Do what you will with me, O my God. Whatever suffering it may mean for me, let thy will be done, O Lord ! " '

From time to time she would allude to a particular person, it might be to one of her brothers :

' . . . It would be your delight, my Hubert, to give guidance to consecrated souls.'

' . . . Georges will be true to his vocation. By him I am understood.'

' . . . Because my father is wholly humble, God delights in him. None but God knows the sufferings of his secret soul. For this God is well pleased in him.'

Characteristically considerate for the feelings of others, she said too :

' If there be any whom I have forgotten to mention, let him not be hurt. In my thought I have forgotten none.'

At intervals she asked for more holy water to be given to her. From time to time seemingly she sought to keep at a distance some invisible power. For at these times she threw a few drops of holy water into the air, or made the sign of the cross.

Marie-Antoinette had expressed the wish that her

favourite friend, Thérèse, should come to see her. Thérèse accordingly stayed at la rue Faure from the 7th to the 9th of April, and there—a privilege shared by no other—had long talks with Marie de la Trinité. Her account of these talks is of the first importance :

'I confess to you that I have never doubted that she received extraordinary grace from God. At the same time I have been at pains to beware of illusions. Nevertheless, to Nénette even in our most intimate talk I gave no hint of my cautiousness in this respect. For that would have seemed to violate something sacred, something that was of God himself.

'On my return to Le Hâvre I was impelled, against my usual practice, to set down in writing what had impressed me most. I had no intention of allowing these notes to be read, written as they were while the inspiration of those talks was still upon me, and treasured by me from that time to this.'

Here are these invaluable notes in all their eloquence :

'April 1915 : You have allowed me, dear God, once more to see Nénette, whom in you I love so greatly, and who is close to death—my beloved sister, Nénette. The hours which I spent with her from the 7th to the 9th of April were such hours as might be spent in heaven. Not she, but you, O God (it seemed to me) talked with me then ; as it is not to Nénette but to you in her that my love is given. For she is all dissolved in you : she lives rather in your heaven than upon this earth.

'Her room is holy ground ; her life is in continuous union with yours, O God. She spends all her time in prayer, it seems. Her crucifix never leaves her hands—it is as simple and as inexpensive as the rest of her few possessions. Even when she is most weary, she never fails to find the strength needed to hold it. Her eyes seem always to seek you out, O God. The humility in her modest bearing, the peace in her smiling face : in her these speak of you, O God. You have given me a saint to be my friend : for that my grateful heart gives thanks, O Lord.

' . . . I reached the house at eleven o'clock on Wednesday. On Thursday morning I received Communion with my dear Nénette. I went into her room a few minutes before the priest came. There I saw my little saintly sister with a great peace upon her face. Her spirit seemed remote from all that took place about her. I saw her make her Communion, and her mother after her. Until it was time to go to Mass, I stayed, that in her I might adore you, O God.

' Nénette was lost in you. A few minutes went by. Suddenly, as if in a transport of love, she began what her young brothers and sister call " her big prayers " : with a loud voice and in tones that no words of mine can describe, she prayed—" O God, I love you. None but you know how much I love you. Yet would I love you still more than I do. I would love you beyond the bounds of my desire to love you—even of the desire which I shall know in heaven. Had you not died for me, O God, I should have loved you, even as I love you now. Though you were never to know that I love you, I would not love you less.

' " Would that I could love you more than the Cherubim and the Seraphim—more than you have been loved in all eternity before ! O God, be your will done on earth, as it is in heaven ! Be it done at all times and in all places ! Be it done by all of us and by each of us ! How sweet is your will, and how little loved of men ! "

' This transport of love of my little Nénette moved me to the depths of my soul. I remember that, despite my attempts to prevent them, my tears flowed unrestrainedly.

'The remarkable thing was this. The rapture in her eyes, the ardour in her breast, found expression in the strength of her voice. Yet at all other times her great weakness permitted her to speak only in tones little above a whisper. We might have talked a great deal during those two blessed days. In fact we had no wish but to talk of you, and of you alone, O God. All Nénette's speech, all her heart's great tenderness, were concerned with but these : your will, O God ; your glory and what may serve it best ; the surrender of all to you.

'She talked to me in utter simplicity of what she called " her little aids." These were they. To give back to Our Lord in humility that which he has given to us in recollection ; at night, before seeking sleep, to devote brief moments to meditation and so to put ourselves in tune with the will of God ; for then all our sleep becomes a prayer, a union with him ; at confession to accuse ourselves of those little things in which there is no real fault, yet the confession of which brings great peace.

'These were other thoughts that she expressed to me :

'Our weaknesses themselves make only for his greater glory. They subtract nothing from it. For he is the more glorified by the confession of our pitifulness and powerlessness, than by any notable things that we may have done for him.

'I have tried always to ask of him that through all my days I shall remain insignificant : that I shall be as a little child in the Father's arms. This because, when the soul is aware of its insignificance, he becomes its all-in-all, and the devil is frustrated. The very helplessness of tiny children is their strength. Against the strength of weakness it is the devil who is helpless. It is no matter if you cannot meditate. Do not attempt it. Love him merely.

'Humility is truth. Humility is holiness. Of

Mary it is said that she was humble. Little is said either of her courage or of her generosity. These are implied in her humility.

' When the time comes to die ; when the eyes behold only God ; when the lips are likely to shape no more words on earth, then happiness lies in this : not in courage shown, not in great deeds accomplished, but in petty sufferings, in weaknesses, in small defeats. Out of these, when we confess them, he draws his greater glory. For because of these, one time or another time he sends us those sufferings, which glorify himself and enable us to make reparation.

' He will glorify himself by glorifying us. Yet it is not for us to think of that.

' In deeds notable for their courage the self can become assertive : too often pride enters into them. It is rather our weaknesses that serve his greater glory. Formerly I would often suffer greatly, but would conceal my suffering. Now if another hurt me, I do not conceal my hurt. And that for me is the better part.

' For sometimes the truest humility hides itself under a show of pride. At times it is well to make a pretence of pride, when it is but a pretence.

' Shall we take pride in living for a hundred years, when centuries of centuries are ours ?

' Let us cling neither to life nor to death ; let us cleave only to his will. If our desire be for ever centred in his will, though there be tears in our eyes, there is joy in our hearts. In his will there is all of God : love then his will.

' . . . She spoke of her life's past years, and said : " In those days I withdrew myself too much into my soul. I failed to let its light shine forth."

' She told me that in 1911, when she faced one of her life's great spiritual crises, I had surprised and comforted her by saying that in her I saw God.

L

'We talked of a photograph, taken at the Sacred Heart at Le Mans. She told me that the mistress of novices had made fun of her, because she had hidden most of herself behind her companions, as any shy young novice might have done. She had been ashamed of herself for this. "For," she said, "it has always been my wish to do as others do."

'I offered her a souvenir from Rome, saying : "You can leave it to whom you choose." "Oh, no ! " she answered briskly, " I shall make no bequests; for I have nothing to bequeath. I would prefer not to have it."

'Once when we were speaking of the will of God, she kissed me warmly. "How happy I am ! " she cried, "you too understand it all. It is indeed as you say."

'These also were her sayings :

' " O God, be it with me as you will it to be, so only that out of your poor little nobody you may draw all the glory and all the love which it is your will to draw."

' " Let Jesus possess me."

' " My task in heaven will be to give God to himself and to the souls of men."

' " It is my faith that in heaven you shall give God to me, while I shall give God to you, and that in this we both shall know increase of blessedness."

' . . . In no kind of order I have set down, as I remember them, the thoughts which struck me most during those unforgettable hours spent in Nénette's company. She is a model for me. Her little body clothes a soul so single and so surrendered to your will, O God, that, with heaven open before her, she has no desire but to do your will, looking upon her recovery or her death as things of no importance. She suffers. Suffering, she makes no smallest complaint. On earth she lives as though she lived in heaven. In her company I have understood, as never before, how lovely and adorable is your will, O God.'

Any outward manifestation of a mystical nature in the life of Marie de la Trinité occurred at this period of her life.

In the small hours—at about one o'clock, to be more precise—of a Saturday morning in April 1915, she called out to her mother : ' Mother ! Mother ! come quickly. The angel is here.'

Mme de Geuser, hampered by the plaster cast which she had worn following her fall, set about giving the invalid her wish. The nurse intervened, saying that there was nothing wrong. Then for a second time Marie-Antoinette cried out : ' Come quickly, Mother ! ' When, after a delay that circumstances made inevitable, Mme de Geuser stood by her child's bed, the girl said in a calm voice : ' Oh, Mother, if you had come at once, the angel would have given you Communion, as he gave it to me.' This happening took place upon a day when the parish priest could not come to the house. When her mother asked what she meant, she said : ' An angel came into the room, and went round my bed. He carried a little host. I called out to you : " The angel is here, Mother ! " For I thought that you would have had the time to come, and receive Communion as I did.'

There were two or three repetitions of this occurrence. And that was all. What was the nature of these strange happenings, and of those mysterious states that her doctor called ecstasies ? Were they to be explained, at least in part, by the girl's physical and nervous exhaustion ? The question is irrelevant—though the statement may astound those of limited understanding. ' Ecstatic phenomena of a visible and exterior nature, despite the popular belief, are neither astonishing in themselves nor essential to the mystical state. They are the mere concomitants and effects of it. They are the price to be paid for it. Their primary cause is the weakness, the imperfection, the insufficient spirituality of the human instrument. As the latter is made more perfect, they decrease in number. Ecstasy—by which is here to be understood the phenomena of inhibition, of temporary unconsciousness, of immobility and muscular rigidity, of words automatically spoken and gestures automatically made—is in itself never a divine favour nor an evidence of mystical power. There are occasions when it marks divine possession : yet in itself it remains a tribute, paid by the mystic manifesting it, to human frailty.'[1]

These visible interventions of the supernatural in the natural world may not be the highest form of such intervention. Yet they are rare favours which God reserves to the few. It is the merit of those whom he thus favours, which commends these manifestations to our belief. Accordingly we shall be at no pains to make a detailed enquiry into the facts thus baldly narrated. For the saintliness of Marie-Antoinette in no way hangs upon them. Her uncle, who as her director spoke with authority, declared truly : ' Whether these happenings were miraculous or a God-sent solace, is known only to heaven. Sufficient for us that only good came of them.'

Actually the supernatural manifested in Consummata was of a quality to justify the interpretation of these phenomena as wholly real and truly exalted in nature. In spirit submissive as were other mystics, and more patient than many in the disabilities and depressions of illness, Marie de la Trinité enjoyed, equally with them, an inner strength, an intellectual vigour and an extraordinary expansion of spiritual vitality. This book's previous pages have failed of their purpose, if they have

[1] *Cf.* L. de Grandmaison's *L'Elan mystique*, in *Etudes*, vol. cxxxv, May 5, 1913, pp. 328 *et seq.*

not convinced the reader that this girl, proved by word and deed to be faithful and generous and constant and heroic, possessed magnificent moral health, an exceedingly well-balanced mind and an exceptionally exalted soul : a combination as admirable as rare.

The noblest soul has its vicissitudes. Human weakness can sometimes play the traitor. The old Adam's wounds have been known to open again. The story of S. Christopher has a moral for men. God is no light weight : he sits most heavily upon the shoulders of those who love him most and most are aware of him. There are inevitably times when the body flinches and momentarily betrays the secret of the work which God has wrought within it.

Upon her recovery Marie de la Trinité grew aware of the facts already narrated and of those words of ecstasy spoken when her agony was at its height. She was abashed. Yet abashed, she remained serene :

' Mother has, I understand, written to you. I asked her to tell you everything. So you will know that when I was dying, a few of the secrets of God's love were made exteriorly manifest. At first I was troubled in mind. I spoke to my confessor who had been a witness. He reassured me : these things, he said, were the will of God. I am now once more happy and at peace.' (To Avignon, November 13, 1915.)

The Prioress, in case of need seeking to buttress her correspondent's humility, suggested delirium as a possible explanation. Marie de la Trinité replied simply but very forthrightly :

' You suggest that it may have been a case of delirious hallucination. I do not think so. I do not believe that I was delirious. It is true that I was not always conscious of the self. But this was willed by God, I do believe.' (December 1915.)

She had good sense and discretion enough to treat as no great matter these exterior manifestations. Not in them but in spiritual union her interest lay :

'Let me be quite frank with you. I have perceived no marked change in the life of my soul, since that of which I wrote to you in July 1912. Does this particular soul-state fit in with the passage from *The Spiritual Canticle*,[1] quoted by you ? It may be so, but I am not quite convinced. There was a time when in S. John of the Cross I found set down with absolute fidelity my soul's spiritual phases, both past and present. Now once more I find in the following passage a faithful rendering of what I felt, so far as I remember, on that evening when Extreme Unction was given to me. Here it is : "Those who love thus die in ardent ecstasy. The love which floods their hearts threatens to break all barriers, and to sweep on into love's sea. Delight rolls over the soul like a wave, as the hour draws near in which, as God's heir, it shall enter into its heritage. Avid to know release from the body's bondage, glimpses of heaven's glory dazzle its prescient eyes, and the very stuff of its being is dissolved into love."

'Thus it was with me—or so I think—upon that Friday night and again on the Saturday morning upon which they said the prayers for the dying. My strength ebbed soon afterwards ; my faint breathing had begun to fail. They gave me Holy Communion. It was then that that happened, which brought me back from death to life. According to our priest this was an ecstasy or a transport. As to that I cannot say. At that hour I had experiences, which it would be sin to tell.

'Though, I repeat, I have no new perceptions to convey to you, I can assure you of these two things :

[1] *The Spiritual Canticle* of S. John of the Cross.

first, this illness of mine is no more than the love which I have for God made manifest, while its outward physical symptoms, which the doctors fail to understand, are to be referred to the present state of my soul ; secondly, various pains in my head and my limbs are direct results of supernatural union with God.

'In a word God has wrought not only upon my soul, but upon my body and upon the relation between them. Until then I had not realised how closely physical and spiritual phenomena are linked together. It is my belief that the beginning of my illness coincided with the date of my conversion, September 21, 1906, that day upon which his love first pierced my heart.'

In a postscript dated March 4, 1916, following upon a request for details from the Prioress, she made explicit and final reference to the incident of the angel :

'Last time, when writing to you, as you asked, of the crisis of my illness, I forgot, I think, to tell you that three times Jesus the Host came to give himself to me without human intermediary. In each case this happened on a day when Holy Communion had not been brought to me. On Wednesday of Passion week and on Good Friday he came alone ; on Easter Eve an angel bore the Host. If I loved him enough, it might well be that he would come more often in this guise or another. Pray that I may grow to love him enough to bring this to pass.

All this is incidental. Not so Marie de la Trinité's attitude towards seemingly imminent death. In many letters she makes this attitude clear. Thus (in a note written during convalescence to her Carmelite cousin Marthe) :

'Will you tell all at Carmel how grateful I am for

the prayers offered for me when I was dying? And to you also for your prayers I am very grateful. Your prayers helped me to make full use of those precious hours for the glory of our great God blessed in Three Persons. Those days brought me unimaginable blessedness. Death came to me in shining glory. Nevertheless I am happy to be left upon this earth. For there can be nothing more lovely or loveable than his will. Continue, therefore, to give me the help of your prayers. For I would put to good use the lessons learned of death, when I saw him standing so near at hand : I would be no more than his will made flesh and blood.'

She finished :

' Good-bye. I am now going back to the silence which I love—that silence which possesses all my spirit and in which he dwells, my crowned king. This silence, compounded of humility and adoration, has become my life's core. By this silence I am enabled to live in him.

' Death would have been joy. Recovery was joy no less. For the one, as the other, is God's will made manifest.

' Make no mistake. It was no grief to me not to die last year. In truth it was a great joy. For now I can continue to suffer for him, and to wax in love. Our wills are ours to make them his. His will, loved with passion and to the exclusion of all else, so sates our souls' needs that we long for nothing beyond it. For heaven itself we lose our desire.

' Yet the great call shall come. His adorable will shall ordain its coming. And then with exceeding joy we shall follow the call. For we shall know that on earth we cannot add to his glory, since our hour is come.' (To Marie-Suzanne, at Le Mans, July 15, 1916.)

A few months before her death she returned to this thought :

'I understand you. To envy others their sufferings is sometimes a temptation. Yet—eternity is so long ; time so short. To use time to the uttermost by any means open to us, that we may glorify our God, is our great need. Accordingly we would toil and suffer to the limit of our strength for him, who in himself is " our reward exceeding great." We would live longer as well as more intensely, if by that the value of our life to him were increased : as little Théophane Vénard of his martyrdom, we would cry out : " The longer the suffering, the richer the offering ! "

'Then reflection makes us pause. To be eager to toil and to suffer for him whom we love : this, we come to see, is not hardship but delight. Time may be short. Yet God, whose " day is as a thousand years," can make time's shortness long. Let us, then, offer up to the Father all those ardent desires which his love has inspired in us, and whose fulfilment the Son makes possible. Let us pray that they may be granted or refused according to his holy will. For so shall all things conspire to a blind and utter surrender to him, who is power and wisdom and love ; so shall all things make for his greater glory.' (To her cousin Thérèse, February 1, 1918.)

CHAPTER THE EIGHTH

TOWARDS CONSUMMATION

THE most adequate formula for the Christian life in its fullness is that of S. Paul : ' For to me, to live is Christ.'[1] Elsewhere he says : ' And I live, now not I ; but Christ liveth in me.'[2] In brief, the self dies ; while Christ—a living member of whose Body, the Church, each is—lives as richly and as fully as we permit him to live.

Again, Christ ' emptied himself.'[3] To ' be about his Father's business '[4] was all his life. His own desires he never consulted : ' My meat is to do the will of him that sent me, that I may perfect his work.'[5]

When the soul so identifies itself with its Lord, that all which it does is done as Jesus Christ would have done it, it achieves the Christian ideal.

Marie de la Trinité, the name chosen by Marie-Antoinette de Geuser, symbolised with a curious felicity this ideal, which she had made her own :

' There is such richness hidden in my name Marie de la Trinité. Let me tell you of my own discoveries. In it is implicit the prayer made by Jesus for those whom he had chosen : "Father, I pray that they may be made perfect in one " ; while implicit also is the double conception of the immaculate purity of

[1] Philip. i, 21.   [2] Gal. ii, 20.
[3] Philip. ii, 7. The literal translation of the words rendered in the *Vulgate* by *exinanivit semetipsum*.
[4] S. Luke ii, 49.   [5] S. John iv, 34.

Mary and of the ineffable beauty of God in Three Persons. The ideal which my name holds out to me is that the self shall dissolve and be no more, leaving Mary and the Blessed Trinity supreme in my soul.

'My name not only holds out this ideal to me; it makes clear the way which I must follow to attain it.

'It implies a self-sacrifice so immense and a self-annihilation so utter, that neither could be achieved by merely human suffering and endurance. The consuming fire of God's love alone can achieve them. I yield myself to this love, aware that, even as it called me in the beginning, so it will consume me in the end.'

This is surely evidence enough. Marie de la Trinité in her own life made manifest the 'And I live, now not I : but Christ liveth in me' of S. Paul, and the 'That they may be made perfect in one' of S. John. By her life she had proved the truth of her own saying : 'Where I end, there God begins.' She had reached her own omega. She did not hesitate. She went on to the alpha of God. God gave her, as reward, his ineffable grace, and the privilege of union which approximated more and more nearly to consummation.

1   The Life of Union

The war left gaps in her home circle and the wider circle of her relatives. Each new casualty made Marie de la Trinité more avid of God and more wistful of heaven. After the death of Georges the airman, she wrote with a peace that was not of this earth :

'When we love our dear ones in God alone, God's good pleasure makes one sweet harmony with love, and, though he take where once he gave, our hearts are not seared thereby. For me there is no grief in the thought of Pierre, Paul and Gabriel,[1] but only a gentle delight. As for Georges, he is but one more brother awaiting us in heaven and attracting us thither. "Our city is in the heavens"; how increasingly true that becomes ! How more and more we have no choice but to live in that city ! '

Again :

' Your home-sickness for heaven I can well understand. Nevertheless, God alone knows how I strive to prolong my own pitiful life upon this earth. Eternity has so rare a promise that instinctively we would postpone its rich fulfilment. We feel that earth too must have its richness like treasure in a field. To do his will on earth we would be content that our mortal life should last till the world end. In my efforts to do his will I would be no miser but a spendthrift of all I have. Let each of my petty ailments or their symptoms—fever, coughing, tightness of breath, general weakness—bless the Lord, and magnify him for ever ! In suffering let my gratitude be made known to him, as it makes known to me his vast love ! ' (To her aunt, Carmelite at Le Mans, during 1917.)

She loved heaven : she loved earth likewise. More precisely, she loved God's will supremely and solely, whether on earth or in heaven.

' I have not the least presentiment that I shall die this year. If by chance I ponder upon the possibility of an early death, it is directly due to the state of my health. His will rules all. How good to know that he shall take all he wills, as he wills, when he wills ! How good too to be surrendered utterly to that adorable will which he exercises for his own greater glory ! ' (To the Prioress, March 6, 1917.)

[1] Pierre, Paul and Gabriel Hardouin-Duparc, killed in the War in 1914, 1915, 1916.

Once more :

' Give me your help. Humanly speaking, it would seem that my hour were about to strike. Yet I have yielded myself up to him to do what he will with me. It may well prove to be his will that I shall live much longer yet. So be it ! For me he only is. As he wills, what he wills, when he wills : O joy to think that so shall he deal with all that is ! ' (To Le Mans, March 7, 1917.)

Again—some weeks later :

' Considerable fever and incessant coughing for four months past might have tempted me to forget the Master : in fact they have kept me almost continuously in his presence. Then there are those other small disabilities—my difficult breathing, my bodily weakness and the rest—in them all I wholeheartedly rejoice ; for they make it plain that he has possessed himself of my body as of my soul.

' The fever continues to baffle my doctor, who can trace no lesion or other likely cause. He is evidently astonished that, despite everything, I should go on living. As God wills, so shall it be. His will is best. If he demand that I yield up to him my life in the flesh, drop by drop, it shall be my happiness to see him thus slowly take all from me. If he demand all from me at a stroke, I will be no less glad of heart.' (April 1, 1917.)

A year was to pass before God demanded all from her. In the meantime he took from her her life in the flesh, drop by drop :

' I have tried to write to you on several occasions. Each time I have failed. A state of semi-suffocation left me capable of nothing except prayer. Lulled deliciously by the Father's will into this state that is neither life nor death, I find contemplation supremely easy.

'The alternatives are recovery or paradise ; the present need : to await either in love. Whether it be the one or the other, since we live continuously in his love, you and I shall be at one. With you and me heaven and earth are but two rooms in one house, with only a partition between them.' (To her Carmelite cousin Marie-Marthe, May 13, 1917.)

Yet again :

' Do you talk too much to me of death ? I assure you, no. The thought of heaven spurs the soul to greater holiness. It brings at the same time strength, enlightenment, peace. Across faith's background with what shining beauty falls the promise of that ever-lasting happiness to come ! ' (To her cousin Thérèse, June 7, 1917.)

In allusion to the fire that burned within her soul :

' Let the soul devote itself to the unceasing practice of love. That is the important thing. For so, reaching perfection, it dallies no longer on earth, but stands face to face with its God.'

And again :

' Here on earth we look upon the divine fabric on the reverse side. Hence the sadness which experience frequently brings us. Let it be our endeavour to behold all things on their obverse side, as they are seen from heaven. Then shall peace and joy be our lot, whatever befall.' (To Marie-Marthe, August 12, 1917.)

Marie de la Trinité was drawing upon her reserves of physical strength, that her soul might mount to God in love and unity. Few whose hearts are supremely set on heaven live long on earth. Marie de la Trinité was

yet to know the joy of transcendental flights to God :
for the sake of these he prolonged her life :

' He has made my faith supremely strong. Suffering
itself has seldom power to make me suffer. How
sweet, my Mother, to break free from this finite
world, and to " dwell in love " ! Love is indeed our
dwelling-place ; yes, and the source whence our life's
spring is fed from the wells of God. To live in his
love that she may give his love to him : this is the sole
reason for your little Marie de la Trinité's life. Equally
its sole purpose is ceaselessly to grow in love, and
increasingly to give him more abundantly to himself.

' Looked at from the vantage of earth, my life
presents strange contrasts : my insignificance and his
omnipotence mix ; while that peace which is of
heaven mingles with my petty engrossments that are
of earth. It is as strange that he, the all, and I, the
atom, should come together ; that I, entered into his
peace, should seek to ray forth in all its splendour the
light of truth which is the Word—should seek to
spread abroad the fullness of his love. Lastly, there
is the reciprocal gift from the atom to the All and from
the All to the atom. How strange it is, and how
delightful !

' This is more than enough. These things are too
holy to be spoken—above all with the clumsiness
with which I have spoken of them. For me it all
resolves itself into my need to dwell absorbed in his
love. He does all ; I, nothing. Whether I am active
or at rest, for me there is only peace.' (To Avignon,
March 4, 1916.)

Two characteristic letters of Marie de la Trinité in
answer to questions asked by the Prioress are notable.
Any comment would weaken them :

' In that focal fire of God, in which all his perfections are made one in the oneness of his nature, the

soul is bathed in living light, until the least and smallest of its fibres are steeped in it—until truth becomes its strength and love its life. In that living light which emanates from the Father the seemingly dissimilar is seen to be similar, the apparently discordant to be harmonious, and the soul to make one music. In it action is one with contemplation; nature is made perfect in engulfing grace. The wholly submissive soul lives only in the indwelling Holy Ghost; in utter intensity lives in him and with him. It is active and it is passive. Its dynamic activity is as much of God as its static contemplation: whence it is that the soul's action is as lovely and commendable a thing as its contemplation. They are but the broken lights of God, whose living splendour and active glory fill all the kingdom of grace.

'In God in Three Persons the infinite diversity of the divine mysteries, separate though each remain, is made ineffably one. It is unity without confusion; it is variety without division. The soul, which makes this knowledge its own, is single in its works as in its vision. Made perfect in this calm activity of the divine life, its one purpose is to spend itself in spreading God's kingdom; its one cry is the Master's saying : *In his quae Patris mei sunt oportet me esse.*[1]

'Its own holiness no longer concerns it. For Jesus has bidden it to forget the part in the whole, to sacrifice the personal for the universal. Equally it is aware that the living light from the Father's face dissolves all its strength into active love, and that it is thanksgiving in every fibre of its being, which gives the Holy Ghost mastery over it. The soul leaves to the charge of its overlord the exaction of that thanksgiving which he demands of it, and devotes itself to the apostolate to which he calls it.

'As Jesus lived only to save the world for the

[1] 'I must be about my Father's business.' S. Luke ii, 49.

Father's glory : so the soul would live only for the buttressing of this work, begun in Christ crucified, and, with the co-operation of Christ's living members (of whose number we ourselves are) made perfect in the Holy Ghost. The soul's whole existence derives from this unique act, which is both life in God and life of, though without, God. That existence is ordered tranquillity ; it is equally unfettered action.

' The soul, because its work is in tune with God's, shall know his peace at the last. It is aware that God's will shall know perfect fulfilment, since divine omnipotence makes of human limitation one more instrument to serve his glory. Our wills are ours to make them his : God's plan has no more adorable design than this.

' The soul, living in the Holy Ghost the life of Christ and walking the ways of God the Father, is increasingly aware of his ineffable reality, and increasingly urged to surrender to him all that is his : that is (ultimately) all that it is. It must exalt its belief, its hope, its love, until their exaltation matches God's. In a word, it is only in God that the soul can deal with God ; it is only by putting off the finite that it can be made free of the infinite.' (April 27, 1917.)

On November 12, 1917, she defined further her conception of God's life in us, and of the mystery of the Eucharist. She continued :

' Now for that saying of S. John, to which you have alluded : " But you see me, because I live and you shall live. In that day you shall know that I am in the Father, and you in me, and I in you."[1]

' As usual in S. John, the word " life," used of the soul, implies not merely *a state of grace*, but *a fullness of grace*. The grace which we receive at baptism is the

[1] S. John xiv, 19-20.

M

seed only of the supernatural life. This seed perforce develops under the action of the Holy Ghost aided by the soul's own co-operation. For " by the spirit you mortify the deeds of the flesh."[1] S. Paul's insistence that at baptism only an earnest of " life," thus defined, is paid to the soul, is admirable. Incidentally, this surely explains how it is that certain estimable folk tend to lack God, in the sense that God does not fully possess them. To such these stages of grace should be made known, that they might be stimulated in grace to go from strength to strength.

' As S. Paul expounds with characteristic force and richness of illustration, Christ by his Blood liberated once for all the human race from the bondage of sin, yet to each individual human being offers the freedom born of grace, by progressive stages only. On Calvary he freely saved the souls of all men in his own person ; now he makes each soul holy proportionately to the response it makes to his Spirit. But enough ! S. Paul gave us inspired clues to the mystery of the Redemption. To discuss them now would take too long.

' Reverting to that text from S. John : for him " the living " are those, made rich in grace, who live only in the Holy Ghost. By the action of grace they live the life which is of God, not passively but actively —not in the core of their being merely, but in every fibre of it.

' Experience teaches that these indeed see Christ. They know that Jesus lives in them, and they in him. Nor (as S. Paul says) is their knowledge of the flesh, but solely of the Spirit. Of the Spirit they see the Father in the Son. Jesus himself declared this. He promised his disciples that the Paraclete, the Holy Ghost, should come. He went on to speak of that further return of himself, and of their hearts' rejoicing in it—rejoicing of which no man should rob them.

[1] Romans viii, 13.

In that day (so his promise was to them, as now it is to us) he will speak " plainly of the Father."[1] The soul which lives only in the Holy Ghost is surely a syllable, a tiny fraction of a syllable, of the Word that is God.

' Such a soul does indeed live only in the life of Christ—that life of love for the Father and of zeal for his glory ; that life which derives from the Blessed Trinity ; which makes for each soul's measure of predestined peace, and which knows an increasing sense of triumph in the glory accruing to him who " shall be all in all."

' Itself perfected in its unity with God, in itself it becomes for him a pæan of praise. One means only is left to it by which it may add to God's glory : it may strive that " all may be perfected in union with God." Accordingly it allows itself to be swept into the mid-current of the divine life, that thus " all things may be given back to Christ." In this striving it is as ardent as it is serene, aware that thus it adds to the glory of God and to the blessedness of its fellow-souls ; conscious of the towering whole to which it has contributed its pigmy part.

' Such a soul grows without cease in grace. For this growth is automatic with the incursion into the soul of the divine life in which it lives and moves and has its being. For ever it brims with God, and yet never is over-brimming. For no longer has grace to strive with the natural man : all things help—no things hinder—its growth. The urgent beauty of its call to praise increases with the increasing ripeness of its apostolate. Busied no longer with its own insignificance, nevertheless it has its share in the mighty whole in which it functions. It lives, part of the living God, part of the living Christ, part of the living Church —for Consummata what consummate union ! Blessed

[1] S. John xvi, 21.

be he, who by grace has made us that which he himself is by nature ! '

Consummata—Marie de la Trinité here uses the name of herself. For long it had epitomised her inner life with an increasing faithfulness to facts.

Marie-Antoinette—Marie de la Trinité (with, for variant, *hostia laudis Trinitatis*)—finally, *Consummata*. The name is supremely right. Its seeming audacity is recognised at once to be essentially scriptural. ' *Ut sint et ipsi consummati in unum* '[1]—that they may be made perfect in one—there is its ample justification.

How nearly did Marie de la Trinité attain to perfection ? Good judges deem that God, donor of great gifts and overlord of time, in a few brief years vouchsafed to lead her privileged soul to the high peak of the mystical life—the marriage of man's soul with God.

II   *The Consummatum est*

One of Marie de la Trinité's last letters of any length was written in January 1918 to Sister Marie-Suzanne, Carmelite at Le Mans, who had given her details of the death of one of the community :

' How good for us is this close contact with the elect ! Heaven seems the nearer for the share which we have in their life. So much and so many await us in heaven, that at times it is as if it were already our dwelling-place. Nor can we easily do a better thing than to permit the radiant light of eternity to shine upon the gloom of time, to the inspiration of our souls.

' Yet I smiled at your exhortation that I should postpone my death a while. Do not fret. Nothing shall make me wish either to prolong or to shorten the time which the divine will has ordained that I

[1] S. John xvii, 23.

shall spend on earth. I can conceive no greater joy than to trust myself wholly to his might, to his wisdom and to his love.'

She signed herself : ' Your little sister, Consummata.' In truth for her all things were finished, or about to finish. Let this last note to her brother Louis reveal how near to perfection Marie de la Trinité had drawn :

' The week of his Passion is upon us. In this holy time all my soul cries out that I am one with you. Ceaselessly I pray to God that he may grant you his greatest gifts of grace. Do you too aid me to be faithful unto death—to remember without cease that, in regard to God's adorable will, to the " fiat " I need to add the " amplius," in order that from me he may have all the glory and all the love which he may wish. Ask our Father who is in heaven that he consecrate me host of love by that divine grace, which the Son died to give us, and which the Holy Ghost has made ours indeed. For then shall he, perceiving Christ in my soul, again be well pleased with his own Son. Lastly and supremely, thank him for all things and for ever—for what he is, and for what he does.'

Towards the middle of May her slow decline was interrupted by a sudden crisis. Fever weakened still further her already weakened body. It had no power to weaken her soul. Fr. Léonce de Grandmaison, staying at the time in Le Hâvre, marked and wondered at the divine peace which wrapped her round. Had she, he asked, any wish to express, or any confidence to make ? She answered him, No. ' I am now alone,' she said, ' with God, and with none but him.'

Her cherished contemplation of God was all but unbroken. Her recollection of her absent brothers and her care for the young children alone interrupted it.

Of them she was wont to say with wistful whimsicality that ' they no longer come to say good night to me '— this was that she might not be wearied—' and that's rather a blow.' On June 5 she wanted to give the children their usual religious reading—a tiny yet significant fact. Throughout she was eager that any letter from Jersey, or from Switzerland where her brother Henri was then a prisoner, or from the Front, should be read to her. On June 22, the day of her death, when her mother began to mention them one by one by name, she murmured : ' There is no need : they are always in my thought.'

On Friday the 8th she asked for Extreme Unction. It was thought that this could be postponed till the 10th, in order that one of her brothers, called up at Le Hâvre and about to leave with his unit, should be present.

On this Sunday of the 10th the *Magnificat* and the *Te Deum* were recited in chorus by all in the house. A few days earlier this touching incident had taken place : ' Mother,' she had said suddenly, ' I am going to God. Tell me that it is with a glad heart that you are about to give me to him.' Much moved, her mother answered : ' My darling, I give you to him with all my heart.' And joyously she : ' O Mother ! . . . Let us say the *Magnificat* together.'

When the last breath had left her wasted body, all who kept vigil in her room straightway recited the *Magnificat* and the *Te Deum*.

The relation between father and daughter was a beautiful thing. For the ceremony of Extreme Unction M. de Geuser had adorned with the flowers which he loved to cultivate, the altar which had been erected. It was he (it should be said), who never failed to bring fresh lovely blooms in slender bunches for the sick girl's statue of the Madonna. He knew how greatly Marie-Antoinette loved lilies. Accordingly he had planted three large clumps of them. In this, the last of her summers, anxious to bring them to his daughter, he watched them day by day. On the morning when Nénette was to die, not one of these clumps bore a single bloom. Her body was scarcely cold, when Mme de Geuser—to quote her own words—' for the sake of breathing the evening air leaned from the window for a moment. I noticed that three lilies had bloomed. I called the others to see them. They came : we were all much moved. She died—the lilies flowered. We knew that it was a coincidence. Yet it touched our hearts.'

One more charming episode : M. de Geuser had trained the branches of a vigorous vine, so that they reached the sick girl's window. During her last months he fastened the vine branches, so that they made a green tracery before the window, and by suggestion brought the garden itself into her room. To Marie-Antoinette the symbolic vine had always given a peculiar delight : for this thought she could find no words to thank her father sufficiently. ' None but father could do so delicate a thing,' she exclaimed. ' How humble he is, and how good ! Only in heaven shall I discover all his worth.'

During her last weeks he spent much time in his daughter's room. There he would say his Rosary, with a special intention at each decade. She would whisper the responses, or when towards the end her exhaustion made that impossible, she would listen with shining eyes, glorying in the praise given to the Virgin of her heart's love. Her rosary held in her hand or hung about her neck, her eyes fixed upon the *Pieta* of Michelangelo, which looked down upon her bed, she would become absorbed in her devotion. Often her eyes would shine with ecstasy, and, lost in prayer, she would seem neither to see nor to hear the things of this world.

On June 16th, in a handwriting that was still firm,

she wrote two separate notes of farewell to her parents. That to her father ran :

'My beloved father,

'If my heavenly Father had not of his goodness already made the choice for me, of all the fathers of this earth I would have chosen you for mine. I feel that I have never let you see how my heart has brimmed with love for you.

'Let me tell you of my love now, once and for ever. You believe as I that, living in the will of Jesus, we shall live his life and share that one life together. In all that you do your little Nénette will be for ever near you, wrapping you round with her no longer earthly love, and by God's grace helping you in all things.'

To her last hour her love of truth persisted. A few days before her death she spoke to her mother frankly of its approach. It happened thus. Left alone for a moment with her doctor, she questioned him about herself. He, pitying her youthfulness, answered conventionally : 'You will get better yet.' When her mother again came into the room, she asked with a hint of sadness in her voice : 'Is it true that I may still recover ? ' Her mother, much shaken, did not hide the truth from her : 'No, it is the end, my darling. You are going to God.' Her old serenity returned to her. She thanked her mother, and added : 'So the doctor deceived me ; he did wrong to lie.' It was not that she asked for death, but merely that she wanted to face the fact of death and not to be deluded by kind falsehoods.

It was not death for which she asked, but for the opportunity to do God's will God's will—it was her one thought. Till the end she forced herself to eat. The nurse was touched to see the effort that it cost her : 'Mademoiselle is very brave,' she said. Marie-

Antoinette answered her : ' It is not that. For my parents' sake I must do everything I can to live as long as I may.' At this time it was agony to her to eat any solid food, though but a crumb or two. True heroism can indeed be shown in life's tremendous trifles. This girl showed it.

A priest from Paris, M. l'Abbé Rabeux, mobilised at Le Hâvre where he divided his time between hospital work and the care of souls, paid frequent visits to the sick girl, that he might give her both company and consolation. When he could no longer pay these visits, Fr. Duriaux, a Dominican, continued this work of true charity. Till the day of her death Marie-Antoinette was able to receive Holy Communion, and on several occasions to hear Mass.

On June 17 Mme de Geuser wrote to her sons :

' Our little Nénette is foretasting heaven's bliss. Thinking of our grief, she checks her heart's rejoicing. Yet she knows that her life's work is done. " I am, your little Consummata," were her words to me, " and my mission on earth is over." To you she sends this message : " It is for you, my brothers, to take up my apostolate on earth, where I am putting it down. In God's own place my work shall go on for ever. *Laetatus sum in his quae dicta sunt mihi ;* that is, I am glad at heart, because I know that I go to my Father's house."

' Father Duriaux, to whom God in his mercy has made known our sorrow in the loss which is about to befall us, comes every day. He does much to confirm her in that state of glad acceptance of death and of serene peace, to which she herself had previously come. He tells her not to check her soul's joy, since it is God's will that she shall know it. He bids her to allow it to possess her wholly, since the peace which is upon her is altogether of God. Thus, you see, in our sorrow we are comforted. God is in the house, giving us his succour. Your sister, my dear sons, has been almost a mother to you. In these, her last days, you are constantly in her thoughts. She takes communion every day ; while to-morrow we shall have Mass, we hope.'

On the 8th she wrote to her seminarist son :

'Heaven hovers near to us : the hours go tranquilly by. Suffering has lost its power over her soul : in God she is made consummate. I have but now been talking with her : she spoke of the way which leads to God. She told me too that from her discussions on theology with you, she had had much profit and had gained much peace. It has been made plain to her (she told me further) that her way was not the way of the extraordinary mystic. It was the way of truth, as taught by Catholic doctrine. "I am a Catholic," she said. And then again in a moving voice : "I am a Catholic." I cannot remember all the lovely things that she uttered : this will be my lasting regret.'

Here are a few of the most characteristic sayings of Marie de la Trinité during her last days on earth :

'On earth my brothers will carry on my mission. From heaven I shall give them my aid. I would like to think that the tiny seed of my apostolate shall be brought to fruition, and the great truth of love spread abroad.

'Until this world shall end, as my brothers know well, I shall continue my apostolic work.'

On June 20 :

'In heaven I shall understand you better than on earth. In heaven I shall not know death, but only life. Though you be unaware of it, I shall be with you ; I shall help you.'

'Cling to his will. So shall a noble work be performed in you. Though we do not see it, this work is like leaven within us. O my mother, you and I are truly *one*.

'Let us but put on Christ, and grace shall ceaselessly grow within us. Let us but welcome that grace : it is all that we need to do.'

Again :

'Your soul is my soul, mother ; so utterly at one are we. God was good indeed to have given me a mother like you. Of all earth's mothers I would have chosen no other.

'Let nothing be denied to him, who is Love. In small things as in great let all be done that may content him well. Let him be praised that I have suffered greatly. My flesh must die, before my soul may dwell in unity with his. I would have all my fellow-men share the peace and joy that now I know. To God I would give love and thanksgiving : the nearer I draw to death, the stronger is this yearning upon me.

'Earth and all earthly things are less than shadows. The self in me which suffers is of no account. Why should I regard it, I who can behold in my own soul infinite love—God himself ? '

On June 18 or 19, her brother François, recently called up, had to return to barracks at Le Hâvre. Overcome by his grief that he must leave her, he stood dumbly at the foot of his dying sister's bed. He gazed at her in silence : in his sorrow he could find no word to say. She looked back at him. Then she smiled, and her smile was as the smile of God. She murmured : *Laetatus sum in his quae dicta sunt mihi : in domum Domini ibimus.* Still he could not sufficiently master his emotion to speak. She smiled again. ' So,' she said—and it was Marie-Antoinette who spoke—'my little François has forgotten all his Latin. Let me then translate for him : I am glad at heart, because I go to my Father's house.'

On the date fixed for the marriage of one of her cousins she was at the point of death. She begged that on her account there should be no alteration in the arrangements made. By prayer she gave herself part in these joys reserved for others. She told her mother how pleased she was that the latter had sent good wishes despite her own imminent death. Thus to the end she was considerate of others, and solicitous for their happiness.

She was now no more than a shadow. On June 21, S. Aloysius' day, Communion could not be given to her : even a crumb of the Host was too much for her—indeed throughout that day she swallowed no more than a drop or two of water. Henceforth for her only one communion was possible—the great communion of heaven. She lay unstirring in her bed, her eyes gentle, her face shrunken—almost transparent. She made efforts to stretch her arms cross-wise out. It was beyond her strength. When her crucifix was put to her lips, she kissed it, and kissed it again.

The extraordinary phenomena accompanying her critical illness of 1915 did not recur until a particular day, when her death was near. On that day the former state of seeming ecstasy was reproduced. Again her eyes grew fixed and shining, her face glorified, her body rigid, her arms extended towards something or someone ardently desired and seen close at hand. Again a few phrases escaped her, that were not of this earth. The Sister and M. de Geuser were summoned. Marie de la Trinité, returned to herself, must have known that once more her secret was betrayed. Supported by her mother's arms, she shed a few swift tears, and said : ' I have been . . . talking again, have I not ? ' It was as if she reproached herself for having fallen under the spell of God—or so it semed to those about her.

On the 22nd, sighing almost inaudibly, she died. These were her last words : ' Jesus ! Jesus ! For you I have forsaken all. Consummata ! '

CHAPTER THE NINTH

AFTER DEATH

1 *Prevision*

IN 1912 in a letter to the Prioress Marie de la Trinité wrote :

'He has revealed what he has in store for me : much suffering, the complete crucifixion of the self, my soul's identification with Jesus sacrificed, lastly union made consummate and the beginning of my work for the Father's glory.'

She had no mission in the official sense of the word. Yet her apostolate-urge was so strong that she could not conceive of death as the end of her opportunities for service. Her zeal, ever a bright fire upon earth, would, she imagined, be but a brighter fire in heaven :

'Eternity is surely the beginning of our true life. Equally only in eternity will our true mission commence. As it was with Jesus, so surely will it be with us : only when we have risen from this earth shall we yield up to him all that we have.' (To Pontoise, 1913.)

In June 1914 :

'When I am in heaven, it will, I think, be my delight to draw souls to God. I shall make known to them that in him is all their need ; while they—they will purge themselves of all that is not of him.

' It is sometimes said that in heaven there is no toil, but only joy. For me this idea has no attraction. Even in heaven could there be happiness, unless there were also service and the opportunity to turn this joy into a gift to God and to other souls ? I like to think that only then shall the highest service be possible for us ; that then through all eternity we shall seek his glory and ensue it. In the liturgy to-day I came upon these words : " The youth of the saints shall be renewed like the eagle's ; they shall bloom like the lilies in the city of the Lord." I rejoiced at this, since it implies that in heaven as on earth our work goes on, and with richer results than here on earth.' (To Marie-Marthe, February 18, 1917.)

Marie de la Trinité was richly endowed to give that service here upon earth. The power of prayer was of course hers, as it is that of all good Christians. Then too she had her own peculiar gift, whose exercise resulted in those writings of hers, which are now extant. Like a beacon set upon a hill, those writings give both light and warmth to men. They illumine the soul ; they warm the heart : this light, this warmth, mark them out for the inspired efforts which they are.

' They warm the heart '—on two separate occasions with a gap of years between them she expressed this thought :

' When I am dead, may only a tiny heap of ashes mark where once there burned the great fire of divine love, which I aspire to be on earth ! ' (To Pontoise, November 10, 1912.)

When she heard that war was declared, she looked beyond the rivalries of the belligerent powers to the tragedy of individual men of all nationalities, whom God had created that they might be supernaturally one in Christ, and whom the nations had crucified by those same rivalries :

' I am one with you in love for the spreading of love. My love for my country is the love that would have Christ crowned king of France. Nor should this love know national frontiers. For we are Catholics, and our charity should reach out over the wide world. Dear God, may all men in love of you come to love their fellows, and all the earth know peace.

' All minds made one in truth, all hearts made one in charity : that is my dream. The spreading of truth and love through all the world : that most surely is my mission. I have said it before—I will say it again—when I die, may I be utterly consumed in a great fire of love ; may there be nothing left of me but a trail of shining truth ! Would that men loved one another, as I love all men ! ' (To Pontoise, August 5, 1914.)

Again—two years later :

' Would that before God's supremely adorable will all men fell in reverence upon their knees ! Oh, let me live in love ; let me grow from love to greater love, that so without cease it may be spread increasingly in men's souls and more abundantly given back to God himself. This and no other is surely our goal ; to possess God and him alone, to possess him only that we may share our possession of him.' (February 28, 1916.)

Once more :

' I prefer not to keep jealously secret those things that have helped me to glorify God. To do so is as if a sower kept a seed stored in the house, instead of casting it abroad upon the fields, that it might come to fruition.' (To Marie-Marthe, May 13, 1917.)

Yet again :

' To magnify him is not enough. Let us be apostles ; let us cover the wide world with our prayers ! Let us not by any omission of ours limit the limitless gift, which our Father has made to us in Jesus ! Let the Spirit be bestowed upon all men, that all men may be God's !

' Let us believe in Jesus ; let us count only upon him ! Thus shall there be performed in us works greater than our own, since he himself shall perform them, that the Father may be glorified in the Son ! ' (February 18, 1917.)

As she lay dying, Marie de la Trinité maintained with emphasis that she was before all things a Catholic. Using the word in its richest sense, she gloried in it. Few have had so notable a grasp of the Church's universality. Her thought like her love embraced the wide world. Limitation of any kind irked her. Her constant need was to go onward and upward : onward in apostolic work, upward to union with God.

As her existence in the flesh approached its end, her soul's radiant life spread limitlessly out. She could not love enough ; excess of love was her death. Though doubtless the image was faulty, she was made, this Marie, in the image of Mary, Mother of Jesus, who died because her love for God was overmuch for her human heart.

On February 1, 1918, she wrote to the Carmel at Le Hâvre :

' The adorable will of our great God of love as gift of grace has given me in an insignificant bout of sickness the opportunity of an excellent retreat. Help me to thank him practically by living a more intensely Christian life. Like the host in the Blessed Sacrament I would be more than the poor shadow of him in whom God finds his glory and souls their grace. And how simple is the way thereof ! His will, than which is nothing more adorable and in which we fulfil our own wills utterly and for ever, shall itself perform all

N

God's desires. Ravaged by his will as S. Ignatius was by the fangs of wild beasts, we shall become the " pure bread " offered to God as a host of praise and at communion given to the souls of men.

'There is delight and splendour in this our vocation. How good it is, and how sweet, to have the power to add to the glory of God and to the life in God of our fellow-men !'

It was in this manner that she reconciled her vocational silence and her loving activities on behalf of souls :

'Increasingly I feel the need to put simultaneously into practice these two exhortations: " Seek to live in obscure humility and to appear of no account," and " Put at the disposal of others the gifts received as almoner of God's grace." Here there is surely no contradiction, but only dove tailed truth. Self-effacement increases the power to do good in the world ; while true humility is " linked with the liberty of God's children." God through the Holy Ghost pours the water of life into our souls : we can but direct its current, that his glory may be served.

'" I have learned without pride," cried the author of *Wisdom*, " and communicate without envy. And her riches I hide not."[1] Selfishly to hold back even the smallest trifle, which might help others to grow in grace, is no commendable thing. To do it under modesty's cloak is to prove humility lacking, no less than large-heartedness and liberality. Essential pettiness of soul cannot be disguised by the trappings of modesty. Silence may be incumbent upon a man for a number of reasons. Let none of these infringe his free right to speech, when the occasion demands speech.

'In all things then let the self be subordinated in the cause of God's glory. You have doubtless met

[1] Wis. vii, 13.

with those notices which run : " appropriated in the public interest." Though I have not seen them myself, the phrase has always seemed to me a striking one. I would adapt it thus : " appropriated in the great cause of Catholic interest—the establishment of Christ's reign in men's souls for the magnifying of God." ' (To her cousin Marthe, February 3, 1918.)

Marie de la Trinité had not only a lofty spirituality : she had also true genius in the ability to crystallise lofty thought into luminous words and phrases. Added to her austere nobility of character and her doctrinal depth and correctitude, it was this which gave her her great influence over others.

Some imagine that profound thought may not be expressed in simple language. This girl, herself no professional writer or recognised theologian, at her best was the match of both the one and the other. It was her great gift, this ability to enmesh in words the love-liness which pertains to the high matters of God and the soul.

The level of her writing was consistent, her style restrained, her phrasing sober, her metaphors extra-vagant neither in nature nor in number, her similes exact and triumphantly faithful to facts. With her language did not hide reality : it discovered it. And this reality was the supreme reality, the sublime mystery of the divine, whether found in God himself, in Christ, or in the souls of men.

We undervalue our rich spiritual heritage. We need to be made aware of it.

Marie de la Trinité by the example of her life—her apostolate, her Christian mission, which she herself defined in set terms as ' the re-establishment of all things in Christ '—shall teach the ignorant and shall recall the faithful to the meaning and the practical application of these great dogmas, the sublime mystery of God, who, blessed in Three Persons, yet lives in us ; and of Jesus Christ whose members all men are, and in whose fellowship all men are brothers.

This girl belonged to those whom God, it would seem, has called to make plain to the men of our day—in the case of certain of them to stir to a first awareness of —the invisible realities ; to show that in them is the sole and transcendent reality ; to prove convincingly, irresistibly, that the true life in Christ makes of these invisible realities the one reality.

Fecit magna. In this girl God performed a marvellous work.

Few of those who read her biography will in all things be able to follow the example of her life, or of her writings' precepts. The way of this saintly girl was not, and could not be, the way of all.

In her life as in her writings there were two distinct elements : that of the special grace which God had given her ; that of the Christian ideal as she herself outlined it.

Of the former no estimate can here be made. Whatever view be taken of the relation between ascetic effort and mystical grace, none can gainsay that such divine favours, particularly when so richly bestowed, are wholly matters of election, discussion of the means of gaining which would be both speculative and dangerous.

The relevance of this biography lies otherwhere. It lies in the fact that Marie de la Trinité in her search after holiness asked only to be a perfect Christian. The phrase has become hackneyed and colourless. In its anterior richness it stood for the fullness of life in Christ and for the perfect knowledge of the mystery of our re-establishment in God by and through Jesus Christ.

This was her own definition of the Christian ideal, made towards the end of her life :

' There are apostles of the inner life, as there are

apostles of the outer. The former spread love more than they publish truth ; the latter publish truth more than they spread love. Others are called to an apostolate combining both of these. There is, I conceive, no higher call than this. It is our own call.

' . . . To carry out this high mission we must become as children, God's true children, made perfect in his love and living altogether in his Son's life. The Scriptures declare that from the mouths of children God draws perfection of praise.

' Let us then utterly and for ever yield ourselves to him, who would have us attain by grace to that which he is by nature. Then shall our perfect praise, more and more abundantly given, make of us apostles truly profitable for God's greatest glory.'

(To her cousin Marthe, February 3, 1918.)

God lives in us ; this divine life is ours through Christ, in whom is its increasing strength ; we become as Christ only in the measure that we slay the human and the sensual self (*Jam non ego*) ; the nearer we approach to Christ, the more we are permeated by the life of God in Three Persons ; this for all of us is the one supreme concern of our souls, though to each be given his differing particular grace and personal vocation : this is surely the core of true Christianity, so far as Christianity can be set forth in a brief summary.

It is as surely the heart of Marie de la Trinité's spiritual message to men.

II *Some Tributes*

Because of this concentration upon God's great essentials, Marie de la Trinité, when she becomes known for what she was, will have a notable influence upon no small number of Christian souls.

Immediately after her death one of her friends—a

woman of sound judgement in no way given to exaggeration—wrote of Marie-Antoinette in these terms :

'You would not have recognised her, so altered she was, so wasted, so pitifully shrunken. Everything about her spoke of long and almost limitless suffering. She has burned her body to the end, as a candle is burned. Now that the flame is out, the candle is done : she held nothing back ; her sacrifice was complete and utter.

'To see her again moved me profoundly. Now she has gone from us, and we do not yet realise all that we have lost in losing her. Her prayer was comprehensive and Catholic and abounding in charity. None visited her but had the irresistible impression that it was a saint whom he visited. And in her saintliness how clearly a saint she was ! Never any more shall we be able to pay those dear and delightful visits from which we came exalted away, much as did those pilgrims, who at Emmaus met Our Lord. Yet our memories are ours : in them she lives and will go on living. I pray for her, because I must—too often and too easily one ceases to pray for such a soul as hers ; but for her I pray not of my own volition.'

Another friend, to whom had been lent some of the notes used in the preparation of this book, returned them with the following account of the impressions which their subject had made upon the reader :

'My long intimacy with Consummata has been a great inspiration to me. Close contact with so pure and so surrendered a spirit made livelier my own desire for greater perfection, for nearer union with Our Lord, and for eventual total transformation of the self into Christ's self. Would that by faith I might in my life know a measure of those sublime realities, which Marie de la Trinité knew and lived experimentally ! '

A third, who had to do with the manuscript at a later stage, cried admiringly :

' Beautiful stuff ! truly beautiful stuff ! And full of spiritual meat ! There must be no delay in giving as many as possible the opportunity of benefiting by it.'

A nun of the Marie-Réparatrice community wrote thus :

' What do I think of Consummata ? My emotion is too great to allow me to tell you all that I think. These pages have set my soul on fire. In no other life have I found such a parallel to the work, which God has wrought in me. Let me hastily add that my life has been less difficult, my sufferings less keen, my love less rich, my surrender less complete, than were hers. I have not been " perfected "—far indeed from that. Nevertheless, what she has known, I have known, though less abundantly—the same call, the same attraction, the same forms of grace.

' . . . I can but feel that her example comes to me now as a reassurance, as a challenge to go on, as a call to steadfastness now and for ever. Constantly I dreaded lest I had fallen into illusion. For there have been long periods, when for me there seemed to be no more light and no more peace, no more desire for suffering or scorn or forgetfulness of self, but only the one great and increasing need to possess God solely and to give him to himself. And now I know that all this can be ; that such a life a soul may truly live. Now I know that this life of union and of love, savouring as it does of that lived in heaven—this life that is mine in my constant communion with God, with his works and with his will : is no delusion snaring my soul. *Magnificat !*

' This is Consummata's gift to me : a new accession of confidence, a new glow of love ; a yearning like her own to climb as high as God would have me climb ; a longing that, become steadfast and unshakeable in him, I may pour into the hearts of men the love which I have drawn from my close communion with him, to the end that I may set their souls ablaze with a great fire of divine charity. I know that merely to have such a vocation is not enough. I need, as she, to feel a sense of urgent responsibility. If I am to be at peace, I know that I must fix my eyes upon the Host, realising that it is my strength and my holiness.

'. . . I have never in my life before written a letter like this.'

It is no very surprising thing (it will be said) that definitely religious minds should find delight in the example and the writings of Consummata. The following letter, written intimately by one woman living the secular life to another, is a tribute from another sphere of life :

'About Consummata. I have not yet read the whole book. What I have read has so lifted me up to God, that I want to stop and ponder it. Other heaven-inspired women have given me glimpses of God's sun of splendour : Consummata has given me that sun itself. The chapter entitled " In the darkness—God " has given me supreme help. It came when most I needed it : another proof to me of the loving-kindness of God, who gives his succour when most his succour is required.

'For I find my own spiritual experience reproduced in Consummata's : not when upon the heights she stands in shining loveliness, but when in the depths she gropes in the darkness of the pit, crying aloud in her soul's desolation. There is a great gulf between us, nevertheless. I am not yet clean enough of heart either to see God face to face, or to quench the thirst for him which parches my soul. Thus for me it is natural to yearn for suffering and for all else that may purify the soul and vanquish the self. So only may I break down the barriers, and reach my goal. How true it is that this spiritual life, which comes of carnal death, is of all things the most desirable ! '

Men no less than women have paid their tributes— men most eminently qualified to appreciate true spiritual values. Thus a venerable priest, a noted director of souls and learned scholar in the science of mysticism. wrote thus :

' I have lent the manuscript (this referred to a first draft of the present work) to a woman peculiarly fitted to draw profit from it. She wrote to me shortly afterwards saying that, once more at home, she took down this work and was at once conscious of the scent of roses and of violets, although there was in the house at the time neither the one nor the other.'

Upon this detail no stress need be laid : it is perhaps a trifle too reminiscent of certain incidents related of S. Thérèse de l'Enfant Jésus. The end of the letter is to be preferred :

' Another woman (living the secular life) found in it very great comfort and notable consolation.'

The superior of an important religious house in Paris, regarded by his colleagues in the light of a saint, declared after a first acquaintance with the writings of Marie de la Trinité :

' When I had finished my reading, I felt both abashed at my own unworthiness and seized by the love of God.'

The head of a mission in China on his return to Europe made an immediate personal visit to express his thanks that the writings of Marie de la Trinité had been given to the world, and his gratitude for the profit which they had procured for his own soul. It delighted him to recount this scrap of dialogue between himself and Dom Louis Brun, Abbot of La Trappe of Yang-Kia-Ping :

' A soul of this quality atones for millions of sinners,' declared the Abbot.

' Isn't that rather an exaggeration ? '

' No. I say deliberately what I said as deliberately before : a soul of this quality atones for millions of sinners.'

To add other such tributes would serve no useful purpose. If this brief biography give a reasonably faithful picture of its subject, its end is attained. God disposes. If it pleases him for his glory's sake to exalt Marie de la Trinité, any of man's purely human proposals will be negligible.

For almost ten years the biographer has known the writings, the spiritual quality and the influence of this girl, who is his biography's subject. In those ten years he has become convinced—deferring always to the overruling judgement of Holy Church—that the most exact estimate of Consummata's spiritual worth is that which her dearest friend condensed into a phrase : ' In her saintliness how much of a saint she was ! '

PART II

LETTERS AND EXTRACTS FROM THE NOTE-BOOKS OF MARIE-ANTOINETTE DE GEUSER

MARIE-ANTOINETTE, AGED 12

INTRODUCTION

IN Part II recourse is had to two series of documents : extracts from the intimate Journal of Marie-Antoinette, and her correspondence with one of her two Jesuit uncles, Father Anatole de Grandmaison, who had been her leader in several retreats.

In Part I little is drawn from these two sources. Parts I and II, therefore, are complementary : each should shed light upon the other. The whole makes articulate a girl to whom God made rich gifts : the gift of initiation into the secret of prayer and of his own immanence in man's soul ; the gift of insight through grace into the true nature of man's life in Christ. And this one gift more : the gift of great human artistry in expressing in lucid language, quick with beauty and instinct with truth, the knowledge which God had entrusted to her of his ineffable nature.

All Saints' Day, 1928.

RULE OF LIFE

(Retreat of 1907, *completed in* 1909.)

NONE BUT JESUS.

1. *Strength.* Never to be influenced by first impressions. Always to plan ahead. Never to be swayed by impulse or to come to hasty decisions. Never to relax in a task till the last minute assigned to it has been used in its performance. Never to fail to employ my time to the best advantage and in the service only of God, and to spend all my courage and all my love in so employing it (this because God cares less for quantity than for quality, less for achievement than for the will to achieve).

In making a decision always to make the hardest, unless charity or obedience demand otherwise. Never to shrink from a sacrifice, but always to seek it out. Never to procrastinate. Never to allow myself a purposeless pleasure, unless again charity or obedience demand otherwise. Always to guard against those bonds that would attach me to earth, to my fellow-creatures, or to the self. Always to repress indulgent thoughts, indulgent affections. Never to day-dream ; always to remember that heart and mind and inclination belong to Jesus, that he is the overlord of all three.

Always to find new courage in Love, that always I may meet Love's demands upon me. Always to hide with a happy smile, reflecting my soul's happiness, the spiritual disturbance and destruction that I may know within me. Never to allow others to suspect that at all times and in all things death and my soul are at grips.

Always to endure suffering in silence ; to accept defeat ; to stumble and fall, yet always to cry *Sursum !* Always and with all my strength to show my gratitude.

Never to cry ' enough ' but always *Fiat ;* ever to be ready to suffer yet more, if God will it.

2. *Charity.* Always by publishing Jesus to all, to allow him to be apparent in me (I need to live less in my soul, to give more service to the souls of others. I need less to make closer my already close union with Jesus, than to resist its attraction for me—my confessor's advice).

Service for others. If possible, always to do a little more (or the little less a little better) than is asked of me—this to make it known that I do it with a glad heart. Always to forestall my own desire—*agendo contra.* When I offer to do a service, always to set about doing it, as I make the offer ; for then my offer is more likely to be accepted, while, if it be not accepted, I shall have made some denial of self A.M.D.G.

Always to share wholeheartedly in the interests of others, as though this gave me personal pleasure.

As for the children,[1] literally *to bring them up*, to fill their hearts with God's love. Always to practise firmness, though by this firmness I give up the pleasure of knowing myself loved by them ; make few demands upon them, but seek their willing co-operation.

In failure always to have courage and confidence, since in effort and endurance is service rendered to others. Always to sow the seeds of love—only God can bring the ripe grain.

. . . The farmer : his sole endeavour is to see that all his seed is sown—and to see that it is sown deep in the soil. Once it is sown he does not look behind him to see whether it shoots. . . .

Always to do as the farmer : take thought only to sow ; to sow with all my heart and all my mind ; at

[1] Her young brothers.

seed-time to take no account of harvest ; for harvest is
no affair of mine.

Never to cease my efforts to become joyous, tranquil,
gentle, lovable. In this to put all my mind and all my
strength. I could face martyrdom with a glad heart :
yet I find myself cowering before my simple duty to keep
a smiling face. Mine is indeed an insufferable disposition ! O my Jesus, though they be blood-wrung
smiles, be smiles my gift to you !

3. *Union.* Always to live for him alone, for the
Father's glory, for the saving of the souls of men ; to
perform the pettiest duty with all the love which I
should show, if I were going to martyrdom.

Always and above all to have trust. To have trust
were no merit, if virtue were mine and I knew God
well-pleased with me.

Utterly and blindly always to make surrender of the
self : to be submissive in all things. This irks my
active and impulsive nature. Yet it is essential.

Always to accept the fact of my own uselessness,
since Jesus wills that he alone shall operate in my soul,
and that I shall stand by, while the work of self-
immolation goes on within me.

Always, as penitent, to surrender the self, to abandon
my own will ; never to ask the ' why ' or the ' how ' :
how or in what way I make reparation is not my concern.

Always to accept the humiliation of being esteemed
far too highly ; to accept praise as if it gave me pleasure.
God knows how truly wretched I am made by such
praise and over-esteem.

Always to prevent others from suspecting how much
I suffer from the sense of my own unworthiness : to
hide it is the better part. Always to move undistinguished among my fellows, not by hiding myself from
them but by doing as they do.

Out of humble-mindedness to give up my preference

o

for simplicity, and to pretend to a little more vanity than I possess, if this make for the pleasure of others. For, if poverty consists of being detached from things, it consists still more in being detached from the self.

Always to keep my eyes fixed upon Love. Always to be willing to renounce all that is not he.

None but God.

CHAPTER THE FIRST

(January 1909—*September* 1910)

HE loves me and demands my love of me.[1] . . .
Plunged deep in contemplation of this Love,
who has come into my life. . . .

' . . . And you, my child, whom I love so dearly ?
. . . See how men repay me for so much love ! '

. . . *Ecce ancilla.* . . . Oh, insignificant that I am !
Ecce minima. . . . I am full of impurities, blemishes,
earthly and selfish inclinations. Yet you are able to
destroy them all in the fire of your Love. You are
able and willing to make me of service for the salvation
of many souls.

O my adored Love ! What do you wish of me this
very day ?

' . . . Adore—repent—give thanks—give love—give
praise . . . deny the self, destroy it, rebuild it in me
. . . be one with me through the surrender of your will
and of your inclinations, through the renunciation,
constantly striven for, of all that is not " me alone."
And afterwards, since I will it so, my glory shall find
in you its dwelling-place.'

---

[1] Consummata responded to this demand upon her by a triple
vow ; the vow of *chastity and virginity* on February 2, 1909 ;
the vow of improvement in July, 1909 ; *the vow of complete self-
surrender*, by which she yielded herself wholly to God as host,
on September 8, 1910.

. . . O mine of pure gold that is the will of God, performed for Jesus' sake ! Let me work that mine ; with love as tool let me work it *per ipsum, cum ipso, in ipso !*

Pure love is not of this earth. Yet let me strain every nerve to make my love as pure as possible.

Let God alone be witness of this . . .

He calls me to sacrifice, to destruction of the self in him. . . . O insignificant soul ! God makes use of you to do great things. Give adoration—give increasing love ! Make sacrifice of self, as Love was sacrificed for you ! . . .

My Lord God, my Father whom I love and who loves me, truly performs all. My soul is utterly insignificant still. For the great things done are all his work. In the edifice of his glory he is all ; he is unique. Nevertheless, this small pebble, which he has chosen and which has given itself to become part of that edifice, rejoices in the glory of its beloved Master.

Unaided, deeds, aspiration, even love itself, are all beyond me. Therefore, O Jesus, *my Jesus*, be with me and keep me in atoning unity ! . . . O Mother of the crucified heart, I would be crucified with you ; I would become a sacrifice to the crucifying will of ' my Jesus.' I would have myself made pure, made holy, made new, though I may not understand the need—above all when I do not understand the need.

Formerly, God designed to have me serve his glory by the way of tribulation only. This was his will. Now, though he bring tribulation upon me still, that is not enough. He demands action of me also. He urges me to take the initiative ; he calls upon me to climb upward.

Therefore, O my soul, insignificant as we be, you and I must climb—climb for our great God's glory's sake !

We must climb by the way of *poverty*.

We must climb by the way of *mortification*.

We must climb by the way of *obedience*.

How splendid is our goal ; to be sacrificed with Jesus —to have share in his abjection in order to make atonement with him, in him, and for God alone ; to be in atoning union with Jesus for the Father's glory !

To-day has been a day of *illumination*. Of love. Of trust—of boundless trust. I have heard Jesus—I have heard my adored Love's voice. He has demanded my love of me. He needs[1] his little nobody to add to his Father's glory and to make atonement with himself. He has shown me his love repaid by ingratitude, and this has come home to my heart. He has called me, and I have come to him. I have sought him ; I have listened for his voice, and I have heard it. This was what he said to me : ' *I love you—I love and choose you.* I in my heaven love you, even you. In you I would do great things for my Father's glory.'—I have listened and understood. Understanding, I find it sweet to surrender the self, and to share the supreme sacrifice of him, whom I love. And when my understanding falters, because I love him, I *live* his will, though I understand it not.

Audivi.

' . . . Lo ! only later shall you know what glory I, Jesus, draw from souls. Only later shall you realise how holy is this vocation.'

The Cross

I have *seen* the light, which Jesus has so many times shown to me. I have seen—as in November, and now still more clearly than I saw it then—the unfathomable deeps of love to be found in the heart of ' my Jesus.' I have heard his call to me.

I have *seen* the unfathomable deeps of wrong, dug by the sins of mankind—sins for which I am utterly unable to atone.

---

[1] ' Needs ' is used relatively. Christ's sacrifice is in itself all-sufficient. Yet he asks our co-operation in it. For so only shall the supreme worth of his sacrifice be made known to individual men.

I have *seen* God's gift of his Son, his love of the world that is the uttermost love ; I have seen ' my Jesus ' *tradidit semetipsum.*

I have seen the very Heart of God, his Heart that brims with love, with merit and with grace ; his Heart that would pour itself upon the world—and this grace and this merit the world would not permit to be poured out.—And I have become aware, *I have seen,* that something was lacking, an utterly insignificant something, yet significant in its insignificance and definitely lacking, something for the lack of which atonement is hindered ; I have seen that for the lack of this something souls are left unsaved. This utterly insignificant something is the channel by which God can pour forth the infinite treasure of his Heart's grace.

Audivi. Yes, I have heard ; I have heard ! . . . ' Are you willing to be this insignificant something ? Know that such a channel is a *surrendered* and *consecrated* soul that has no desire, no prayer, no life, save for the glory of God ; a soul that puts from it all personal inclination, and works only for the inclination of the Heart of Jesus. This does not need a soul of exceptional nobility : it needs only a soul that shall be *surrendered utterly.*

' My little insignificant child, give me your heart.' . . . Yes, Lord, I give it. . . .

. . . Accept, O Holy Father, this little host that my soul yearns to become ! Accept it with the oblation of your divine Son's body ! Grant that ' by him, with him, and in him ' it may be purified, stripped naked, sacrificed, utterly destroyed, and afterwards made holy, made new for your glory's sake.

What peace, what happiness I know in this knowledge that *verily* I am nothing, and can do nothing—*vere nihil sum, vere nihil possum*—and yet that God makes use of me, *vere.* . . . Yes, that he has need of me to pour his grace upon this earth. *Vere,* out of my insignificance shall God draw great glory, so only I dwell in union with him. *Qui manet in me.*

Nor is it enough to dwell in Jesus. I must be the lantern of which he is the light. This that men may praise him, love him, adore him, give him thanks, because of me ; this that men's hearts may expand at my approach.

I have seen what surpassing glory is rendered to God by the immolation of a soul that loves him—of a soul that, in trust and in love, *permits itself* to be stripped naked and utterly destroyed, and afterwards is made holy, made new *by Jesus.* Of a soul that humbles and sacrifices itself with Jesus ; that, seeing, desiring, seeking *none but Jesus*, strives with all its strength towards love at its purest, shrinking from nothing that may unite it more closely to him.

Let my prayers be full of praise, of adoration, of thanksgiving ! Let me petition too for grace to be given to my fellow-men ! Again and above all, let me watch ; let me listen that I may hear !

When vision flees and intuition fails, it is not easy for my soul. Yet may it never cease to *strive !* It pleases him that I shall owe him a debt of love.

With Mary at the foot of the Cross

It is she ; it is Mary. She gazes upon earth's children, whom Jesus has called to come to her. She cries : ' Who will have share in my sorrow ? ' And I : ' Oh, I will share it, my beloved Mother. I will not avert my eyes from your abysmal sorrow, O my cherished Mother, who are immaculate yet crucified. By your side I will willingly stand as sacrifice, even as you still stand. Even as you, I offer the Holy Father the sufferings of my Jesus.

Even as does the priest, I offer the Father the host of sacrifice which is mine to offer. With this Host that is pure and divine and adorable, I offer the little host of my soul to make atonement with him.

Stabat Mater. Be of good heart ! With all her own heart Mary still endures. She has this double comfort. She knows that suffering is a gift of love, that love may come of it. She submits therefore with courage and with trust ; once more she makes offering of her love to the Holy Father. Lo ! now she sees—our blessed Mother—at the foot of the Cross John and Magdalen —purity and penitence. She sees them there. Jesus sees more than them. He sees also those atoning souls, which in days yet to come shall share his crucifixion— and hers.

O Mother, look upon your little redeemer and all her sister redeemers ! Let your sad heart be in a measure comforted to see before the monstrance the brides of your Jesus, who make atonement with him, even as you at the foot of the Cross. . . . O blinding light of revelation ! I to be the bride of Jesus, to share his sacrifice ! Oh, who may touch even the fringes of these *uttermost truths of love*, and fail to be enraptured by them ? . . . *Si scires.* . . . ' My Jesus,' how abounding is this grace, that you give me—this grace that enables me to forget all things, even my own soul, and to lose myself in your abysmal love.

This has been a day of great and dazzling illumin- ation. A day upon which I have glimpsed the *uttermost truths of love*. A day of surpassing happiness. A day upon which, in contemplation, the self has been obliterated within me.

Vision upon the Mount

I am alone. Jesus draws near. . . . Jesus draws near ! So my God is not beyond my reach. He lives, he loves, and yet he is my God—Jesus, Emmanuel. . . .

O adorable mystery ! God—Jesus, ever present in the Blessed Sacrament, calling me, claiming my love.

. . . Let me make a void of my heart ; let my heart be one great solitude, that Jesus may draw nearer yet ! . . . ' I go away, yet I remain with you.' So be it ! When I see him no more, I will yet stay with him ; I will live as if I still saw, since ' he is for ever there, claiming my love.' . . . ' Jesus Christ is my sufficiency.' . . . Be strong, my soul ! He is *my* Host, and you are his host, O my soul ! I can offer them both to the Father. By this offering is the pit of my unworthiness filled wholly in.

NONE BUT JESUS.   *February* 2, 1909.

Laudate Dominum

To-day, the Feast of the Purification, I have made the vow of virginity and of chastity. I have taken this vow until the Assumption, subject to the overruling discretion of my confessor.

With this new consecration of myself this is my relation to God :

On April 24, 1889, I became a Christian ;

I was later dedicated to Mary ;

On June 14, 1900 (as at all times since and for all time to come), I gave myself wholly to God to do with me what he would and all he would ;

On November 13, 1900, I was made a soldier of Jesus Christ ;

On October 31, 1906, I was betrothed to Jesus ;

—and now to-day, in a nearer, dearer union, I am become the bride of my Jesus, sufferer with him in his work for redemption.

Henceforth I would be more than ever about my Father's business ; I would serve his interest in all that I do ; I would with Jesus be a perpetual sacrifice for God's glory.

I am a debtor, whose debt is infinite. I am God's bankrupt, who may never discharge her bankruptcy.

And yet my adored creditor, not content merely to forgive my debt, which would in itself be an unsurpassable kindness, is eager to *love me*, and *actually* to make me his bride. This that in a true union he may make my debt *his own*, even as he makes his glory *mine*. Thus he is at once debtor and creditor. . . . Overwhelmingly conscious of my complete insignificance, I was utterly without worth in my own eyes, when Jesus offered himself to me to be my sufficiency. He—he himself—loves me beyond the bounds of love ; loves me thus to-day, will love me thus for ever.

Overwhelmed with gratitude and with love, I can only adore. Enlightened by this truth that dwells in Love's unfathomable well, over whose edge I peer and into whose depths I may not see, I can only adore. *Jesus loves me*—loves me beyond the bounds of love.

Quid retribuam ? . . .

Though I were martyred many times over, it would be nothing compared to the vastness of my love. Let me be strong in the unity of atonement *ad gloriam Patris*.

Si scires donum Dei—let me live, as if indeed I knew it !

Let me adore—let me give thanks—let me make oblation—let me pray—let me work !

Misericordias Domini in aeternum cantabo. . . .

O truth ! *O mystery* that defies understanding ! *Qui manet in me . . . hic fert fructum multum.*

Wholly surrendered to God's will that he may do with me all that he may wish to do, I have an overpowering desire to know extreme suffering for his sake, and immeasurably to magnify him. I hold myself in readiness, *indifferent* to all else.

My Jesus has made it plain to me that he is well pleased with this oblation. For by it he is made overlord of my surrendered soul, as out of it he draws all the glory, which it is his wish to draw. Ah ! now—now ! —I have seen Jesus, suffering, agonising, dying, with none to comfort him. I have seen him abased, deserted by all. I have seen *the Cup—his Cup*. I have heard his voice crying to me : ' Are you willing, even you, little child, whom I love well ? ' At the sight of such infinite anguish I flinched ; at the thought of my unworthiness I faltered. And then he declared : ' *It is my will that you drink my Cup.*'

Convinced that it was his will, with a glad and grateful heart I drank of the Cup. It is my faith that he shall give me grace.

He has promised to give me the maximum of suffering and to destroy me utterly for his glory's sake. He has promised to bring me into *the closest union* with him, and to have of me *the maximum* of glory. He has promised me things that are beyond the understanding, and that no words can express. Once more he has spoken, and I have heard : ' Be not afraid ! I have promised you suffering and grace and revealed wisdom. All these shall be given to you *abundantly*. For all these are needed that you may be strong, strong to endure. Love shall be your strength , for of yourself you can do nothing. In grace and in the light of wisdom I shall be one with you. Your own suffering in no way serves the Father's glory : it will be I, who will suffer and be abased in you, and I, who will be your *strength* and your *worth* to God.'

Further, he has repeated his earlier revelation, and renewed all his promises of these past months. It is his wish that I shall be a little host, altogether consumed for his glory's sake.

Calicem accipiam et nomen Domini invocabo, laudans invocabo Dominum. . . .

These words too seem intended for me :

> ' *Fac me plagis vulnerari,*
> *Fac me cruce inebriari*
> *Et cruore Filii. . . .* '

I have become convinced that all this shall be *exactly fulfilled* in me.

Further, he has shown me what my oblation will mean for me—a headlong plunge into suffering's fathomless depths.

He has gone on to show me the fathomless worth of this oblation for his glory's sake.

Lastly, he has shown me many other things, which may not be written in words, but remembrance of which he will make mine, when I shall have need of that remembrance.

Mar. 1, 1909.

' My dear Uncle,

' For the first few days after the retreat the great revealing light continued to shine for me. On the 2nd I made my vow. That vow has brought me great happiness and great peace.

' Afterwards the light grew dimmer. Becoming again as I had been during the preceding months, I knew a painful sense of loss. I no longer saw truth clearly. Yearning for spotlessness, I felt myself once more spotted. With all my strength I sought to give God my love. Loving him, I knew the urgent need to love him more. And I could not. I felt the desire to mortify myself. It was a vain desire. For when I had satisfied it, I felt that it had been no mortification, but indulgence. I sought to humble myself, and found no means. On each occasion I grew sensible that my motives were suspect, and finally that the self had entered into both them and my actions, my knowledge of the fact coming too late for me to drive out that self.

' In this state of mind I strove with all the courage that was in me. My faith has not faltered ; for I perceive that in all this Jesus has wished to test me a little. Wherefore, as frankly as I may, I have accepted the humiliation of being unable to humiliate myself, and the mortification of being unable to mortify myself.

' When one is wholly possessed of God, as in times of great illumination, there is no risk that the self may enter in. Equally when the self is aggressive, it remains plain-sailing : the soul has only to oppose and rout the self. It is when the self lies in ambush that the difficulty begins. It is then that I fear always lest the self shall make an alloy of my intentions' gold.

' On the third evening of the retreat Our Lord gave me a clear call to enter l'Adoration Réparatrice. Unless he gives me as clear a call, countering the present, I am convinced that thither I must go. Thither I would go unquestioning.

' On Mar. 25 last year, believing myself truly weaned from earthly things, after a Communion admittedly less inspiring than some, I declared to Our Lord (whom interiorly I saw) that my love was ready to meet all his demands. As so often before, I heard his words claiming my love : " Adore—atone " —those two words, that so constantly I hear, again sounded in my ears, this time with a note of challenge. Vividly before my eyes I seemed to see the walls of l'Adoration Réparatrice, and to hear the question involving my freedom without those walls put to me in the words : " Do you love me enough to follow me there ? " At once I discovered, I assure you, that I was still very much in the power of the self.

' Nevertheless I determined to do as he would have me do.

' One evening at the beginning of December as I was preparing my meditation, the thought of Carmel's mortifications made a sudden strong appeal to me. I have come to realise that if l'Adoration Réparatrice be Our Lord's will for me, since suffering serves his glory, greater suffering will be my lot there than it would be at Carmel.

'On Feb. 19, after I had received Communion, Our Lord made me the promise that he would give me what best should serve the Father's glory. This I perceived to be suffering. For he revealed himself to me in his agony. For ten days the revelation lasted : during them the sufferings of Jesus, dying with *none to comfort him*, were ever-present with me.

'At first I was a little afraid, too much afraid to accept. I felt myself too insignificant and too weak. Then conviction came that, since Our Lord called me to that agony, in it he himself would be my strength. This great revealing light of love still shines about me : I avert my eyes from no anguishing detail of all that agony ; from this revelation I get for my soul what strength I can. My strength and my trust I am hoarding against the hour, when his cup shall be mine to drink.

'For several reasons I have not told you of these experiences before. First, I had not the courage. Second, I was not sure that I ought to do so. Third, I feared that imagination might have played some part in them. However, this last experience has been more vivid and more unmistakable than any that preceded it. It lasted from ten to twelve days in all.

'Years ago, when I was seven or eight, I prayed to Our Lord that I might have a share in his agony. After this prayer for long I was extremely unhappy, believing myself to be damned. You may be sure that since then I have not prayed for suffering, although I have often yearned for it. Now it is otherwise. Our Lord himself has asked it of me. So I can accept it with a glad and grateful heart, can I not ?

'I have looked upon a truly shameful death. Our Lord, making me no promise and no appeal in regard to it, asked me whether I too would be willing to face it. Whereupon I answered him simply that it should be as he willed, whatever his will proved to be.

'Mortification has a strong appeal for me. In moderation I practise it whenever possible. My heart, I feel, is void of all that is not solely God ; I see all things in truer perspective : that is, I perceive that God is all and that the rest is nothing. Everything that is not austerely poor I find a heavy burden. I would possess nothing of my own ; I would be able to make no gift to others, since in this there is a wholly natural pleasure. Plainly, therefore, the hardest self-denial for me is to give up my longing for utter poverty. For poverty is but a means, and too great an attachment to it would be a weakness. . . .

'I have never known such close union with Jesus in his agony and with Mary at the foot of the Cross. It brings me indescribable happiness. I am one with utter purity, one with utter love ; I am bathed in living light. In this rapturous union I wait, expectant of suffering and humiliation.

'I am aware of my many faults. Yet this does not in the least discourage me. For the Heart of Jesus purifies all things. I have done little good in my life. This gives me no inquietude. For if I were to see some merit either in myself or in any deed done by me, I might well be overtaken by pride. Or, lacking pride, I might well know satisfaction that it was within my power to give this or that. Not to be able to make gifts would trouble me far more than mere poverty, however utter. But, as I know, it is God's will that he alone shall be responsible for my sanctification, that to him alone the glory pertaining to it shall accrue.

'As for those about me I try to give them some share in this goodness and sweetness of Jesus, with which he has so abundantly blessed me. That they may not feel left out of my life, I try also not to appear too detached or too contemplative.

' In my home-life the self is still too assertive in my nature. God's grace comes to others a little soiled by contact with the self in me ; while, reciprocally, a little of that which they should give to God is lost, in that they give it to me. When I have made myself of less account to them, they will be in closer touch with God.

' Inwardly, I am no more I, but only the indwelling Jesus. I go here and there, and yet it is not I who go : the more whole-heartedly I devote myself to the daily round, the more I am conscious of the presence of Jesus and the more distinctly I hear his voice.

' It is my faith that God will be my prop, when I am assailed by that great suffering and by that exceeding humiliation, which I foresee.   'M. A.

' There is only one thing, which I have never fully experienced and which therefore I am wholly unable to realise : to see *nothing* and to hear *nothing*, merely to live by faith and *faith alone*. The thought is frightening. To have strength to face that test, I shall need God's great light of wisdom. But my faith is strong : this light will be given to me.

I have asked my Jesus to strip me of all that is not solely he, to make pure my heart, to make spotless my love, that I may be more nearly one with him, and that I may magnify him yet more.

' . . . I have suffered in my own person all the vileness of the earth : from this suffering all shrink ; into it none follow me—and you ? '

. . . O Jesus, if it be your will, it shall be my happiness.

' . . . Men would have me give them various attractive and noble qualities ; there are some who ask for suffering itself. None yields himself up to the humiliation of humiliations—none *surrenders himself utterly to my will*. Do you then ask of me only my will, since you *do not understand* in what the Father's glory consists. But I—I know what best shall serve it, and that will I confer on you.'

. . . Yet to pray for priests, does that not make for your glory ? (My confessor had suggested this intention to me.)

' . . . If it be my will that your devotion shall be especially for them, I will make it known to you, and allow your prayers to avail them. Meanwhile, ask only my will. For thus is your prayer *unquestionably pure and acceptable.*

'Surrender yourself in love and in trust to my Love. Take *my Cup*, unquestioning, from my hands, and with me drink it *to the dregs*. That shall *most avail*. . . . I am one with you in the *closest union of all.* . . .

'I will draw the maximum of glory from you—and of reparation. Yet of yourself seek to do nothing : I *would be alone* in the work of your sanctification.

'If men but knew the glory that God draws from a surrendered and reparative soul, however insignificant ! . . .'

And I—I did perceive this glory. . . .

'Men petition for much, yet themselves offer little either of service or of gratitude. There are few who love, who adore, who listen expectant. . . .

'Do you then lift up your eyes and strain your ears —love and follow and praise ! . . .'

What could I say to him ? What but everything ? (She interpellated this to her director.)

' . . . Your debt shall thereby be larger in God's sight and yourself more negligible. He will be aware that in all these things I only am, and the glory of them is mine alone. Be strong in faith ! Say what I bid you say ! Be strong in trust : to you shall be given

P

only humiliation and suffering ; to me *all the glory shall be reserved.*'

Mar. 27, 1909.

'My dear Uncle,

'On the 21st I had a frightening experience. Our Lord gave me a glimpse of the wrong done to God by my sins. I knew such hatred of my worthless self, that had so wronged my God, that momentarily and involuntarily I would have been content to have seen that self damned eternally.

'Straightway I knew horror of myself. I would have been *content*, this time truly, to have seen myself deprived of the Love of God and of eternal happiness, if so I could have made atonement. For even this would have meant less suffering for me than the knowledge of such wrong-doing.

'Throughout the day, out of love for him, I have sought to rid myself of this self-hatred. I have failed. To love others, however uncongenial or repugnant, is no difficult task. To love one so spotted as I, is less easy.

'Thereupon Our Lord disclosed to me that it was this soul, a fraction only of whose impurity I had glimpsed, which he had chosen for intimate union with him and to which he had granted the gift of his love. Usually when God has made me this trans-forming gift, my heart has rejoiced at the union to which he summoned me. On this occasion I would have preferred the favour of God's love to have been given to another purer than myself.

'Drawn thus to Our Lord more irresistibly than at any time before, to break from him I needed to make an exceptional effort. It was difficult ; it seemed impossible. I did my best. I debated whether possibly I had not kept myself too remote from the life of every day.

'I have tried, not (I think) without success, to

seem more light-hearted and more interested in
matters that do not truly interest me. At least I
have made the attempt, or have begun to make it.
For plainly I ought to make others conscious of my
inner life. In this matter I believe that I tend to take
things too easily.   'M. A.'

Mar. 5, 1909.

' I have already told you of the clear call to
l'Adoration Réparatrice, which came to me during
the retreat. Since then there has been no renewal of
that call. . . . Our Lord, it seems, invites me only
to suffering : I am to share his sacrifice.

' Can I by means of a vow still further surrender
myself to the way of sacrifice ?—as so often, I cannot
see the best for me ; I can only do what I *think* to
be the best.

' In regard to the Order I am not troubled. I
believe that Our Lord will show me the way, when
it is his will.

' A few days ago I had a great yearning to die, that
I might be out of men's sight, out of men's thought,
alone with him. Why I had this yearning I do not
know, nor whether it is worth while to allude to it,
particularly in this inadequate fashion. Ultimately it
occurred to me that, dead, I should no longer suffer.
My yearning then left me. The tomb for which I
long is one in which, though buried, I shall suffer still
with Jesus, and with him shall die continually for the
Father's glory. For myself I can conceive no better
vocation.   'M. A.'

Mar. 14, 1909.

I would pattern myself upon Joan of Arc. She
trusted her voices and followed them ; *none but Jesus*
was her heart's cry. Contradictions apparent to the

petty human reason might cause others to misunderstand : they could not hide from her the ' great Truth.' She did not demand to understand : she was content to follow. Still as far from understanding, she died. In his own time God has been magnified in this little saint. To-day Joan stands revealed for what she was : she challenges little souls to follow, though they may not understand.

I must *strain every nerve* to go in the direction in which he would have me go, not knowing whether I shall arrive or even whether I am going forward. For this is his will with me.

From February 19 onward it has been as if he had set me in a skiff on a stormy sea, and, bandaging my eyes, had put the sculls into my hands, saying : ' Pull away . . . be strong . . . whatever befall you, have faith . . . for I am at the rudder.' Then, as if bending to the oars, I had started off . . . in love . . . in self-surrender.

It is my faith that upon the last day I shall have come to harbour ; that in harbour he shall take the bandage from my eyes, and I shall know that my safe arrival was due solely to his guidance.

From time to time he vouchsafes me a word of revelation. On each occasion it is a word of love, of confident faith, of peace. . . .

Oh, how good it is to love truly and to see all things in the light of truth ! Yet if one loved always so, in the things of this earth there would be neither suffering nor joy, while mortification and self-denial would become purposeless. These are but the means of which I must avail myself, that I may win to the more blessed state —they are no more than means. The goal is otherwhere —is beyond the reach of any means. The goal is life lived in him.

I have not the strength always to tread those heights. I need to make use of means. Willy-nilly I fall again to

earth and into earthly inclinations. Then how hideously
I suffer. With each new glimpse of his splendour the
vision, once faded, becomes a more exquisite martyrdom.

I am as a small uprooted and not yet transplanted
plant. All earthly things have lost their sweetness for
me. ' I shall be satisfied when thy glory shall appear,
Lord.' My love has reached that stage, when separation
from him causes me to suffer intensely. My love for
him is so great, that life has become a daily death. . . .

By this love which attracts me to heaven, I am kept
prisoner upon earth. Men have sinned against God.
To atone for their sins Jesus has come and has been
sacrificed. He demands that I shall share in his suffering. I will meet his demand, that his work may go
on. . . .

The purpose of my life on earth is a perpetual dying
to the things of earth, to the end that I may be perfected
in him. Further, its purpose is this : that I may be a
brand of divine love, setting fire to the souls of men,
warming their bodies, kindling their hearts, until the
day come, when my little spark shall be quenched, lost
in infinite love, yet able to spread that love abroad upon
earth.

June 18, 1909.

' My dear Uncle,

' During a particular High Mass Our Lord disclosed a high ideal that might aid to perfect me.
Aware that the time had not yet come, by joining in
the *Credo* I put this ideal from me. Yet its attraction
was strong upon me ; the ideal, remote and lovely,
constrained my eyes to look upon it. Throughout
that day the daily round stood between me and it ;
while, once free to meditate, I found that the light of
its glory had departed.

' I had lost the vision. Yet words of love sounded
in my ears. I knew tranquillity and boundless trust.

Yet the one question remains : I have seen the ideal far off and removed : I have not known how to reach it—what am I to do ? I am, I feel, strong enough to break down every barrier, to make every sacrifice, and yet before me there seems to stretch merely a great emptiness. . . . I am on fire to give to Our Saviour, and I have nothing to give, nothing (since my sufferings are wholly inadequate) with which to prove my love. . . . My cup is full, but it is not full enough.

' I try to control these urgent longings ; for I know that through them I have lost perspective. I seek to be more single of soul.

' I try to convince myself that, where his light leads and as it leads, I have but to follow ; that present seeming contradictions are but the means which God uses to reach his end ; that Our Saviour, unable at the outset to reveal his true purpose to me, will disclose it glimpse by glimpse ; that, his ultimate truth and his ultimate perfection being so infinitely beyond my understanding, he needs to reveal to me such transitional truths and such transitional per-fections as my soul may grasp. The things of God are so far beyond my comprehension that God, if I may say so, to reveal himself to me needs to hide his purity ; to make me understand he needs to descend from the heights.

' Ultimate truth and ultimate perfection are hidden from me. Yet it is Our Saviour's will (I believe) that I shall seek and come to understand them. Hence the appeal for me of Carmel, and my gratitude to him that first he made me wait, and then called me thither.

' This letter stumbles among words. They are too poor, and I am too stupid in the use of them, to trans-late truth. Truth is beyond me, but my trust is in God : he will give you guidance that you may give it to me, insignificant and impure as I am, when thus confronted by his vast love and mercy.

'How may I reply? Tell me if there be anything, anything at all, that I may give.

'For myself, having nothing, I can but surrender myself to his love.   'M. A.'

July 11, 1909.

'I am in great perplexity. Constantly God gives me glimpses of his truth, and as constantly I fail to perceive their meaning. I know increasing strength and love, but have no comfort of them. Our Saviour lifts me up, only to set me down in the place where before I stood.

'The vision is given to me. Momentarily I seem to see aspects of it with clear eyes. Then it fades. Latterly, exterior things seem no longer to lead me to God, but away from him.

'Last Sunday, for example, the vision returned : not until it had vanished, did I perceive that it had been given to me. I had an engrossing desire to serve his glory, and yet knew that within me was lacking the wherewithal to serve it. I asked myself whether there could be contact between him and me ; whether in this new and hitherto unsuspected union, to which I was conscious that he had called me, the inequality between us was not too great.

'When I consciously search for him, I do not find him. Reasoning and meditation seem to be but barriers between him and me. When I make my soul a void and my heart an emptiness, I am brought near to God and to perception of his shining truth. At such times I am in fear, lest I may be able to do nothing for him. Yet, following your advice, I am content to strive no more, but merely to endure in this light-in-darkness, and by my endurance to be made clean.'

July 16, 1909.

ALL IN UTTER LOVE.

For your greater glory, O my God, this day, the feast of Our Lady of Mount Carmel, I vow to do what I *believe* most shall perfect me. This vow shall serve :

1. At ordinary times to strengthen my love and my trust, and to keep me from earth's vanities ;

2. At times of illumination both to comfort me, conscious of my previous lack of insight, and also to keep me, as God wills, aware of my own paltriness ;

3. At times of hesitation when *reflection* would draw back my arm extended to take his cup, and my *will* would forbid me to drink of it, that I may not shrink, but, with courage made strong by love, may perform my duty, nor know the grief that comes of failure.

This vow, made subject to my confessor's overruling discretion, shall bind me from now till the Immaculate Conception.

You know, O Jesus who are both man and God for love of me, that I make this vow, as I live my whole life, to the *sole end* that your glory and your love shall be the more greatly served by it.

I would die daily for you. It is sweet. There are difficult days, which are full of pain, when this daily death seems not for me ; when in the grip of anguish I fail to see the cup. It is for such days that I must make mine greater simplicity, greater tranquillity, greater trust. The way which my Jesus has shown me is the way of *boundless trust* and loving surrender. I need to have *heroic trust* in his love.

It is not enough to die daily. This daily death needs to be compassed *simply, naturally and wholly calmly.* . . . Though I may not see the cup held out to me by Jesus, yet let me drink of it. . . . Exteriorly, this daily death needs to manifest itself by a joyous tranquillity. Its compassing must be *unconscious on my part* if I may express it so. Inwardly, I must be above the spiritual battle. With the same calm love I must welcome equally tribulation and truth.

Out of love then let me die daily, until that day come, when, for the last time dead—dead for love's sake still, I shall be at one with my beloved God and wholly lost in his love. . . .

Aug. 9, 1909.

' My dear Uncle,

' On Sunday I am to make perpetual my vow of Feb. 2nd, then taken till Aug. 15th only. What do you say to this ?

' My soul continues to know vicissitude.

' On the 27th Our Lord gave me an hour of insight. Since then I have groped in darkness.

' I am no longer conscious of God's love for me, or of mine for him. My heart is cold ; my eyes are blind ; my soul has lost its assurance that it is watched over by God. I seek suffering, but do not find it. Or if I do perceive how I may make it mine, I am not sure that it accords with God's will. I am in torment. Yearning for passing joy, that I may deny it to myself, I experience none. I am dead to joy, dead to pure desire, dead to spiritual need.

' Yet at bottom I know peace and trust. For Our Saviour has been merciful to me in the blackness of my soul's night. Though he has withheld vision, he has given me suffering.

' Solitude and suffering—they have an ever stronger appeal for me. God seems to call me to absorb myself in him. I see more and more plainly that Carmel is my place. As was not previously the case, I now definitely desire it.

' Outwardly, everything indicates that my entry will not be immediate. However . . .

' Either God gives me this desire because it accords

with his will, or he gives it to me merely to take it from me.

'If by God's will there be more delay, so be it ! If the time be come for me to enter, equally I am prepared : already I have put this world from me.

'M. A.

'P.S.—Here, nettles would be good things to use for purposes of mortification. May I use them ? They have the advantage of leaving no mark, and of in no way impairing the health.'

Sept. 26, 1909.

'Latterly Our Saviour seldom seizes my soul during my hours of meditation. So, as you have advised me, I have gone about my everyday life— have even sought this diversion or that—in an endeavour to find Our Lord in acts of love.

'What am I to do when, as often, his light comes to me at times other than those given up to devotion ? The other day, for example, a walk was suggested. Feeling within me some stirring of the divine, I told mother that I was thinking of going to Vespers. Mother bade me accompany the others on their walk : this, she said, was best. I went, heedless of my inward urge. This sounds a trifle. Experienced, it is more than a trifle. It involves resistance to God, and yet the resistance is a sacrifice made for his sake. What should one do in such a case ?

'The contemplative states which Our Saviour permits me to know become increasingly rapt. Often I have to strive against their rapture. To surrender myself to it would mean too complete a surrender. When I do yield myself up to it, I put my head in my hands : quickly it is as if I were in a cloud high above the earth. Temporarily all things are blotted out. Then the cloud clears, and I am in a new world, a world walked by God.

' My roots are not here. Since the revelation of July last I have had this sense of uprootedness. I realise that Carmel itself will be but a half-way house. The true goal is otherwhere. 'M. A.'

Sept. 29, 1909.

' The more complete consecration of myself which I made a few weeks back has brought me much happiness.

' As I have told you already, I believe that in February last Our Saviour made me his host of praise. At the time I failed to understand, chiefly because I am a coward and because my nature is exceedingly stubborn.

' Within two or three days of that time I went to the Carmel here[1] that I might know definitely what their decision was. Chatting, the Prioress told me among other things that she had just received photographs of a young sister, who had died in the odour of sanctity at Dijon a couple of years previously.[2] She offered me one of these. Though I took it, I scarcely glanced at it : only one thing interested me then—was I, or was I not, accepted ?

' I was not accepted. I had expected this refusal ; I had even wished for it, since for some time Pontoise had had an indefinable attraction for me. Yet I felt tremendously disappointed. Leaving with, in my heart, a murmured " O God, is then Carmel to be for ever closed to me ? ", I chanced to glance at the photograph. As I looked at it, the face of its subject seemed to spring into life, the eyes to smile at me, while within my spirit I heard most distinctly the words : " No ; as I, you shall be a host of praise."

---

[1] At Le Hâvre.   [2] On November 9, 1906.

In the word " host " I perceived an abyss of suffering, and knew that in it I should have my lot. For me the phrase had an implicit meaning far richer than its explicit sense. It was implicit of God's will for me. My way is a way of austerity, and I thank God for it.

'Since then the old Adam has been less assertive. More and more my union with the Blessed Trinity embraces also union with the Blessed Virgin and with the little Sister Elizabeth de la Trinité. Though through the latter God has vouchsafed me both light and strength, I am aware that this particular devotion is in no way authorised by the Church. The revelation made to my soul is the only evidence I have of her saintliness.   ' M. A.

'A year ago you promised me an iron bracelet for mortification. Could I have it, please?'

Oct., 1909.

'Just now I am much troubled. I have doubts whether my life and my prayer do not leave much to be desired. Though I have sought to regulate both by submissive responsiveness to your guidance, I have had fears lest I may have explained these things badly, and unintentionally deceived you as to what is passing in me.

'Further, there are experiences which no words can *transcribe*. Again, although till now your advice and my confessor's have always coincided, what if this were not always to be the case?

'During my frequent experience of what I have called light-in-darkness, it is rather as if the soul and the self begin to disintegrate: I become unable either to perform acts of love, or to make resolutions, or to realise what may be happening about me.

'I am conscious of myself as a spotted thing,

estranged from God. It is he who gives me this consciousness. Had I not seen him, I should have a better conceit of myself. Our Saviour gives me vision, that my lack of humility may be corrected. My one need is to be resolute in my trust in him.

' There are times when Our Lord gives me such excess of love that by no one suffering can I make response to it. Accordingly I seek to make larger my suffering's oblation. But my soul is not equal to it ; an inner fire seems to burn me, my heart to be about to burst.

' In my own despite I yearn for union : the yearning makes me long either for death or the cloister ; for in either more perfect union should be possible. On reflection I perceive that suffering unites me to God, as neither death nor the cloister may do.

' I do not find mortification in any way painful. So I practise it less frequently. I do not wish to risk shortening my life : for others' sake I ought to prolong it.

' Whether I enter Carmel, or whether I need to wait yet longer, I can still glorify God. But I do believe that for me Carmel is the way, and that Our Saviour bids me to follow it.

' In obedience I find great peace. I would neither hasten nor delay my entry.'

Nov. 1, 1909.

All Saints' Day.

' A few days ago in the cloud, which was above me sitting contemplative below it, a narrow shaft seemed suddenly to open. Through this there came light so pure and clear, that it can only have emanated from God. In a matter of two or three seconds it had vanished. While it lasted, I had the impression of being one with him. The experience brought me surpassing happiness. Of itself it repaid all conceivable sufferings.

' For such union separation from most earthly things is essential ; for in the world they make it difficult to follow the way which leads to union. These are :

' *Separation from my fellows :* let me be no longer anxious to give souls to God ; let me seek him by climbing upward—let me not look backward as I climb. Union with him will procure more grace for souls than any exterior effort of mine.

' To make this further separation of myself : by every means in my power except those which would involve scandal or sin, let me make men think contemptuously of me ; to this end a general confession is, I think, a good means.

' *Utter poverty :* let me strip the soul of all it has. I used to order my life to the one end of being able to give to others, and so to do good. Now I know that it is not exteriorly that I can serve souls. Hence my needs are none. In the secular life is it possible to renounce all and to have nothing—nothing—of which to dispose ? If not, the religious life seems to be marked out for me.

' Should I leave pictures, papers, etc., as they are ? Or should I burn the pictures, which I have cherished for certain graces associated with them—or possibly find another use for them (I might for example use them as illustrations, when I question the children on religious subjects ?) My personal papers were better without exception destroyed, I think. Of what use can they be, now that my own way is so plainly Carmel-wards ?

' I have expressed myself badly. Yet you will understand. These shackles must be broken at all costs. They bind me to earth.

' This vow of poverty, assuming that it can be kept

in the world, implies the surrender of my right to dispose of spiritual things no less than of material things. A year ago Our Lord taught me that I must propose no more, since in all things God would dispose according to his pleasure, and by my complete surrender would add to his glory. 'M. A.'

Nov. 23, 1909.

'For a month past that light of God's truth, of which I have written, has been notably mine : in my prayers God grants me no other.

'God demands to be alone in his work in my soul.

'My intelligence is a tool of which he makes no more use. He intends to reveal himself to me without it. Then let it go, since God does not wish for its help. 'M. A.'

Dec. 16, 1909.

All lost to me—Jesus alone left to me : here is plenitude of peace and of joy.

'But when God's night of darkness closes round, all then is lost to me, and with it Jesus : here is abysmal anguish ; here is his *cup*, his promised cup. . . .

In this night let me yet know peace and joy and trust and love !

. . . Let me know trust in God's infinite mercy, and let me seek nothing that is not of him ! Though I be ignored, disdained, forgotten, it matters not to me, who am alone, alone in this dark night of indescribable suffering.

Let me have trust . . . so only souls receive God's seed in abundance, the rest matters nothing. Be there none but you, Love, O Love most cherished ! Pitiful Jesus ! . . . God most pure ! . . . Eternal Truth ! Life more excellent ! . . . Be there none but you ! . . .

If you depart from me in the night and the tempest, then would I dwell alone. For I would have none other take the place, which I seek to keep sacred and reserved for you.

Alone in my night of sorrow I shall await you. For I know that your work for the souls which you cherish goes on, though they be unaware of it.

Dec. 27, 1909.

' My dear Uncle,

' The light of truth grows stronger. I hesitate to credit this summer's call to complete surrender of self, since the attraction of and desire for Carmel entered into it, and inclination less spiritual than natural might have misled me. Later, perceiving the potential suffering in this surrender, I doubted still, since I have a great desire for suffering.

' The other day, however, Our Saviour gave me a foretaste of the anguish, which is to be my lot, and I was sated by it. It was an anguish given of God, and like no ordinary human anguish. It a little resembled that other, which I had known at eight or nine years old, when I begged the Jesus of the Agony to allow me to share in his agony. It was of God, and yet at the same time God seemed to have forsaken me, leaving me only with a horror of such suffering. I was tempted once more to give myself to the world of men and things, feeling that this oblation, which Jesus asked of me, was too great. Yet I made it in the end, with much reluctance, I own, and with too little gratitude for his grace. From that day God has seemingly used all things as means to draw me to him.

' I am once more tranquil of spirit : indeed, Our Saviour having given me a special access of strength, my deep-seated peace has remained with me throughout.

' Since June, when God began to manifest himself

to me in forms not readily recognisable—forms that can only be conveyed by the use of such inadequate symbols as the words " cloud " and " darkened light "—I have failed to see how heaven and earth can be in tune. By this I am convinced that my understanding has failed me.

' On the 24th during the night office God's light came to me once more. In this close union I was isolated from earthly things. Jesus in his divinity came to me in a glimpse of new truth. My body became weak like water ; my soul grew sure that from me he asked all, and that those I left would profit by my leaving them.

' It is his will that my lot shall be removed from men's earthly habitation. He has made men dwarfs in my sight. In heaven my part shall be (I believe) to sow upon earth that seed of love, which I shall have of God in infinite abundance.

' To my earthly place I no longer belong. Jesus calls me elsewhere. Notwithstanding, I have abounding trust that in his little nobody God's glory is served. By his grace and at his slightest nod I shall leave this external world with a glad heart. Meantime I am content to accept as much as I must accept of this somewhat false position in which I find myself. Whether it cost me little or much, I will consent to forsake my plain vocation.   ' M. A.'

Feb. 19, 1910.

Sacrificabo hostiam laudis

These words rang in my ears. Part of his truth, they were rich indeed in their meaning for me. In this *Sacrificabo* I have come to see that it is he and only he, who must make of me a sacrifice ; that my sole part is to yield myself into his hands, and to accept all from

him. In this work he is all ; I am nothing. . . . In
this *hostiam* I perceived nameless, intense, surpassing
suffering. I perceived that the host is to become a
holocaust ; is to be destroyed, body and soul and mind
and strength. . . . And that *laudis :* the word is like
a deep-voiced bell, calling to the life hidden in him !

Laudis. . . . In an anguish *known to him alone* I am
to be sacrificed, that in his poor little nobody his work
may go on.

So let me not pose as a victim ; let me rather with the
aid of my old secluding ' joy and peace ' preserve my
soul's immolation for him alone !

In my soul let annihilation and absorption go hand
in hand : let the host be consumed beneath ; let the
soul's more worthy elements be lost above in him !
Let me seek to sow his seed neither by word nor deed
nor even by example ! Let me take thought only how
I may bury myself more and more in him !¹

Feb. 20, 1910.

' My dear Uncle,

' Last Wednesday I once more knew tranquillity on
the one hand and tribulation on the other. This
evening, seized again by the old spiritual suffering, I
heard once more a voice ask the question : " Is it
enough ? Are you this time at the end of love ? "

' God gave me strength. I answered that my love
was not exhausted but excelling ; that if it were God's
will, I would be tested further, then and always.

' My soul's torment did not, as is its wont, grow
greater. On the contrary it left me. Our Saviour
made himself known to me in such sweet fashion as
I have not known for two years past.

¹ It must not be forgotten that Consummata had definitely
a specially contemplative vocation. The generality of the
faithful are called rather to initiative and to action. Prayer
has not so exalted us ; we must seek to ' sow the seed by word,
deed and example.'

'I was amazed : I had so little expected this. I had so often made sacrifice of similar grace, that I thought it was never any more to be mine.

'He looked at me, and his eyes were shining with mercy and with love. He uttered these words : "How may I make use of so clumsy a tool?" I knew at once that the tool was I, and that the clumsiness was my exaggerated attachment to suffering.

'Not by words, but by his expression—his indescribable expression—did he reproach me for my belief that this suffering would always be my lot ; for my forgetfulness that his yoke is mild.

'Of old, when Our Saviour showed me his sorrows, he told me that I should share them all. I knew that I should not experience them to the extent of his capacity, but only to the extent of mine. Now he made it clear that of these sorrows I should have all the grace, but less than all the suffering. This excelling love I had not foreseen.

'In regard to all this, following your advice, I reserve my judgement.

'You are right. God would not have me hurt by offering resistance to him. If it be his will that my life shall know strife and sorrow but no peace, his will be done.

'M. A.'

March 1910.

'Since God has made me perceive his *essential* goodness, I no longer perceive his love for me. My own love for him grows in strength : if he did not love me ; if he had not given his Son for me, I should love him no less ; for he is love.

'I have come to feel that he is content with me, because I have sought to do all that might help me to follow him.

' Still more clearly, and this time finally, he has shown me my vocation : I am to be a sacrifice, for his love's sake. For me the way of sacrifice, as I conceive it, is a triple way :

' 1. The sacrifice of things implied in my vow of poverty ;

' 2. The sacrifice of my time involved in my vow of obedience ;

' 3. The sacrifice of all my intentions by a special oblation, that leaves him free to dispose of my soul's life wholly as he wills.

' He requires from me a vow that shall cover this third sacrifice. Is there such a vow ?

' I do not think that the first and the second are sacrifices that can be made in the secular life.

' It is for him to crucify. I believe that for me Calvary's mount will be Mount Carmel. I have faith in him, all powerful that he is. If, not through my will, Carmel be closed to me, he will find another way.

' In this waiting time is there anything that I can do to further this oblation of my intentions, and this surrender of myself as host ? '

March 9, 1910.

Magna opera Domini, exquisita in omnes voluntates ejus.

' Your life is my concern. Neither men nor things can thwart the work which I perform in you. . . . You are my sacrifice, *body and soul and mind and strength.* . . . I am drawing you into the *closest union of all.* . . . '

Strive with all your strength towards the goal, which I have revealed to you. If you fail to reach the goal itself, be not astonished : to strive is to arrive—is a means to the goal's end.

March 25, 1910.
Good Friday.

*Si exaltatus fuero a terra . . . omnia traham ad meipsum.
. . . Qui manet in me . . . hic fert fructum multum* (that grace of Christmas last year) and *Qui habitat in adjutorio Altissimi, in protectione Dei coeli commorabitur* (that other of January 1 this year) : they are all of one piece.

' . . . He who dwells in God . . . ' and the rest. Ponder it, O my soul ! For you—for you shall be the protection of the God of heaven ! . . .

March 28, 1910.

Oh, there is nothing that is hid from you, O God whom I so love ! Neither the depth of my suffering, nor the end of thanksgiving, which it serves. Oh, let me be dissolved in a canticle of praise, *hostiam laudis . . . laus Amoris purissimi !* . . . Let, I pray you, the sacrifice of your poor little nobody ascend to you like a psalm of pure love—pure because it is your work. . . .

Amazingly this shining truth of February 19, 1910, *laudis*, gives me new strength. His solely is the knowledge—his solely is the glory—of my exceeding suffering.

My Beloved has revealed to me the wisdom in his truth.

Without reservation he identifies me with his sufferings. . . . I shall follow ' *usque ad mortem crucis !* . . . ' To suffer now and always to suffering's limit—it is no small thing. Yet it matters not : given his grace, *I will go forward.* He has put division between me and my fellows ; between the earth and myself he has dug a great pit ; for me he has robbed all earthly things of their sweetness. So let me press onward ; let me climb upward ! On the heights he stands, and sends me burdens beneath whose weight I sink. . . .

Fiat, O God, my adorable Love ! . . .

To follow Jesus, what untold sufferings ! Notwithstanding, in peace, in love, in trust, I am climbing Calvary ; I am become his sacrifice. . . . This sacrifice he shall continue to make, until my soul is *identical* with his : of this *I am assured.*[1]

' . . . Be of good faith ! Accept all at my hands ! Of yourself do nothing ! I will make all things serve your immolation ; I will keep its glory wholly for myself. . . .'

Each day this promise is fulfilled. I do no more than follow him with a single heart ; while all things do indeed serve my immolation.

Misericordias Domini in aeternum cantabo. . . . ' Who is like to thee ? ' Indeed, ' the mercies of the Lord I will sing for ever ! For the Lord is my Love.'

March 30, 1910.

In the fire of his love let me be destroyed ; in the light of his wisdom let me be made new ! Let him sweep into my soul like a wave ! That is all I need to do. . . .

The shards of my broken self, become a canticle of praise, are given to God, and in him are lost. Like two waves meeting is my existence become : his wave that pours into my soul ; my soul's ebb-wave that turns again to him. . . .

May he pour himself into my soul, until the I, which is I, know consummation in him—until we are not two, but one !

Borne away to this union by his love that calls to my love, may my soul seek only him ! For his glory's sake may it be lost in him !

His poor little nobody to be made consummate in God ! . . .

---

[1] Mystics refer frequently to an identification of their soul with God's. The expression is not to be taken literally. It is an hyperbole, by which privileged souls seek to translate untranslatable experiences.

At the thought my need is silence—silence and solitude. . . .

I have seen the *Word*, which is God . . . *the light of men*. . . . God and the Son and the Holy Ghost. . . . I have seen it condescend to me, that I may be one with the Three in One. . . .

' . . . If anyone love me, my Father will love him, and we will come to him, and will make our abode with him. . . .'

Absorbed in the Three in One . . . lost in adoration.

Apl. 2, 1910.

' My dear Uncle,

' I wrote to you, the other day, of my vocation. I no longer merely believe what I wrote to be true—I know it. God has called me to a life lived with him, given up wholly to silence and solitude. I must no longer resist this call—if I would, I could not, or so I think. How can I answer his clear call here in the world ? There is no doubt that it is the Master's will : the light and love which have accompanied it declare its nature unmistakably.

' Imperfectly I have seen that God in Three Persons would possess and absorb me. I have come to understand that God has chosen this poor little heart, which has but the one merit of loving him very greatly, to make it his abode.

' I am aware of myself as brimming with God. In me, it would seem, Christ has become incarnate[1] in me to be sacrificed again for the Blessed Trinity's sake.

' What am I to do ? I shall continue to be obedient. Yet truly I have no more strength with which to resist. This lack of strength I take to be further evidence of his will in regard to me.

[1] It is obvious that here there is no question of hypostatic union, but of an exceedingly close union—and of no more than that,

' I am not allowed to leave the house. The doctor insists that I must rest, and refuses to allow me to go to Communion. But He, who understands that rest for me is communion with him, comes to me now that I cannot go to him : he comes, and he sates my soul. I take advantage of this rest that has been ordered me by living in solitude with God. In silence and solitude to permit him to possess my soul is rest indeed !

' Yet that rest soon comes to an end. For here are the children back again, and my everyday life begins once more.

' If I cannot go to God, I do not know what there is for me to do ; for I have done all that I can.

'M. A.'

June 1910.

' I am again in doubt, but since the last grace given me by God (that of the 15th) I am increasingly perplexed as to whether there be not a better way to keep them, than that which I have so far used. Till now, seeking to surrender myself to him as host, I have tried to make choice of that aspect of his will, that was likely to be most painful of performance.

' I have now come to see that it is he and his love, to which I am surrendered without reservation, that shall make choice of what is best for me. I see clearly that such a passive state is without the ordinary way. Yet God clearly calls me to it : I can no longer resist. Please tell me, can I keep my vows in their entirety, and yet make use of this new way ? Myself, I believe that I can, and that I should.

' Formerly my strength was in suffering. By it I was made one with Jesus first, and then with the Blessed Trinity—often consciously and always by that conviction of faith, that has remained with me since Easter.

' Suffering was now no longer my support. Seemingly there was no sensibility left in me. To suffer I should have needed to revive sensibility, and this something prevented me from doing.

' The void in my heart filled with love ; his all replaced my nothingness. I knew the spirit of Love's indwelling presence, and by Love I was changed into the Trinity itself.[1]

' My soul had lost its bearings completely ; I was oblivious to the nature of the experience, through which I was passing. I had but one desire : to unite myself to Jesus in his work of redemption—I had had no thought to make myself one with the Holy Ghost : this is the explanation of my reluctance to leave my old way of life. The excuse is a poor one. Henceforth, I shall seek to be more amenable to his will and work. Because I was wanting in devotion to the Holy Ghost, doubtless God has given me this grace.

' During the first phase of my union with the Trinity my former relation with Jesus remained unaltered. This is no longer the case.

' In this latest union love uses my senses and even my body itself. It comes, now rippling like a stream, now rushing like a torrent. No suffering accompanies it, and no ecstasy. It comes in peace : in peace it is love. Experiencing it, my soul remembers the words of the Psalmist : *Convertit petram in stagna aquarum*. . . . In brief, me who was once cold and dead to love, he has changed into love itself.

' This evening my heart seemed hot with fever. This is, I think, the first occasion upon which the fire in my soul has reacted upon my body. This physical state lasted a short time only. Yet it has given me a lively sense of the indwelling Holy Ghost, as once I had it of Christ and of the Trinity in general.

' M. A.'

[1] See previous note, page 234.

' We suffer tribulation ; but are not distressed. We are straitened ; but are not destitute.' Here is truth.

I have gone under, but I am not drowned. For the breath is still in my body, the breath that is my All ; while in the depths I breathe with ease.

Let me preserve my suffering for God alone ; let, as of old, ' peace and joy ' be my seclusion ; let me give joy to souls, and to God love and thanksgiving ! Last, with a great *Sursum corda !* from out the depths let me emerge ; let me float in the sunlight of love !

Yours be my love and yours my gratitude. I would willingly die daily now and for ever if that might serve your glory. . . .

My trust in you is great, O my Love !

July 18, 1910.

I shall drink of his cup : I *shall not stop to ask what the cup may hold*.

Let me not seek to sow, but rather myself to become wholly seed for sowing ! . . .

Let me plunge deep and still deeper into God, till in him I am come to rest ! . . .

Out of love for you, O my God, I surrender myself to your adorable will ; I give myself as host to be wholly destroyed for your greater glory.

On the Feast of the Nativity of Our Lady.
September 8, 1910.

Most Blessed Trinity, indivisible Unity subsisting in all your plenitude in Jesus ! O God of love, my Lord and my All ! I love you—you alone know how much I love you ! I love you, because you are love itself. If, to suppose an impossibility, you were not to love me, I should love you still. If you had not died for me, it would be my desire to die for you notwithstanding. If you knew nothing of my love, I would love you no whit less.

Because I love you, O my God, and because you are my sole love, I have but one desire : to give to you as greatly as I love you ; to glorify you in the highest. And my desire is so intense that, to realise it, with your grace I am ready for all.

Yet I recognise that it is impossible for me to give you one tittle of glory. Therefore, boundless is my trust in you, O my God, who are able by your power to work in us infinitely more than either we ask or understand. I surrender myself, through Mary, to you and your adorable will. Do you then draw from your poor little nobody all the glory and all the love, which you may wish.

Love divine, let me be wholly absorbed in you, so that I may be no more than a little host, made perfect in your Unity.

Jesus, my adored love, dwell in me as I in you, that it may be no more I who love, but you in me, for your glory's sake, and your Father's, and the Blessed Trinity's.

Heavenly Father, consecrate me a host of love, that in this gift of my surrender I may recognise that there is only Christ, and so may be well-pleasing in your eyes.

If my innate cowardice betray my will, and I allow suffering to swamp my soul, I retract in advance all shrinkings on my part, which may lessen my oblation. Let these be changed, O God, into an unbroken canticle of praise and of perfect love, that shall last through every hour of all my earthly days !

CHAPTER THE SECOND

IN THE DARKNESS—GOD

(*September* 1910—*early* 1912)

September 11, 1910.

WHILE my soul, torn and crushed, drops blood, I must give men my smiles. . . . I must be calm and peaceful and joyous. . . .

September 19, 1910.

' My beloved, if you partake of the sufferings of Christ, rejoice ! '

How greatly do I rejoice !

How intoxicatingly sweet is the cup of which I drink !

October 22, 1910.

In the darkness let me act as if there were light ; in the storm as if there were calm ; in suffering as if I knew joy ! . . . Let me seek now and for ever that which most shall immolate me—let me seek it in joy, in tranquillity, in thanksgiving ! . . .

November 13, 1910.

Sacrificabo hostiam laudis. . . .

How completely this promise has been fulfilled ! . . . What graces were given me in 1909 (that unforgettable February 19) and in 1910 ! Each was the complement and the confirmation of the other. . . .

And that further grace by which I surrendered to him the charge of making sacrifice of me ! The suffering which I can find for myself is infinitesimal compared with the suffering given of God. . . . And oh ! how faithful he is ! . . . indeed he sacrifices to the utter and bitter end . . . *hostiam laudis*. . . .

It is he, and only he, who sacrifices. My part is but to stretch myself upon the altar. . . .

If my cup be gilded ; if my Calvary be locked in a tomb—in the cup you know what bitter beverage, at the Calvary you know, and only you, what suffering is mine ! what love ! . . . Make of me Love's seed, that I may fall into the hearts of men ; make of me a canticle of your own praise ! . . .

Love fills me ; love grows big within me. Love destroys all that is in me, that in me there may be love, and only love. Let me wane, that Christ may wax to his full stature in me !

Oh ! there is nothing that your grace does not do ! . . .

Misericordias Domini in aeternum cantabo. . . .

November 9, 1910.

When my soul's skiff drives into the dark night ; when it starts to sink ; when it floats, a wreck . . . despite all let me be strong in trust ! . . .

Glutted with suffering, I stretch out my hand to take his cup, though I see it not. I seek to lay myself upon the altar, though the altar be hidden from me.

In manus tuas. . . .

Dec. 29, 1910.

' My dear Uncle,

' The greatest comfort, when one loves, is to prove love by gifts and self-surrender. This comfort is not for the nothing that I am. I have nothing ; I am nothing. The fire—it seems like fire—in my heart is, it may be, love. It craves for fuel—for fuel upon which it may feed—and I, it seems, have no fuel with which to feed it. This state is one of indescribable torment. There are times when it threatens to kill me. At such times I need all my self-control to turn a tranquil face to the world.

'This fire shall burn itself out. Jesus shall take the place of my burned-out self, and shall thereby glorify the Blessed Trinity.

'I feel the call of obedience most strongly: my way has particular need of its power to curb. I have only the pale glimmer of my soul's dim lamp of faith, by which to guide my steps. The lamp of obedience burns with a brighter light, it seems to me. And obedience in its fullness is not possible without Carmel's walls. In the world I should need to break my soul's seclusion, and that I know not how to do.

'Between him and me is nothing any more, save sorrow and grace that has no name. Now that there is nothing, should I find my strength in memories of graces given, or in self-surrender simply? Probably the last is the better way, the more so as often my memories escape me.

'When am I to have your "yes" to my entry? I wish it only because he makes me wish it. It is Love who prompts my wish. I would be dead in Love, and so am eager for that "yes" to be spoken soon.   'M. A.'

January 3, 1911.

My vocation is to live my life not on earth, but in heaven. . . . *Splendor gloriae*. . . . To suffering let me surrender all that I may surrender; to the sword of God let me bare my bosom's inclinations; to the last tittle let me be his sacrifice! . . .

Then, *Sursum!* Let my soul, made new, live in Love. . . . *Splendor gloriae.* . . .

January 19, 1911.

God is my plenitude. . . . I am dead to all but Love, this ' consuming fire ' that devours me whole, and wholly has its will of me. . . . Let me burn, till only ash remain.

January 23, 1911.

I am changed into the Trinity itself. . . .[1]

My soul looks upon God exactly as he is ! . . .

Not in divine stirrings within me, not in light from without me, not in vision itself, but in a state, *in which the senses have no part, I see God!*

The round world rolls away beneath me . . . all earthly things dissolve . . . there remains the Blessed Trinity, the Blessed Trinity itself. . . .

All things dissolve, the perception of the I, which was I, with the rest. There remains *only God, God who is very God!* . . .

Into him I am *changed!* . . .

Jan. 23, 1911.

' My dear Uncle,

' On Friday evening I had a spiritual experience that must surely have been a grace given of God.

' I neither prayed nor meditated. Alone, I thought of him, as is my instinct. Suddenly it was as if I were changed into the Blessed Trinity. I know that this is a venturesome thing to say. Yet I cannot otherwise express what passed in my soul.

---

[1] Of all such phrases the precise meaning needs to be remembered. ' When I speak of man's unity with God, as I have said before and as I repeat now, I mean not unity of nature nor unity of essence, but only unity of love '—to quote Ruysbroeck, speaking for all Catholic mystics. Marie de la Trinité makes clear her own thought in subsequent passages, *cf.* the explicit reference in that of August 19, 1912.

'Since the end of March last year, when I first knew the inpouring of the Trinity, I have known "Christ to live in me." From that time the two words *Splendor Gloriae* have given a new richness of meaning to my prayer.

'In this there was light; there was vision; there was the faint stirring of God within me. In this there was, and I perceived it, plenitude of glory for God and plenitude of grace for souls, and for me increased love of suffering, increased desire for still closer union.

'This new grace was otherwise. In it was neither light, nor vision, nor glory, nor grace, nor the I which was I. There was only God, God as he is, God in Three Persons. . . . In this experience the senses had no part, and it cannot be described. Yet it was beyond doubt, beyond mistaking; it was reality.

'Since then I have had but one prayer : that I may be " changed into him." It is a " state of soul," not a happening from without : it is God, God solely. When I recall that state, I remember above all tranquillity, unity, immensity; I remember that I had a sense of infinity and of eternity. . . .

'What is this state ? Is it good for me ? I would like you to tell me. 'M. A.'

February 27, 1911.

Let me be as wax in his hands, that he may mould me into such state of identity with him, as he may will ! . . .

I know of a certainty that he leads me into that Unity, which transcends all union, and that he consumes me utterly in his love for his glory's sake.

March 12, 1911.[1]

'My understanding gropes. His Word tells me that he is justice, and that he acts only upon those souls who are in tune with him. Yet I—I am never in tune. My faith for ever fails. Yet his work goes on in me. He has me go before him : he heaps me with favours more and more abundantly. . . .

'Let your sacrifice of me go remorselessly on, my Beloved ; let the holocaust be complete. . . . I will bring myself into tune. . . . I will no longer think of your demands as too intolerably great. . . . I will no more ask even to see the sacrifice made of me.

'Once, when in our Latin translations we met the word "Amor," I needed all my strength to repress my inward ecstasy. . . . Yet now in this work in me, that is so notably of God, I remain cold and unmoved. . . .

'This state profoundly humiliates me. Surely one should not grow accustomed to such things ? To hear his commands as though they were a matter of course : is this not a lack of respect for God ?

'. . . O my God, though your touch—though your grace—move me no longer to the old enthusiasm, you know that my soul is on fire with love and with gratitude ; that your loving-kindness confounds me and plunges me into wretchedness. . . .

'For me is the dark and the consuming fire, which burns in the dark : the heights are not for me, nor mystical transformation, nor even his old magnetic attraction.

'A little light has been given me direct from God.

---

[1] This letter is addressed to the priest, who was her confessor at that time. At this period of mysterious purification—such periods are known to most mystics—Marie de la Trinité had an urgent need of counsel : her soul was adrift ; for it she needed anchorage. Hence the increasing frequency of her letters 'to her director,' as they are indicated in these pages, where they are to be found under their respective dates.

'As on a moonless light the stars reveal the deep purity of heaven : so this little light assures me that I am still in him. . . .

'On a starlit night the utter blueness of the sky cannot be fully realised : just so, despite the little light, I fail to see God ; I am in the dark. . . .

'The stars, despite their own shining, do not illumine the earth : just so my little light, though it be steady and in a few matters revealing, leaves my soul in the dark. . . .

'Let me fix my eyes *only upon heaven!* . . . *None but God.*

March 16, 1911.

'My dear Uncle,

'I have fallen again into my old state : I stand before God with neither emotion in my heart nor strength in my soul. I can do nothing of myself. I am capable of neither prayer nor exalted thought. Between those moments in which I am wrought upon by God, I remain close to him, sightless and mindless.

'After the heights—the depths. You have warned me that so it is. The warning comforts me. For I had begun to doubt the truth of God's graces given to me, so little time did I enjoy them ; so low am I fallen since.

'Let me try to answer your questions : my normal state at present is a kind of night of the soul. It is not that light-in-darkness, that leaden cloud, which wrapped me suffocatingly round, before my union with the Trinity. It is as though I stood in the light with sightless eyes ; as if I had God, but had no joy in him ; as if I saw him, but only in rare glimpses— I know not why.

'Yet consciousness of God's indwelling presence at no time forsakes me, nor, more recently, that of the Holy Ghost ; while always, however faintly perceptible it may sometimes become, I am aware of a leading towards Pontoise.'[1]

April 5, 1911.

Let me seek to follow none but God ! Let me follow him directly !

None but God . . . latterly, his strong compulsion is for ever upon me, drawing me towards the heights and transformation into him. . . .

None but God. . . . It is the old compulsion of my childhood. Now I perceive that it can be a lasting state, only when the soul is *in its essence* detached from all that is not he. . . .

April 6, 1911.

Let me follow him directly . . . to do so let me sustain my soul *in him !* . . .

Let me climb upward in peace and in love whither he wishes me ! . . . let me with a glad and single heart be content with that measure of holiness, which is his desire for me ! . . .

With this complete detachment as my staff, let me climb upward, that multiplying grace may bring forth abundance of thanksgiving ! . . .

Apl. 1911.

' My dear Uncle,

' Since I wrote to you last, God, it seems, has scattered the mist surrounding my soul. I am now as if changed into him ; as if the senses, the intellect and the will were no more concerns of mine.

---

[1] As related in the first part of this book, she hesitated between the Carmel of Le Hâvre and that of Pontoise. It proved that her vocation was for no particular cloister or set rule, but for the most absolute renunciation in the secular life. To her director on December 22, 1911, of God's (humanly speaking) conflicting calls upon her she wrote thus : ' It is God's will, I do believe, always to ask of me only those things which I cannot do.'

'In this state it is as if the self in me were dead, and God living in my stead—his Unity, his Immensity and (in some incomprehensible fashion) his Immutability substituted for that ephemeral and infinitesimal " I," which now is dead and become uniquely God.

'Afterwards this " I " resurrects, and suffers much before it is again destroyed.

'For some time past the nature of this suffering itself has altered. On February 15 Our Saviour gave me the promise that I *should suffer and remain unconscious of my suffering*. This promise has now been fulfilled. My suffering has no relation to the senses. It is as if that which God sacrifices in me neither is myself, nor belongs to myself.

'I am as though without a soul. Thought, emotion, volition are all beyond my reach. God wholly possesses my soul : in it I have no foothold, no support, not even the support of suffering experienced. When I stand upon the heights, God is all. When God is no longer with me, life is one vast void. . . .

'M. A.'

May 13, 1911.

'I have emerged from the dark. God bids me leave the secular life : he seems to fix the date for next Autumn.

'I am transformed—" transformed " is a clumsy word : there is no word which may render this experience—into Mary. I seem to have lot and part in her, the Queen of martyrs, Virgin most pure. . . .

'Incidentally, he would, it seems, have me call myself " Marie de la Trinité."

'M. A.'

May 15, 1911.[1]

' In my dark night just now there are stars. . . .

' One such star makes plain to me the profundity of this " true holocaust " . . . this perception gives me great strength . . . of me nothing shall be left . . . that nothing has a vast implication. . . .

' God immolates elements in me, of which I had no previous knowledge. Now that I have lost them, I perceive that I once possessed them.

' His word—the self become the " seed of love "— that seed planted in men's souls—extreme suffering —daily death—that suffering unseen, except of God—that death by me uncomprehended : this is my lot and my vocation.

' Let me then seek to make no more sacrifices ! Let me sustain my soul in sacrifice itself ! Of this and of this alone can all the glory be for God, all the grace for men's souls, all the holiness for mine own.

' In the measure that my soul knows expansion, God gives it plenitude.

' The only happiness which God gives me is a share in his own. Such happiness cannot be offered as sacrifice. For it is God.

'. . . This is the second of my stars : in his merciful love he has repeated his message, given so notably to me in July 1909—*Expedit vobis ut ego vadam*. Of me too his words shall prove true : it shall be for their advantage that I go. When the holocaust shall be complete—and only then—will they receive love and grace in plenitude. To-day in reading S. John I have been greatly reassured. I am certain now that when I am with him, it shall advantage those I leave in the world. For, as I may not, the Paraclete shall teach them all the secrets of his love, according to his will.

[1] To her director.

' May the holocaust be speedily completed ! For I would begin my mission, that shall publish to souls God's boundless love.

' . . . And my third star is this : " Mary and the Blessed Trinity—these are my soul's objective. . . .

' . . . Since Saturday I have written several letters. Each of them I have been impelled to sign " Marie de la Trinité."

' It is fitting. Marie-Antoinette is a dead woman's name, not mine. My name is Marie de la Trinité. In such an old-established and numerous community as that of the Carmel at Pontoise, so obvious a name must already have been assumed. Nevertheless, it is my name : I am convinced of it. . . .

' These three stars of mine sustain my soul in God himself. At intervals they brighten. Where they are, God is. Nothing can interrupt our converse, which is already in heaven.

' Once the light of his truth absorbed me. When I talked with men, I could not pray to God. Either I gave myself to God, or I gave myself to men. Now, almost without effort, I can talk with both at the same time, since now I can make my conversation with men a prayer to God.

' A day or two ago I was a little troubled to hear God speak to me while I continued an ordinary conversation, and to receive his most solemn communications, as though to do so were the most natural thing in the world. To-day it is all plain to me. For me God is in all things and in all men : his will, expressed in men and things, most surely can be no barrier to my union with him. . . .'

May 16, 1911 *(evening)*.[1]

' For the first time in many weeks I have known a

[1] Addressed to her director

measure of active peace in my relation with God. Momentarily he has made me share in *his own* happiness.'

May 17, 1911 *(evening)*.[1]

' This blessedness is infinitely greater than any earthly joy. Alas ! it is very fleeting. It comes but to go.'

May 18, 1911.[2]

' To know happiness is not to experience joy : to receive God's greatest favours is often to have no comfort of them.

' Last evening I stood upon the heights. No words can describe them, or their remoteness from the fashion of earthly things.

' . . . I will put fear from me. I will climb as high as he wills me to climb. In climbing, it is my strength to remember that I climb not for my own sake, but for God's and for the sake of men's souls.

May 26, 1911.

' My dear Uncle,

' Darkness is about me, much as it was before my union with the Blessed Trinity. It is darkness more desolating than the old. I grope blindly : nowhere seems there any light of truth. My existence is rather hell than purgatory. How to pass through this hell I do not know. So I stand, unstirring, and allow the flames to devour me.

' I know neither whether I am in tune with God's grace, nor whether I am true to the faith which is in me. I know nothing. ' M. A.'

June 10, 1911.

' I have told my parents of my proposed entry into Carmel in October next. They have put no obstacles

[1] [2] These two letters were both addressed to her director.

in my way. It is understood that when I go, I go
experimentally.

'As for my inner life there is little change : the
little light and the great darkness alike persist. My
entry in October, my definite divine call to the
House at Pontoise, my name " Marie de la Trinité "
—these may be but trifles. Yet they are tremendous
trifles.

'At Pontoise there is at the present time no other
Marie de la Trinité. They are willing that this shall
be my own name, because I love it so.

'The altar of sacrifice is no longer far off. I soon
shall reach it. Since my journey to it began, I have
sung my *Magnificat* upon the road. I may well sing
it now. For it is always good to rejoice and give
thanks at the setting-out : the arrival can take care
of itself.
                          'MARIE DE LA TRINITÉ,'
                                  Carmelite Postulant.

                                  July 22, 1911.

'You have heard what has happened. At sight of
mother's suffering I thought first of postponing my
entry. This is not, I believe, God's will for me. He
sent this passing thought to prove my faith.

'My soul's night continues. I suffer indescribably.
Occasionally, like stars in a dark sky, shining points of
his truth flash upon me. For the most part there is
only the dark and my sightless suffering in the midst
of it.

'For me there is only submission at all times and
in all places to his *Fiat*. In prayer I am as one
dumb and paralysed : yet God has made me understand that this inability either to speak or to act shall
in my surrender count as thanksgiving.

'Thus surrendered, I wait till exterior circumstance

and Our Lord's call shall conspire together to permit
my entry.   'MARIE DE LA TRINITÉ.'

September 18, 1911.[1]

   ' On the 8th in my old dilemma —called by God to
go ; myself unable to go—I was impelled by God to
make this prayer :
   ' " Grant, O God, that if I do not go, it shall be
but one more suffering for me, and no diminution
either of glory for you or of grace for men's souls."
   ' God has given me the conviction that my prayer
is granted.'

Obedience like a lighthouse has marked out my way
. . . despite everything I am not to go. . . . 'My
Jesus, though I resist you, be sure that it is because
I love you, because I obey you. Only teach me how I
may reconcile your demands with obedience.'
   I am not to go either now or in the future. I am not
to go. I am to stay in this life, for which I feel myself
less and less fitted—in this life in which everything I do,
I do badly—in this secular life in which I show no
skill. . . . God does not ask postponement for a few
months, but indefinite postponement. To be uncertain
indefinitely is now to be my lot. Though it crush me,
it shall serve me well, since it rids my life of one more
fettering attachment.
   God is indeed good to me. The more I thank him
for the suffering which by his will I am now experiencing,
the more suffering he visits upon me.
   I am at the end of my strength. My suffering may
not be told in words. I would give him thanks without
measure. . . .
   My heart is filled with love and with gratitude. I
can only cry ' Lord, of this I am not worthy ! '

      [1] To her director.

My blessed Mother, *Regina Martyrum*, particular
patron of Marie de la Trinité, gives me part in her own
sacrificial lot. I cannot share it wholly, since my own
immolation is not yet complete.

My joy is abounding. Often I have cried, *Fac ut
portem Christi mortem, Passionis fac consortem!* often I
have yearned for suffering—now I have his promise ;
now I have suffering to the limit of my capacity ! . . .

September 22, 1911.[1]

' God in his wisdom ordains that for me all things
shall make for " consummation in unity." I need to
surrender myself to God's work in me ; to remember
that for me as *hostiam laudis* God is his own priest ;
that as a host destined to be a holocaust I must expect
intense suffering, nor be astonished at the fierceness
of the fire, which shall consume me. . . .'

Sept. 1911 (*end of*).

' My dear Uncle,

' My soul's call to Carmel grows still stronger. I
am convinced that my mission here at home is
finished. The life of silence and of recollection, which
God demands of me, cannot be reconciled with my
present life in the world.

' In the world I am stifled by the air I breathe.
God does not want me here. I cannot resist his will
for a great time longer.

' On June 11th the Blessed Trinity was again
manifested to me. About this there was no illusion.
The manifestation was neither through the senses nor
in the soul's exaltation. In the course of it God
revealed to me his wish that the Feast of the Blessed
Trinity should be more solemnly celebrated than it
has been hitherto. I grew convinced that for the

---

[1] To her director.

feast of so great a mystery the rank of double of the second class was not enough.[1] What was the object of this revelation I do not pretend to know. I try to dismiss it from my mind ; for what the Church ordains is right. Did God wish for an alteration in this matter, he would enlighten those in authority. Eventually I decided that it was in the soul of Marie de la Trinité that this sublime mystery must receive greater honour. I have made efforts to this end—but in vain. Yet I am certain that a day shall come, when God's will shall be fulfilled.

' Afterwards his light once more departed from me ; his sword pierced me afresh ; no star shone in the darkness of my night.

' I yielded all my senses to God's devouring fire. I transcended them. I knew transcendent peace. I knew—I was become—*Splendor Gloriae*. . . .

' In earth and my fellow-men for me there is no comfort left. Nor am I wistful of such comfort. In my soul is no exaltation. God is the one refuge remaining to me. And from God my imperfection shuts me out.

' I can neither pray nor think. Desire is dead in me ; understanding fled from me. I grope in darkness ; I am consumed by fire. I am altogether given over to death, and in this death there is *no comfort*.

' Between a dark sea and a dark sky I have my being. I need to meditate, but the pressure of my daily occupations precludes meditation. Oh, my need to enter Carmel is great indeed ! . . .

' The evil in my disposition, for some time less in evidence, has reasserted itself. Taking advantage of my weakness, the devil tempts me. Often, it seems, I am without strength with which to resist. In the

[1] Since that time the Feast of the Trinity has been elevated to a double of the first class.

grip of relentless suffering I frequently permit impatient words to escape me; while often, as I am well aware, I am far from amiable.

' I need to be taught both how to pray and how to live. Untaught, I know not whether I do God's will. Yet I am so eager to be faithful !

' The truth is probably this : while I am no more I, I have not yet been changed into him.

' MARIE DE LA TRINITÉ.'

October 3, 1911.

During this week much grace has been given me. God has lit stars in my sky. But my everyday life and its duties leave me neither the time to gaze upon them, nor the opportunity to be tranquillised by their tranquillity.

Thus, on one particular day I had neither Mass nor Communion ; three days when, apart from Mass, I did not spend a moment in church ; while on Sunday I could not go to Vespers. Yet what matters it ? For you to be glorified by them, O God, it is not necessary that we shall enjoy your favours.

To know the light of truth we must know the darkness of suffering. The river must brim before we who, like corks, are borne upon its current, may see above its banks the far horizon, or may escape to God.

October 5, 1911.[1]

' I need not to suffer merely ; I need *to die*. I must not stop short at immolation ; I must go on to consummation.

' The self must be slain in me, that in me he may live his life in plenitude. Only through suffering— such suffering as ends in death—can this come to pass.

' I must surrender self—the higher self no less than

[1] To her director.

the lower self—without reservation, till for me there
be only love's light-in-darkness. Not spiritual nakedness but spiritual annihilation shall discover *Very
God!* . . .

'By his light-in-darkness he has shown me new
horizons. Till the holocaust be complete, I may not
attain to them.

'I am free from my fiery furnace. I am come out
of the cloud, which was like a black shroud about me.
I am emerged from the darkness of the pit, and the
torment of my suffering in it.

'Though I have not yet come forth into God's light
of truth, my few stars shine for me in the dark sky.

'It is in God's light-in-darkness that I shall know
transformation and consummation.

'In this dark light I must seek to remain, that I
may identify myself with God's will, and reach at
last that utter spiritual death, which I must know
before I am " transformed into God." '

October 9, 1911.

Yesterday at Vespers, during the chanting of the
hymn of the Rosary, at the words ' *Ave redundans gaudio,*'
the Blessed Virgin gave me insight into the mystery of
her sacrifice : her joys, I now perceive, are not personal
to herself ; they are the part which she has in God's
beatitude.

O Mary, dead to self ! O Mary, absorbed in God !
She has made me aware that, as it is with her, so it
shall be with me. My lot shall be not personal joy, but
part in God's happiness.

October 9, 1911.[1]

' On the 4th, during Mass I stood on the threshold
of a new world. Before me stretched those wide
horizons, which I had seen first upon the evening of
the 3rd.

[1] To her director.

' I felt an urge from God to penetrate into the secret soul of Jesus, and there for ever to establish myself at the centre and core of the divine mysteries ; to identify myself with the mystery of the Redemption ; to contemplate it at its focal point, the soul of Christ, in making my own soul one with Christ's.

' I glimpsed then the union, which has been promised me—that consummation into his unity. Yet on the threshold something held me back. There remained one fetter from which I was not free : the self was not dead.

' I needed to suffer once again, if that fetter were to be broken. As those souls, who standing before God's perfection are conscious of their own yet too great imperfection, plunge themselves of their own will into purgatory, so I plunged myself once more into suffering's pit.

' My way is clear before me : I must have eyes for none but God.

' I must shut myself from things : I must neither see nor desire them ; neither enjoy them nor be hindered by them. I must stand alone. In an even greater measure I must shut myself from men. I must turn to them neither for support nor help. I must stand alone. I must shut myself from the divine—yes, even from the divine. I must shut myself from all that is. I must stand alone.

' Only so shall I discover God who is Very God. I must shut myself from all that is.

' In a word my need is *to die*. To possess God I must desire only him—I must be only he. In a word, the self must die, and, dead, must know no resurrection.'

November 7, 1911.[1]

' The contrast between the beauty of God's work and my own pitiful shortcomings is overwhelming and

[1] To her director.

a little frightening. It plunges me into humility and stirs me to gratitude. Truly it passes my comprehension. One thought only comforts me : this contrast is designed to keep me humble and in the knowledge that he alone is all. With this design God *allows* me to be evilly inclined.

'His glory is in no wise diminished by my shortcomings. In me as "*hostiam laudis*" he takes his pleasure ; to me myself he is oblivious. The Blessed Trinity is not grieved but glorified by that which I am. In me as in the Host of the Tabernacle it beholds none but Jesus. It has no more regard to my shortcomings than it has to the grains of wheat making part of the Eucharistic Host. As God, so I must behold none but *my adored Christ ;* I must be oblivious of my shortcomings. I am not worthy even of scorn. Oblivion is my lot.

' God's will is that my soul shall constantly discover new fields of humiliation. Once I hoped to suffer public humiliation. Now I know only the suffering which comes of increasing awareness of my own imperfection and of the obliviousness of others to it. My sin is too subtle, as my evil inclinations are too deep-seated, for men to perceive it. Neither the extent of my shortcomings, nor the measure of my suffering, will ever be known.

' Yet in that, I see now, there is comfort ; for in that there is true humiliation. In public humiliation my self-love would find satisfaction.

' Let me then surrender my desire for such humiliation ! Let me seek only oblivion ! '

November 13, 1911.[1]

' During this week I have been consecrated " host of praise." My sacrificial soul has had part in Christ's surpassing sorrows. The sacrifice was utter. The

[1] To her director.

cup brimmed. My suffering was pure suffering—the suffering which Jesus knew and which glorifies the Father. It has filled my soul with peace.

'When first he gave me to drink of his bitter cup, I was sorely troubled, and my soul wrestled strongly against God's will.

'I can neither pray nor love nor give thanks; desire is dead in me, understanding and vision fled from me. Like one distracted, I walk in hell. Unlike the souls in purgatory, who suffer in God according to his will, I do not suffer as a Christian should, but as might some hurt dumb brute.[1]

'I am afraid to confess to the passion in my soul. Had I not been seized of God's love, I might well have developed into a notorious criminal. It is with passion that I love God's will. Its performance alone can give my passion peace.'

Nov. 30, 1911.

I am in God's fiery furnace. It is my faith that I shall emerge from it with my soul made new and splendid.

This earthly exile weighs upon me. Would that I could die! On earth all is dark; were I dead, all would be light. *To die*—those two words are the loveliest in the language. To die is to see God. Oh, to die, that I may see God! . . .

I have a great thirst for truth and justice. I have no fear of justice; for it is one with love and mercy. O merciful justice of God! O God's eternal truth! I love them and I long for them.

December 2, 1911.

'Most of the work which God performs in me is beyond human conception. It has no relation to the senses. It is beyond the understanding.

---

[1] Hyperbole, of course.

' By his near presence I am so dazzled that I can distinguish nothing. His light of truth needs to narrow and to dim, before I am able to look upon it. To express it differently : I can interpret only what, and only when, his truth permits me to interpret—and this is but a fraction of the whole. . . .

' Constantly I am caught up in a dark cloud—often during evening prayers, almost always at Communion. Then I pass beyond the world of sense into a kind of nothingness of the spirit. Only afterwards do I realise that I have left the self behind. It is as if for a moment I ceased to be. In those moments I am not conscious of receiving any grace from God.

' In this state I cannot pray. When Jesus thus possesses my body, I am out of it. Yet it is vain that I try to hold back my fugitive spirit. For it is caught up without my perceiving it.'

December 9, 1911.[1]

' On the 4th God with the light of his wisdom not merely dazzled but blinded me.

' His glory had dazzled me before ; it was he himself who blinded me then. For in this " still dark " he stood face to face with me.[2]

' In this " still dark," remote from earthly things, in nakedness of spirit, absorbed, obliterated, utterly sacrificed, my soul stood before its God. It could not see him, because in the darkness was no light. Yet between him and it was no separation.'

December 11, 1911.[3]

' I heard both the first two sermons of the retreat. The stimulating thought, which they contained.

---

[1] To her director.
[2] As before, this is hyperbole—a mystic's hyperbole. In fact God stands face to face only with souls in heaven.
[3] To her director.

S

spurred me to prepare a meditation. But God made
it plain that this premeditated intellectual concentration on specific points was not in accordance with
his will.

' His wish was that I should remain in his " spiritual
twilight," that " still dark " in which he can best and
most directly perform his work in me.

' In this " spiritual twilight " my soul stands alone,
remote from all earthly things, without stay and
without comfort.

' In the black cloak of this " spiritual twilight" my
soul stands secure. Nothing can touch it there,
neither the devil, nor men, nor things. The cloak is
open only on the side upon which God is. On that
side is darkness, and in the darkness—God. When
eternity begins, the darkness will disperse, and God's
splendour shine forth in all its glory.

' It is a fleeting state. Now it is God's light of
wisdom, and now some specific suffering, which drags
me from the black cloak's shelter, and from my
isolation with him, who is my all. Light of wisdom—
specific suffering : they are but two names for a single
thing. I need to experience the one and to endure
the other, and, as soon as may be, to re-enter that
spiritual twilight, in which, with the self destroyed,
I may reach the focal point of God.

' Alas ! I know that state too seldom and too
fleetingly.'

December 11, 1911.

' At the beginning of this retreat, in God's twilight
and under his direct action, I knew an " inpouring of
truth."

' I do not know the exact nature of this grace. I
think it must have been that which inspired the
Psalmist's : " *in excessu meo omnis homo mendax !* "

' For in the light of the truth given me then, I realised how small a place pure truth holds in the souls of men.

' Truth—how simple life would be, if each were wholly *true* !

' Yesterday evening at Benediction, a thought which occurred to me was : if all those here present were in the truth, how changed would be this congregation, how lovely in the eyes of God ! For each would then have eyes for none but God. . . .

' Again : truth is one with charity.

' God in his goodness has filled me with an abounding love for men's souls, with a love that is a little like his own love. God in his charity has given me charity towards my fellows, and at the same time revealed how short my love falls of his own.

' Truth and charity, though they leave me detached from my fellow-men's affections, bring me nearer to them in a way which, because language is so poor a thing, I cannot describe.

' This love for my fellows has no earthly affection in it. Rather, it is a sense of mutual sharing in the love of God.

' Detached from my kind, I have desired from them neither help nor love. I have desired none but God. Yet in him I have re-discovered them. In his love I love them with a surpassing love, in which is no fettering affection.

' If each, dead to self, love only God : then each, transformed into this one love, is one with his fellows, themselves likewise transformed into that love. It is no less than perfect consummation into God's unity, not only of each with God, but of each with his fellows themselves in God. The second commandment is indeed like to the first. Love of our fellow-men derives directly from our love of God.'

Dec. 19, 1911.[1]

' At present I am in great distress of soul. It is as
though I were caught fast in hell itself, powerless to
stir or escape.

' The devil discovers my soul to me as too impure to
be purified. And the impure thing discovered by
him is indeed my soul. As to that the devil speaks
the truth.

' Oh, what torment so to have sinned against God !
The devil is driving me towards despair. Yet no !
Satan begone ! He lies. I have received absolution.
I have disclosed all my sin, and God has pardoned
me. . . . The devil discovers more of my impurity.
. . . My faith holds fast. God can perform miracles,
even this greatest miracle of all his miracles—my
purification.

' " *Non veni vocare justos sed peccatores !* "—for me,
impure as I am, what comfort and what joy in those
words ! I will turn this temptation not into despair,
but into humility.

' The devil persists : he accuses me of lack of
charity, of keeping silence, when others would have
me speak. This temptation is more difficult to resist.
Our Lord's words are my best defence : " he that
shall receive one such little child in my name, receiveth
me." Let me add this : the leper shows no lack of
charity, when he permits a Sister of Charity to care
for him.'

Dec. 20, 1911.[2]

' In my soul's distress I have gone to my books.
They have not helped me to understand. Neither
books, nor counsel, nor sermons give me new ideas :
they merely confirm and give me increased understanding of what God has taught me already.'

[1] [2] Both letters to her director.

Dec. 22, 1911.

Suffering, sorrow, agony, distress, desolation, torment, martyrdom, temptation, again agony, death, dissolution —these words are but faint shadows of my soul's state.

I am dumb : I cannot even call upon God. ' Suffering ' is far too weak a word with which to describe this state.

On re-reading these notes, this evening, I perceive that they convey not the dark, but the bright side of my life. Only blank pages could convey my life's dark side.

For when I write, it means that the darkness has in a measure lifted. When the darkness is greatest, I cannot write.

I am again in the dark. Let a blank page follow this.

Dec. 23, 1911.[1]

' I am not so sore beset. This comfort has been given me in the midst of my soul's travail : I *know* that I love God purely ; that I believe implicitly, hope ceaselessly, surrender myself utterly. I *know* that I would choose to suffer to the limit of suffering, rather than of my own will to yield myself to *the smallest imperfection.* I *know* that I would not shun martyrdom, but seek it. This faith is rooted not in myself, but in him.

' I know too that this comfort may be taken from me at any moment.

' Since at this particular moment I, dumb no longer, can call upon you, O my God, let me implore you, now and always, whatever my soul's state, to perceive in it faith, hope, love and boundless trust.

' When I have lost this knowledge—when I can no longer call upon you—I implore you to believe that I love you still.

[1] To her director.

' You know my love for you ; you know, no less, my love for the souls of men. I cannot myself prove to them how much I love : I implore you, who see all my heart, to bestow upon them the full richness of your charity ; to make them conscious of your love, till, responding to it, they love you even as I love you, that they and I together may be " consummated into the unity of your love, and made holy in the truth of your charity."

' *Laudate Dominum . . . qui in altis habitat, et humilia respicit.*'

Dec. 31, 1911.

' My dear Uncle,

' I have known seclusion with God ; I have been detached from all created things. I have passed brief intervals in a still dark, in which my soul has been lifted above this life to a selfless absorption in God.

' Once emerged from this darkness instinct with God, I have been exposed to the devil's assaults : he has attacked me with innumerable vague temptations. There are no words to describe the suffering, which my soul has known.

' Yet in the midst of my suffering, perceiving it to be God's will, I have known joy.

' These things have brought me joy infinitely greater : my divination of the secret of Jesus' ceaseless and surpassing sacrifice ; his invitation that I should identify myself with it, and his revelation that I am to be his host, his host destined to be a true holocaust.'

' MARIE DE LA TRINITÉ.'

CHAPTER THE THIRD

'NONE BUT GOD, WHO IS ALL'

1912—1913

Apl. 15, 1912.

IN my suffering there are interludes of vision. They are not frequent. The vision fades; the suffering returns. Though it be my normal and absorbing state, it is beyond my understanding: it is *known only to God.*

I walk strange unknown ways. Personal suffering does not touch me, or touches me only fleetingly: all my petty crosses are destroyed in the fire of his love.

Dead to the world, dead to the self, I am yielded up to his sword. Nothing can prevent my destruction by it.

I have given him all. He has taken all. Nothing is left to me—*nothing.* I am without a friend.

Though he slay me, let me praise him!

NONE BUT GOD. *Apl.* 24, 1912.

' My dear Uncle,

' Since I do not know whether I shall recover, at present I am making no plans for the future. I trust myself blindly to the arms of my beloved Father. I wish neither for recovery nor for death. If I live, sick or well, to work and suffer longer, I will rejoice; if I die to-morrow, I will be content.

'When I perceive the extent of the work still to be done in my soul, I cannot but think that I have much longer to live. Yet I know that in a second of time he is able to make the holocaust complete : therefore in ignorance I wholly surrender myself, and rejoice in my ignorance.

'He has set me above exterior happenings, above earthly sufferings, above even the interior suffering of the soul. I am given into his destroying hands.

'In joy, in love, in gratitude, I am destroyed. Though, thus sacrificed, I suffer much ; though I am left uncomforted and unbefriended, my soul knows a deep peace. May our great God of love magnify himself in his poor little nobody ! With her may he do what he wills, when he wills it ! For she is wholly surrendered to him.'   'MARIE DE LA TRINITÉ.'

Let me do God's will without equivocation and with no thought of the surrendered self ! Let me endure all that I may need to endure, without regard to the pain which it may involve !

Let me live out of and above the self ! . . .

None but God—none ! . . .

May 5, 1912.

Is it possible, when possessed of God, to know either suffering or joy in respect to earthly things ? . . .

When my humanity shall be dead and transformed, and desirous only of God, I, become he, shall be not my own but his reward : *magna nimis.* . . .

May 6, 1912.

Let me live as though the self were dead ! . . .

Let me put all my courage and all my love into everything that I do, while *attaching myself to nothing !* . . .

Let me do things, and yet be no slave to the things which I do ! . . .

May 7, 1912.

Let me continue to be lifted *out of myself !* . . .

Let my share in the work performed in me be *complete detachment !* . . .

When my humanity desires only God, it shall be glutted with his divinity. . . .

May 8, 1912.

Let me continue to be without the self ! . . .

Let me apply myself not to those things which God desires, but to God himself, who desires them ! . . .

Let me have eyes for none but God ! . . . Let me not depart from him ! . . .

1912.

' My dear Uncle,

' For some ten days they have made me keep more or less to my bed. I have had Mass and Communion only on the two Sundays. There is little wrong with me except excessive tiredness. This they attribute to over-work. It may be so, but I doubt it. For lately I have done nothing.

' The trouble, I myself think, is that the constant effort to resist my soul's urgings, and yet to remain outwardly happy, is something of a strain upon me. It is the body, and not the will, which is a little weak.

' However, I am going to struggle on. I want merely to give you a passing warning on this subject. For I do not believe that the time has come for me to die. Yet physically I am near exhaustion.

' I do what I can to patch up my body. For the cup which God has prepared for me to drink is by no means empty yet. I have faith that he will give me bodily strength, that I may continue to be obedient to his will on earth. I do what I can to hold on to life.

'I should do amiss if, out of lack of candour, I did not give you this warning : I must not hurry my death.

'——Though the light of God's truth is given directly to my soul, making me oblivious at the time of all things else, and making me afterwards desolate of spirit : there are occasions, when God possesses himself also of my body, as if to demonstrate to me that he is overlord of body and soul alike. On these occasions I use all my strength to resist him, though I know that, if God will it, all such resistance is futile.'

'MARIE DE LA TRINITÉ.'

June 2-3-4, 1912.

In secret God performs his secret work in me. . . .

Though he leave me detached from things and isolated from men ; though he leave my soul void and my body altogether spent, myself I give him but little. For in my soul he would do all, and be all. . . . '*Ego ero merces tua magna nimis !* '

It is true—only too great a reward in fact ! . . .

Earthly things are vain indeed ! . . .

In men there is no abiding surety. . . .

This ' I,' that agonises, is truly contemptible. Though I give up all to find him, this all is nothing ; while he— he is love itself, the true All. . . .

Content that he shall dwell alone in me, in him all things are added to me. . . .

God indwelling in me !—he who is infinite love . . . who is ruler of the world . . . this great living and loving God for ever present in me . . . he, the all-seeing . . . he, the all-knowing : he loves me, even he ! . . .

June 3, 1912.

' My dear Uncle,

' I was craving for silence and solitude : despite difficulties of circumstance he has led me to them. In silence and solitude he persists with his work, to whose secret I have no key.

' For me God is everything, the rest nothing. Would that I could retire into my soul's shut cell, where he dwells hidden and apart, and, so retiring, have knowledge that he is all ; that in my life there is none but he ; that for me life has no meaning apart from the all that is he.

' Alas ! my faith too often falters for me to have this knowledge uninterruptedly. Inconsequent trifles constantly distract and delude me, who should live firm in the truth. Too often I lose my sense of the actual and immediate presence of the living and loving and indwelling God.

' I do not know what my earthly future is to be. I do ask myself whether other than in solitude I can live my life without harm to my soul.'

' MARIE DE LA TRINITÉ.'

June 12, 1912.

Let me be wrought upon directly by God ! . . .

Let me seek him in tranquillity of spirit ! Let me seek him only in himself ! . . .

Let me in no way rely on the intellect to bring me to him ! . . .

I have surrendered all ; I have put the self from me finally. For me my fellow-men no longer exist. Emotion and experience are of no account. I have put them finally out of my life. . . .

My humanity desires only God's divinity. He alone can glut my soul.

July 15, 1912.

With mind and strength utterly spent in the service of his adorable will, let me see only God ! . . .

He alone is all. . . .

Let me gaze upon the Father—gaze upon the Son ! . . .

July 16, 1912.

Let me be transformed *by* God *into* God ! . . .

To me, with mind and strength utterly spent, he gives the fullness of himself.

July 17, 1912.

How wholly vain are earthly things ! . . .

O my Jesus! no earthly spouse fascinates as do you ! . . .

God the Father—my Father ! . . .

Mary, Mother of God—my Mother ! . . .

July 18, 1912.

' *Nostra conversatio in coelis est* . . .'

Let me have to do only with my Father, the all-loving ; with his Son, the all-loving no le.s, whom the Father has given to be my Spouse ; with Mary, *Virgo Purissima*, my beloved Mother ! . . . .

Let my life be lived only with my *new Family*—that Royal Family, which despite my meanness of rank received me royally ! . . .

July 20, 1912.

In absorbing vision I have seen myself received into the home circle of my Royal Family. How good no longer to look upon the earthly scene ! How good to live with the Father, who is Perfection and Plenitude, the Alpha and the All ; with his Son, the all-loving, who is like to the Father, and Spouse to my soul ; with Mary, Virgin most pure, who is my Mother ! . . .

How good to live their life of love ! . . .

How good to join with Mary in that adorable conversation, which continues through eternity, and is shared by the Holy Ghost in the divine fellowship ! . . .

July 21, 1912.

God is ever present. How shall suffering have power over me in face of the fact of his presence ? How shall I count important that which has *no importance ?* Confronted by so great a mystery, have I not far other things of which to think ?

Let me no longer have eyes for the earthly scene ! Let me busy myself only with God ! . . .

Let me live only this supernatural life in the circle of my new Family ! . . .

How fascinating is this converse in eternity ! how fascinating ! how varied ! and yet how harmoniously one ! . . .

It is with this Father, who is Perfection and Plenitude, the Alpha and the All, that I must converse, gazing from love-brimming eyes at him, who is the meaning of all —who himself is all.

It is to him, her Spouse, that his poor little nobody must yield herself up, accepting his outpoured love there in the sight of the Father and of Mary. . . .

It is in company of Mary, my beloved Mother, that I am able to look upon him, who has made queens of us both. . . .

Further, it is the mystery of the Word made flesh, of the Redemption and of Jesus the Redeemer, of Mary ' *Regina Martyrum,*' in which I need to absorb myself with the heavenly Family for the Father's glory's sake.

All this can come to pass only in the Spirit—only in the abiding peace and eternal silence of the Blessed Trinity.

The Father, in giving me his Son for Spouse, has revealed himself to me as never before. He has made it manifest that in love I am his child, become through love a queen. . .

O Father of my adoration ! O Son beloved of my soul, my Spouse, my Jesus ! O Mary, Immaculate Mother ! O Holy Ghost ! keep me one of your family ! Increase my love ! Bring me into the perfection of your fellowship ! Break every bond that shackles me to earth ! . . .

O Father, hallowed be thy name. . . . Thy kingdom come. Thy will be done in earth, as it is in heaven. . .

July 26, 1912.

None but God—none !

Let me live in the circle of my Royal Family ! . . .

Let me contrast that Family with all other families ! . . .

July 28, 1912.

Let me live uninterruptedly in God ! . . .

The Three in One and Mary dwell with me always ! I dwelling with them ! . . .

July 31, 1912.

Jesus . . . in him is the plenitude of the Godhead.

Let me live the divine life . . . through the Holy Ghost . . . in the fellowship of love ! . . .

Let my soul be a ' house of prayer ' indeed ! . . .

July 31, 1912.

' My dear Uncle,

' . . . As for my soul, I am earth's happiest living
creature. God, and none but God, is my all. In
him my soul is at home. It is so glutted with him,
that it seems at last to have realised its true nature,
its essential divinity.

' This sense of beatitude is far from being continuous. If this union with him were always thus
absorbing, I should have no more suffering, and
suffering is still his desire for me.'

'MARIE DE LA TRINITÉ.'

Magnificate Dominum mecum. . . .

August 5, 1912.

Secluded from the world. . . .
Secluded in him. . . .
In him, Jesus of the Threefold God !
Secluded in God, the ever-indwelling. . . .
' He who sees me, sees the Father.'

August 7, 1912.

One with God in prayer. . . .
Nothing shall interrupt it. . . .
Nothing shall interrupt it. . . .
They are there now and for ever. . . . Let me live
their life ! . . .
Jesus of the Eucharist. . . .
Of the Eucharist and of the Trinity.
How fascinating is their company !

August 15, 1912.

We are in the care of God himself. . . . For me, I
have no care but to concern myself with him. . . .
When he departs from me, let me love him as before !
Let me believe as implicitly in his love—yes, and in his

presence, though he seem to have departed from me ! . . .

I have but one duty : to remain remote from the self and from all created things ; to remain in intimate union with God and with none but God. . . .

This is the nature of the union reserved for me :

Perfect purity . . . purity that excludes every emotion of the flesh, and in fact devolves into unity with him. . . .

Perfect solitude . . . shut out of the earthly scene, I am secluded only with him. . . .

Perfect silence . . . all my converse is with him. . . .

Perfect mortification. . . . I am altogether abstracted from the self. As host, I stretch myself upon the altar, that I may have no concern save him. . . .

Perfect obedience . . . my will, my heart's desires, are one with God's ; for now I have no will and no desire apart from his. . . .

Perfect poverty. . . . I am stripped of all, that is not he, and only he. . . .

Perfect humility. . . . I live in him with the self obliterated. . . .

Perfect trust. . . . I have lost all trust in myself : in him my trust is infinite. . . .

Perfect strength . . . of myself I have no strength : in him my strength is immense. . . .

Perfect patience . . . since my life is lived in eternity already, there is nothing for which I am over-eager. For in him I have all. . . .

Perfect simplicity . . . to see only God—only for him to work : this is my simple rule of life. . . .

Perfect good-temper . . . if in him I live his life, I can be capable of no human irritation. . . .

Perfect charity . . . for in this state of union I can do

no other than love love's fellow, charity, that is beloved of him. . . .

Perfect truth . . . for he is truth—he himself ! . . .

Perfect love . . . for the completed holocaust leaves me ' transformed into him,' and he is very love. . . .

To such union I can attain only by *perfect faith*, by truth's compulsion seeing in all things only him.

Let me then live out of myself—live only in him : so I shall of necessity practise every virtue that is.

Aug. 24, 1912.

' A.M.D.G.

' My dear Uncle,

' In celebrating in love and in gratitude, as I have been doing in these last few days, the sixth anniversary of my conversion,[1] I can do no other than allow a faint echo of that gratitude to reach yourself as the instrument of which God made use to turn me from my life of evil inclination to the things more excellent.

' Oh, when I think that once I lived every day of my life with the secret apprehension that at the last I might not go to heaven . . . !

' Despite this apprehension I had a certain uneasy peace of mind. Yet though I sought to love and serve God to the best of my ability on earth, some impediment of soul prevented me from drawing nearer to God. Then you assured me that God's grace was in me and that most certainly he loved me, and gave me my faith in the fact of God's love. By this confidence that you inspired in me, you made my soul expand " and I have walked in his ways."

---

[1] ' *Her conversion* ' : by this should be understood her definite entry into the mystical life—*cf.* Chap. 7 *et seq.* of Part I of this book. September, 29, 1906 marks the beginning of that experimental union with God which reached the very high degree of perfection which the preceding *Life* has sought to depict.

T

' Of the rest you know a little, and I cannot tell the whole. Enough to say that it seems to be his will to make swift use of me for his own purposes.

'——For seven weeks past, through the mediation of the Immaculate Virgin, in the light of truth I have lived my life in the Blessed Trinity : *nostra conversatio in coelis est* has had a new and almost literal significance for my soul.

' I have been exalted above the self and its sufferings ; I have escaped from the bondage of the exterior life into the blessedness of his life.

' In his holy will I have known peace. By its performance I have never failed to find him.

' The old bonds are broken. His light-in-darkness has become full day. In him my soul stands fast.

' God is my all ; God is my desire and my delight. In silence and in solitude I converse with heaven's Royal Family ; through the Holy Ghost I know their fellowship of love.

' My indifference of these past few months, as to whether I live or whether I die, has left me. Now definitely I yearn to die, and to find in death the satisfaction of my urgent God-given need to go to God himself.

' Our Lord has revealed to me that a stage has been reached in my spiritual pilgrimage. Till now my way has been a way of destruction, with transformation into God as its goal. Now he wishes that I shall make outward manifestation of his indwelling presence : he wishes my life in the world to declare his life in me. My course of conduct remains unaltered. I am passive in his hands : as before I left him free to destroy the self in me, so now I leave him free to manifest himself through me.

' Perfect purity—isolation from men and things— absorption in God : union with him will, I believe, add all these to me, and with them every virtue that he requires me to practise.

' When in the light of his truth I contemplate God, I enable him to perfect his transformation of the self in me. Through love of suffering, humiliation, and the rest, my thought and my love and my desire have come to be centred in him alone.

' This life in the light of his wisdom and in the peace and fellowship of the Blessed Trinity is now more, now less, conscious to my soul. My own lack of faith accounts in part for its oscillation between the more and the less. When my faith is weak, he in his love recalls me to his love, and I am once more purified, once more transformed. Wholly abstracted from the self, I make God my one concern.

' This converse with the divine Persons has infinite diversity in its essential unity. It fascinates, it en-raptures in a fashion that no words can make plain. None may reveal " the secret of the King." Yet what joy it would be to publish abroad the loveliness of the divine mysteries ; to convey to men's souls the delight of converse with the Father, with Jesus the Spouse, with Mary our Mother, the Immaculate Virgin ; to discover to their eyes the profundities of the mystery of the Jesus of the Eucharist ; to lead them also into this life, in which the Spirit of Love is all !

' All these favours notwithstanding, in his goodness he treats me still as host. For this I give him un-bounded thanks.

' In him now and always, and in none but him, for the glory of the Father,

' I am,

' Hostia Laudis Trinitatis.'

August 29, 1912.

To have *implicit belief* in the presence of Jesus in the Blessed Sacrament is to have :

Love . . . gratitude . . . happiness . . .

—' He who sees me, sees the Father '—

Jesus desires that I have no fellowship save fellowship with him—desires too that this fellowship shall know no intermission—desires lastly that it shall be that same fellowship, which subsists between the divine Persons in the circle of heaven's Royal Family. . . .

September 1, 1912.

No more in the slaying of the self, no more in vigilance lest the self know resurrection, but in increasing resuscitation into him : must I follow him. . . .

To turn my back upon the self that I may turn my face to God, is my purpose no longer. My purpose is to dwell in him. . . .

I must shut my soul upon the side that looks towards earth ; I must *open it upon the side that looks towards heaven.* I must strive less to turn my eyes from his creation, than to fix them upon him, the Creator. . . .

I no longer need to strive after union, but to make *still closer* the union to which I have attained already. . . .

I no longer have occasion to seek transformation, but to make that transformation *transfiguring.* . . .

Ceaselessly and increasingly God discovers himself to me, who dwell in him, *remote from all earthly things.* . . .

Oblivious of the Host on the altar, I am fled away and away ; I am removed from joy and from grief ; I am remote from the self, from things, from men. . . . I see none but God—none ! . . .

The *gulf of a great secret* shuts me from the world. He is my all, and none but he ; the rest is *nothing.* . . .

September 6, 1912.

NONE BUT GOD.

Let me live in him, who is my soul's End, that he may shine through me, as a light shines through a lantern ! . . .

So let me live, unconcerned with means that shall bring either myself or others to him—for others let me take no thought at all. . . .

No thought, since upon them the light of my soul's End shall shine directly—a means to the end, which is he ! . . .

(The beams of a beacon-light lead us more surely and more accurately than the directions of passers-by, who may come our way.)

Therefore *let me live in him :* so shall the direct and shining light of his truth, falling upon men's souls, draw them to him in accordance with his will. . . .

September 7, 1912.

None but God. . . . God who is all ! . . .
May he be *increasingly my own all !* . . .
As the light of truth grows stronger, my vision widens. I see the heavenly world, in which the divine family move and have their being. . . .
. . . I see *the Trinity more clearly.* . . . The Father . . . The Son . . . The Holy Ghost . . .
I see . . . the mystery of Jesus . . . of the Blessed Virgin. . . . I see the wide world of heaven, and the angels, and the saints and the blessed souls, who praise and adore our Thrice Blessed God for his great glory's sake, and for the sake of his boundless love. . . .
Oh, how infinitely petty is this earth by comparison !

September 9, 1912.

In close communion with Jesus, the 'Word made flesh,' my Beloved, my all. . . .

' My delight is to be with the children of men. . . .'

As the Blessed Trinity is more completely and more worthily made manifest in me, so my thirst for communion increases. . . .

Though I be privileged to contemplate him uninterruptedly, I thirst to possess God in his entirety in the shape of that small Host, where in the person of Jesus God in Three Persons subsists in his unity. . . .

September 10, 1912.

O mystery of the Eucharist ! . . .

O mystery of Jesus ! . . .

. . . For ever Three, yet for ever One. . . .

O Jesus, who is all ! . . . One (yet Three) . . .

O all-embracing God, who art encompassed entire in the Blessed Host ! . . .

Sept. 16, 1912.

' A.M.D.G.

' My dear Uncle,

' Let me give you belated thanks for coming to see me, when I went through Paris.

'——I am increasingly sustained in God's infinite love.

' Recently he led me to his highest peak.

' There he revealed himself to me, very God of very God. I seemed to be one with every perfection that is his : I feel sure that on earth the soul can climb no higher. Subsequently great powers of intercession were granted to me. By such union as by nothing else infinitely more can surely be achieved for the glory of God and the good of men's souls. In it I have realised the worth of the communion of saints in heaven to the cause of the salvation and sanctification of men's souls.

'Such grace calls forth an overwhelming desire for death, since only in heaven can love enter upon its next stage. The fact that this ultimate earthly union comes to me oftener, and endures longer, suggests that the hour has come in which I am to cry " *Consummatum est*."

'Yet I am not impatient. I desire only his blessed will. Already God is my abiding place : I am safe in my Father's arms.

'This ultimate love by its ardour assists (I must believe) my soul upon its road. If it increase, my happiness will increase with it. . . .

'——I am able to receive Communion only four times a week. I delight in the fascinating mystery of the Infinite encompassed entire in the tininess of the Host.

'——Once more thank you for everything. Thank him, will you, with me and for me. Myself I am no longer able to tell him all that I have learned in the fellowship of love and of truth. There is but one word—one word that only silence utters—which embraces it all. That word is " God."

'In this fellowship I wait expectant of my summons to heaven. May it be not long delayed ! For I would welcome death, that I might love him with the fullness of love.

'In respect,
'Hostia laudis Trinitatis.'

September 14, 1912.

God alone shares all my secrets. . . .
In the Trinity, Unity—Unity eternally. . . .
God in Three Persons subsists in the *Unity of Jesus.* . . .
'You see me, because I live and you shall live. In that day *you shall know that I am in my Father*, and you in me and I in you.'

September 16, 1912.

None but God—none! For these weeks past he has been my abiding place. . . . *None but God!* . . . *Reaching the goal*, I forget the way, which has led to it. . . .

Most surely suffering may not touch me, who am thus *in union with God*. . . . *None but God—none!* My desire is only for him.

Though at times he permit me to fall back into the self, and there to know suffering, yet at these times I have but to go on, till suffering be left behind, and union once more bring me *into direct contact with God*. . . .

Though often a grey veil fall between my God and me, my peace of soul persists. For always I have the certainty of finding him again. . . .

Like the needle of a compass I swing to him, who is my north. . .

October 1, 1912.

The purpose of my life is that my soul shall live and move and have its being in the being of God. . . .
. . . *Is to live above suffering*. . . .
Above suffering that has lost its *sting*. . . .
. . . *Nos vero omnes revelata facie*. . . .
Let me contemplate him now and for ever! . . .

October 2, 1912.

Wrapped in peace . . . brought again into the *Fellowship* . . .

October 3, 1912.

The Word . . . *in him all things are* . . .
In the being of all things he is. . . .

He alone knows truth. . . .
He sees all. . . .
He is *truth. . . .*
He alone is sharer of my secrets. . . .

October 7, 1912.

I am *fast-fixed* in God . . .
I have no desire *but for him.*
For he is all—all ! . . .

October 8-9-10, 1912.

God who is all . . .
In God and *of* God let me live ! . . .
. . . Live as if already in eternity. . . .
Let heaven be my vantage-ground ! . . .
. . . As it is God's . . .
The fire of love devours me no longer . . .
For I am become that fire . . .
Stick of love's kindling-wood, let me burn in God !

October 28, 1912.

One day—one day that is like to a thousand years . . .
. . . Spent now—even now—*in eternity* . . .
Fast-fixed in God . . . and in his will . . .
. . . *In none but God—God, who is all* . . .

November 15, 1912.

Father, I love you . . .
How utter-sweet to call you ' Father ! ' to know
myself in truth the child of your love ! . . .
Father, I am held close in your arms. . . . *I am fast-*
fixed in your will. . . . I am content to continue, de-
prived of all. . . . I am content, because it is your will.
Father, in your unity with Jesus and the Spirit of
Love, for me you are *all.* . . .

December 9, 1912.

To have eternal life is—' to know God ' . . .

Dec. 29, 1912.

' A.M.D.G.

' My dear Uncle,

' My life is simplicity itself. It is of God and in God—and it is no more than that. All that I can tell you comes to no more than that.

' He transcends his own attributes ; he transcends his own perfections. Attributes and perfections are, if I may dare to say so, the less divine aspect of God : in them there is a resemblance—infinitely remote, but still a resemblance—to our own. Therefore I turn from his attributes and from his perfections to God himself, and am plunged into the divine mystery of his being, of his essential life. In that life's immutability is no weariness ; for in his unity is infinite diversity.

' The deeper I penetrate into his unutterable secret, the closer becomes my union with him, and the greater my soul's happiness.

'——As for my health, it has improved upon the whole, though it has its ups and downs. When I feel better, and think once more of Carmel, the fever returns ; when I am not so well, and think of death, the doctor patches me up !

' Spiritually, God gives me assurance that Carmel is still my vocation, and not life lived in the world. When I am free to go, I shall be both coward and traitor, if I do not go. On the other hand, if it continue to be his will to prevent my going, he has made it plain that without Carmel he will give me all that I may find within it.

' He makes it plain too, that all exterior things—

even time itself—are but subsidiary means necessary for the work, which he performs in my soul.

'I live on the threshold of eternity, striving, as he wills, in heart and soul to be ready to leave this earth —to leave it with a soul already emancipated and a heart already glowing with love.

'In love and complete surrender of self I am at peace. My faith is stronger that, when my hour shall come, whether it be to-morrow or years hence, the work in my soul shall then be perfected. I try to live each moment as if it were my last, though at present to all appearances I am on the way to re-covery.

'MARIE DE LA TRINITÉ.'

January 25, 1913.

Into each moment of my life let me pack that *plenitude* of love, which I should show in doing notable deeds for him ! . . .

January 26, 1913.

If one but knew all that he gives the soul !—all that he does in it *in an instant of time*, and that *altogether interiorly* ! . . .

January 29, 1913.

In this earthly exile how could one live but for the comforting opportunity of doing the Father's will ? . . .

February 2, 1913.

How *paltry* is earth, beheld from the vantage of heaven ! . . .

God, who is all . . .

February 4, 1913.

Let me plunge deep into God . . . till I be lost in him! . . .

February 6, 1913.

I am no more I . . .
God who is all . . .

February 10, 1913.

God, who is all. . . .
In God and his *infinite perfection* I behold all that is good, all that is lovely, all that is lofty, on earth. And, these subtracted, there remains *the whole of God, who is all. . . .*

February 17, 1913.

Let me make particular use of solitude ; for *solitude is sacramental! . . .*
Now and *for ever* he *is. . . .*
In the being of all things he is. . . .
Let me contemplate *the Father . . . the Son . . . the Spirit of Love! . . . Let me dwell in them! . . .*

March 5, 1913.

Let me plunge deep, and still deeper, into this *mystery of intimacy,* which he has made mine to fathom during my retreat . . . until I am come to its heart! . . .

March 11, 1913.

Now and *for ever* God *is. . . .* He dwells in me : I am *altogether his concern.* And I—*I have no concern but him. . . .*
Without intermission he gives himself *in his entirety* to me. . . . Keep yourself in tune with God, O my soul!

that you may commune uninterruptedly with *God in his entirety;* that you may remain uninterruptedly ' *in unum !* ' . . .

With my Jesus . . . *in infinite love* . . . *let me lie* in the *Father's* bosom. . . . I am *his child.* . . . It is my *unity with Jesus* . . . in *infinite love* . . . that makes me *the Father's child.* . . .

What matters it that I am poor, insignificant, miserable? Am I not *his child?*

Compared with the *infinite majesty* of the Father, the noblest soul is of no account.

In the *infinite mercy* of the Father do not the sins of the prodigal vanish away, as completely as those of his brother? And those of Magdalen even as those of Martha? . . .

There is but one essential : to be *his child indeed.* . . .

If Judas had had love in his heart—love and trust and humility—if, in short, he had been *God's child,* he too would have been a saint, even as the others. . . .

What is there left for me to desire, whether on earth or in heaven? . . . He is *my Father;* I am *his child.* . . . He is my Father—my Father ! . . .

With Jesus, and in Jesus, I have, it seems to me, *all the rights and all the privileges* of God's only begotten Son. . . .

March 17, 1912.

Now and always my life is his life. . . . ' *in unum.*' How *much* is implicit in this intimacy . . . It is to live life at its profoundest ; to stand in his courts when God gives judgement ; to be *one* with him in every action ; to be part of the *might of God.* . . .

March 27, 1913.

Now and always let me be the little dispenser of the Great Disposer ! . . .

April 2, 1913.

What you alone know, my adored Master, is increasingly my preoccupation. What is known to others as well as to you, I treat as of *no account.* . . .

April 4, 1913.

Between the truth of my soul's experiences and the account which I am able to give of them, there is a discrepancy far greater than that between the ocean and the raindrop. Moreover, while the raindrop is of the same substance as the ocean, my rendering of them is not of the substance of ' these things.' They are utterly incommunicable.

June 20, 1913.

Where the *self has its end,* there God *begins.* . . .
Only in this is holiness : to cease to be ; to become absorbed in God ; to be one with him. . . .

June 21, 1913.

One of life's hardships is the soul's inability to communicate truth. *Truth must be lived :* it cannot be explained. . . .

June 26, 1913.

How unutterable are the soul's experiences when, *its life one with another life,* it is *capable of infinite love !*[1]—how unutterable, when that other is *God !* . . .

July 14, 1913.

Utter sacrifice is the rind : beneath the rind is to be found the incomparable fruit—the fruit which is Very God. . . .

---

[1] Once more this is a mystic's hyperbole. A finite human being is not capable of infinite love. This expression seeks to express the inexpressible. Passage after passage in the present book make its meaning plain.

July 27, 1913.

Suffering is the token coin. With this token the soul can purchase spiritual power. . . .

When the soul would perform *unceasingly deeds of power* for the Father's glory, it must spend its coin, *as a spendthrift does*. . . .

August 3, 1913.

In me may the stigmata be *wholly invisible !* . . .[1]

Though *in the eyes of both God and man*, I be of all men the least, it matters nothing ; for of me my Beloved has *the maximum of glory and the maximum of love*. . . .

August 5, 1913.

How *paltry* is this earth ! . . .
Nothing is hidden from his sight. . . .
He alone knows truth. . . .
He alone knows all things. . . .
He alone . . . alone. . . .

October 17, 1913.

Silence alone utters all. . . .

November 12, 1913.

My soul is his bond-slave, and my soul is happy, because of that indefinable element which makes God, God . . . that element in which created things have neither lot nor part. . . .

. . . That element which is *the essence of God*. . . .

In him suffering vanishes away ; in him desire, no matter how strong, is sated ; in him is abiding peace ; in him the soul is glutted . . .

. . . In him, *my God, my all*. . . .

[1] See note page 290.

CHAPTER THE FOURTH

'HID WITH CHRIST IN GOD'

1914—1915

January 18, 1914.

I AM to be identified with Jesus the Redeemer, the Crucified. It is his will. I am more and more sure of it. Yet not the Son's cross, but the Father's bosom, is to be my abiding place. For there is the Word made flesh, and there the Holy Ghost.

And only there is that '*life hid with Christ in God,*' as it is termed in the epistle for the day of my birth. . . .

'*Hid in God*' : this is implicit of union with the Father. . . .

'*With Christ*' : the purpose of that union is to continue in me the work of the Redemption, and to transform me into Christ crucified . . . He wills that my life shall be as the Mass—a continuation of the sacrifice upon the cross. . . . Consequently for me, as once for Jesus, God intermits that union and its joy—intermits it with suffering that shall serve his glory. Not I, but Christ in me then suffers for the glory of ' our Father ' . . . Though thus my soul know crucifixion, it knows also abundant joy, abundant peace. In full union with him it serves his glory fully. It foretastes heaven— a dolorous heaven, it is true, but still heaven. Each access of suffering brings access of happiness ; for each brings increase to God's joy and glory. . . .

Like a little child held close in his heavenly Father's arms, I am surrendered to his love. He is my soul's desire and my eyes' delight ; he is my all. Just now his eyes are veiled from me, they and their paternal tenderness. Yet I doubt neither that he loves me, nor that he watches over me . . . despite the veil, despite the tenderness withheld. . . .

——You know, Holy Father, how much it means to your poor little nobody to miss the blessedness of your eyes' regard, when she lifts her own to you ! You know too that your blessed will—that furtherance of your glory, which is her desire no less than your will—is indeed her heaven, however dolorous a heaven it be ! . . .

January 30, 1914.

Let me drink of the cup, nor look to see what bitter beverage it hold ! . . . For all things and for ever let me give thanks ! . . .

January 31, 1914.

Let my rivulet-soul join the river of *truth* . . . the river of *charity* ! . . .

February 4, 1914.

Of what great worth to his glory, *the cross known to him alone* ! . . .

In his slightest wish he altogether is. . . .

February 25, 1914.

Your life is *hid with Christ in God*. . . .

My soul has two seals : the one is *Jesus Christ* ; the other the *Trinity*. . . .

U

Could any one phrase be implicit of all the favours with which he has heaped me, that phrase would be : ' *the sign of the cross.*'

In close union with *Jesus the Redeemer in God.* . . .

April 21, 1914.

If only men knew him ! . . .

Oh, now and for ever be he my utter all ! . . .

April 30, 1914.

In suffering and in humiliation : ' *Jesus autem tacebat.*'

In the grace of union, in life intimately shared with him : ' *Maria conservabat omnia in corde suo.* . . .'

Therefore : ' *Me decet silentium.* . . .'

May 1, 1914.

Any source of surpassing suffering I will bury deep in the secret known only to him. . . .

May 9, 1914.

The Blessed Virgin. . . . How great her simplicity ! . . . It is so great that to contemplate her is easier than to speak of her. . . . Surely the clue to all her life is this : she lives with God ' *in unum* ' . . .

Her way is my way : in that deep mystery in which she lives, I too must live . . . plunged deep . . . absorbed in God. . . .

To be ' *Marie de la Trinité* ' in truth : here is the sum of my vocation.

May 10, 1914.

Let heaven be even now my *habitation !* . . . *Let me be plunged deep into the deeps of God !* . . . *Let me walk upon this earth, engrossed in God !* . . .

In God, who is my all ! . . .

June 8, 1914.

The *Blessed Sacrament.* . . .

It embraces all of God's plenitude. . . . In it all things are added to the soul. . . . The *Blessed Sacrament :* it is *the very dwelling-place of the Most Blessed Trinity.* . . . It is by the *Blessed Sacrament,* above all, that the soul lives this life of fellowship with the *Three in One,* and can cry with truth :

' *Nostra conversatio in coelis est.* . . .'

October 15–21, 1914.

Let me give ! . . .

To give is my vocation. . . .

To God, as to men's souls, let me give *the plenitude of God !* . . .

So shall I know *abounding joy.* . . .

Let me vanish away, mingled and lost in you, O God of love ! O God, who are hid ! . . . Let me, living in love, *give out* love ! . . .

It is the joy of my life to feel that it yields nothing—nothing !—to me, and all—all !—to God and my fellows. . . .

O God ! preserve through all eternity the lot, which I so cherish. When my earthly exile is over, and in glory you become my lot for ever, let this too be my gift to you ! . . .

November 24–*December* 8, 1914.

Let me, who am *identified* with Jesus the Redeemer, and with Mary, Regina Martyrum . . . who am absorbed in the mystery of the Redemption—let me search out the supreme dolour of Christ ! . . .

The inconceivable unction of that supreme dolour has its spring in this : it is in love and by love that I am thus identified with him. . . .

Marvellously he has revealed to me my vocation.

⌐ There can be no better lot . . . for it is the lot most like to his.

It is because of my exceeding worthlessness that he has chosen such suffering for me. Because of this too it is his will that he alone shall perform the work in my soul. . . . Therefore my wish is to give myself humbly to this dolorous love . . . with Jesus to be lost in the *pit of suffering and of love*. . . .

With Mary, Regina Martyrum, my beloved Mother, let me bury my life in that of Christ Jesus ! . . . How surpassing is this union ! . . . How complete the identification with you, O my Jesus ! . . . my adored love ! . . . Oh, *the joy so to suffer to the limits of suffering !* . . .

December 13-15, 1914.

He has given me the assurance of his *preferential love*. . . . To know oneself ' the preferred of God ' is to know ecstasy, transcending all words—and with that ecstasy a sweet humility. . . .

Jesus, my adored love, I love you ! Of your own love I do not ask the reason. . . .

He has allowed me to glimpse *his work* in my soul—it may, or may not, be as further proof of his preferential love. . . .

The surpassing peace which he has bestowed upon me, is a burden to my soul : I am weighed down with a great sense of responsibility, and a great fear lest, by keeping ' these things ' hidden, I am failing to put his gifts to use. . . . Are ' these marvels ' to be published abroad, or is it your wish that they shall be kept for you alone, O God of love ? . . .

You know, my soul's beloved, with what great joy I would reveal ' these things,' if to reveal them were your will, inadequate and unworthy though my revelation of them would be. . . . To do becoming honour to your love I should need the voice of an angel ! . . .

It delights me to reflect that, while your work in the Virgin Mary was infinitely lovelier than that which you have performed in your poor little nobody, yet in those simple words ' *Fecit mihi magna . . .*' she has rendered you abundant glory. . . .

It is my trust, O God, that from my silence, as from hers, you draw the plenitude of glory. . . .

December 18-19, 1914.

The glimpsed perfection of his work in us implants the need to praise his mercies. . . .

Yet how in poor words can their *multiplicity* and their *sublimity* be rendered ? To publish the divine secrets of his love abroad, would rejoice my heart. Circumstance and my soul's suffering constantly prevent it.

When it shall be his will, he will give me both the means and the opportunity of making revelation of the abundant grace, which he increasingly bestows upon me.

December 20, 1914.

Because I keep silence, all this grace is not lost. I am to remain upon the heights : to behold them, I should have to descend from them. This is not his will : his will is that he himself shall be my sole concern.

He shall teach me, *living absorbed in him and surrendered to the work of his hands*, what to reveal and when to reveal it. . . .

For two and a half years our union has been constant. *What exceeding grace !*

God and his plenitude remain unchanged, unchanging . . . only his manifestations in our union change without cease. . . .

Let love shine through me ! . . .

December 21, 1914.

For his glory's sake I am to have great *influence* over others : he wills it so. . . .

NONE BUT GOD.

Christmas 1914.

' My dear Unclé,

' Help me, please, to thank our great God of Love for all his favours and above all for those heaped upon me during 1914. Of all the years of my life this has been the richest, both in grace and in suffering. The suffering of other years has been as great perhaps. Yet it has been a different suffering, obscure in its purpose, purging in its nature. Now it has become (may I say it ?) a participation in the sorrows of Jesus, into which love and peace both enter. Even when that suffering is at its worst, direct union with God, that leaves me serene of soul, in a greater or smaller degree is continuous.

' Beyond that suffering, beyond the grace of prayer, beyond all things, " God is." His spell binds all my being. I am like a little child, whose mother gives it pretty things, and yet who has no eyes for those gifts, but only for its mother, their giver. Tell me, is my attitude in this matter right or wrong ?

' My normal union is with God in his unity. Ought I sometimes to make particular efforts to know union with Jesus ? From time to time he makes me sharer in his sorrows, and allows me (to express it so) to participate in the mystery of the Redemption ; I had almost said in that of the Incarnation, since there are occasions when he permits me to perceive where his humanity fuses with his divinity. Yet this union, compared with the other, is rare.

'——Mother's illness, though it grieves me, does not perturb my soul. I have faced the possibilities, and by God's grace am ready for all. I seek to do his will : his good pleasure is my one concern. It is difficult to make plain the state which I have known, since he has given me this completeness of union with him. It is a state of soul in which every inclination of my being is in tune with his good pleasure. It brings me my greatest happiness.   ' M.A.'

January 14-21, 1915.

My suffering is like the sea : my unbroken contemplation is like the clear blue sky above it. . . .

Let me be content for God to lead me on by his *lovely yet sorrowful way*—that way which more and more enraptures me. . . .

January 27—*February* 1, 1915.

As my suffering grows, my *love of and desire for* suffering grow with it. . . . I am like the martyrs, who *in the midst of their suffering saw the heavens open, and their destined bliss and God's glory increase in the measure of their suffering.*

In my weakness and my wounds I am strong—strong to give him glory . . . as *my wounds—love's wounds— widen, my strength grows.* . . .

Let me live *even now in heaven !* . . . Live for *God in the presence of none but God !* . . . In all things let me seek only to be well-pleasing to Jesus, my King ! . . . He alone sees the right side of my soul's stuff ; men know only the wrong. . . .

Love's martyrdom—love's hidden martyrdom—is well-pleasing in his sight. . . .

February 6-11, 1915.

Whether it be a little one who interrupts me, or a visitor's call, or some small hardship, or some requirement of God's will, or even something that *apparently* opposes his will : let me recognise in each of these *the working of that will !* . . .

Whether he make use of a sacrament, or whether he give himself to me directly : so only he come to me, what care I ? . . .

In all things let me see *only* God ! . . .

March 1-3, 1915.

Let me remain *identified* with this divine will . . . *absorbed in silent adoration*, in *praise*, in *gratitude*, and in *love*. . . .

This adorable will is my *heaven upon earth*. . . .

With me joy is one with pain : *in his will I see but him*. . . .

As if in heaven already, let me live, *hidden and lost in him !* . . .

In all that he performs in me, let *silence* bring me into tune with him—that *silence of love, which is at once humble and trusting and pure !* . . .

Let silence pervade all my soul ! . . .

March 3-5, 1915.

No taking of thought will enable me to set down what occurs in this union . . . in this life ' *in coelis*.' . . .

To speak of ' these things ' I need to climb down from the heights. Once the descent is made, the vision vanishes. . . .

These notes are but echoes of words heard when the descent has already begun.

Or : they are thoughts come to me as I write, or as I talk with another ; they enable me to capture faint echoes of those words uttered upon the heights. . . .

The purpose of these notes is not to discover the state of my soul, or even to indicate this or that feature of it : their purpose is solely to help me dwell in God. Their dates, the form which they take, the underlining of the words, the very breaks between the words—have frequently more significance for me than the literal meaning of the words themselves. . . .

To descend the heights or to transcribe experiences known upon them, is not essential. The one essential is to rest absorbed in him, and to have no life except the life ' in heaven.' . . .

March, 1915.

' My dear Uncle,

' I want to tell you something of his will and of my adoration. I see it in its wisdom, in its loveliness and in its love. I am bound by its divine spell ; I am privileged (I dare to say) to enter into its decisions ; I find it adorable ; I praise it unceasingly for its superb manifestations in myself. I yearn to see all men prostrate, as I, before it, and as I, identified with it.

' I echo S. Ignatius of Antioch : " I have broken free from earth ; I look upon my life with men as at an end." So it is with me. As I cannot sing his mercies with the Church Militant, by his will and out of a full heart I sing them with the Church Triumphant. He cuts off my communications with men : I take this as a sign—and am happy at the sign—that he wills his love for his poor little nobody to be known only to him.

' Help me, I beg you, to give him thanks for my life " *in heaven.*"

' M. A.'

May or June, 1915.[1]

'Give me the help of your prayer; for I have great need of both strength and humility to bear in silence and alone my many present burdens.

'May *his will* be done! May his will be loved! In it I am continually one with you.

'I am too weak to write more. What he wills you to know, his will will make known to you.

'May my weakness bless him!

'May my silence magnify him!

'May my suffering utter to him my love! May my life, hidden wholly in him, leave upon this earth seeds quick with truth and love!

'Thank you for all your goodness.

'Now and for ever in God,
'M. A.'

[1] Written at the time when her sickness seemed to threaten death—'her first death,' as Consummata was, later, jestingly to allude to it. *Cf.* Chap. 7, Sect. 3 of Part I.

CHAPTER THE FIFTH

DESIRE OF LOVE'S DISCIPLESHIP

1915—1916

' *Magnificate Dominum mecum.*

' *July* 1, 1915.

' My dear Uncle,

' As for my soul, I have nothing new to tell you.

' A soul to which God is all, can surely sing him its canticle of praise only in silence. In the comprehension that God alone is, and that God is all, earthly things so dwindle that joy is one with pain, and both are nothing. . . . In him is peace. . . . In him earth becomes heaven ; life on earth, life in heaven. Not here but there is now our dwelling-place and our conversation. Of that conversation this only can be said : it is silence kept in love's union ; it is silence in which one word is spoken—the Word which is God.

' Let me tell you of a recent experience.

' Without warning the eagle of God let fall his little prey. Union was broken, the self returned. What were previously molehills of suffering became mountains, mountains threatening to topple upon her. The devil beset her with every manner of temptation, as though to avenge himself for his previous powerlessness.

' In love and in the hope that he would bless me with his glance, I turned my eyes towards heaven.

Heaven granted me no sign. By my soul's dim light —all other light withheld—I saw a great pit, dug at my feet—the fathomless pit of my worthlessness. Into this I was called upon to plunge. I took that plunge, making use of these three means. First, in my soul I acknowledged my worthlessness ; second, I compared that worthlessness with the worth of others ; third, I performed one or two small acts that should discipline my self-love. By this modest way of humility I re-discovered my God. For at the pit's bottom his heights began.

' On this occasion I had no sense of standing upon those heights and looking down from their high place, but a sense of having fallen *beneath* the self, of struggling to my feet in the depths and of looking upward. Even so, I had once more found God, while this union was the more sure, in that I could fall no farther.

' God in his loving-kindness has given me his cross and his cup at an early age, and with them his indescribable grace with which I may bear suffering as indescribable.

' If, as once he did, he were to manifest himself to me in love that is palpable, I believe that I should die of too much ecstasy. For my love has become an exceeding love. Were his love for me made palpable, my joy would snap the threads which bind me to earth. Even now, wrapped as I am in suffering, his mercies transport my soul, thrilling it to silence. I am a little like a lyre, whose strings have been made so taut, that a touch will snap them.

' The hand to give that touch shall surely be death's : faith's curtain shall be rent across ; the hidden shall become the plain ; love's last thrill shall snap the strings of my soul's lyre.'

' Marie de la Trinité.'

Dec. 29, 1915.

' That love which " sanctifies Christ " in us continues to operate in my soul, even as the light of God's countenance continues to shine upon it. The one is as delightful as the other is lovely.

' I get much help from the Blessed Virgin. She, " *abscondita in Deo, cum Christo*," is my ideal. I seek to follow in the train of her perfection. With such a life no other may compare. The soul needs but to be in tune, and grace received breeds further grace.

' My life's purpose is to remain hidden in love, that I may spread love, and lose the self more and more completely in love's intimacy. To possess God is happiness indeed ; to give God is beatitude itself. To live love is sweet ; to give God's life of love to others is sweeter.

' Would that I were so full of grace, that I infected men's souls with it, making them quick with God ! Would that I could publish truth and spread love to all about me—those nearest to me, those not so near, and myriads of others outside my acquaintance ! Would that I could inspire men to holy vocations ! For this aspiration's sake I seek to store in the granaries of God an abundance of seed.   ' M. A.'

Jun. 9, 1916.

' Love is all my life—his love for me, mine for him. Nothing alters. This love, his infinite mercy, his light of wisdom, the increasingly lovely serenity which it confers, intermittent suffering, the absorption of this suffering into that love, the consequent greater intensity of that love, the growing sense of beatitude : in these there is no change.

' If each day brought me Holy Communion, earth would be heaven.

' I hunger and thirst for Communion. Yet apart from it, I am glutted with his will ; I am drunken with the living water of Very God.'

1916.

' For the past two years in particular, there has been much gossip about myself, as varied as absurd. Some of it has come to my ears. It ranges from the ridiculously eulogistic to the vindictively spiteful. I need scarcely tell you that I am influenced by none of it. Men's opinions have neither stability nor consistency. Towards my fellows I seek to show Christ's charity ; to their opinions I am so wholly indifferent that they scarcely exist for me.

' Yet from a friend the other day I received a warning, given in all good faith, as to the general opinion of me. She emphasised that, living in all probability in illusion, I was a stumbling-block to others. At first this left me entirely unmoved. I know what I know : I know God's promises ; I have seen their fulfilment. Then suddenly doubt came : might it not be pride in this forthright fashion to set aside all such warnings and so entirely to dis-regard the opinions of others ? Thereupon, I begged God to believe that never—never—will I doubt his promises, but that I wished no longer to withdraw myself into my soul's strong tower in disregard of warnings, that might possibly come indirectly from himself.

' God answered me that I was to have no fear. I am re-assured and comforted ; for his divine reply was to have me behold himself crucified in me more unmistakably than ever before. My body smarted with his wounds, even as my soul knew his glory.

' Other grace comes to me often. To one who is thus dissolved in love, identified with Jesus, and as if lost in the Trinity itself, things happen, which it is impossible to doubt, although those things glorify him inordinately. In these things is such an utter and unique unity, that there is no possibility of error. For sake of such beatitude better to suffer every conceivable contradiction and every manner of persecution from now till the world end, rather than forswear the gift of God ! At the end of his way for me stands God himself : I cannot doubt it.

'With my life of everyday it is otherwise. Though I do not doubt that the exterior life depends upon the interior, I would not care to claim that this particular phenomenon or that was of divine origin. In these matters delusion is possible, is it not ?

'I never state my own belief as to the nature of what happens in me. I do not seek even to acquaint myself with it. I do not claim to know it with certainty. I know only that my experiences are mine by the will of God. It is no matter to me as to whether they are natural or supernatural or both. They are his will : for me that is enough.

'To revert : it is precisely this calm certainty in which I live, that others seek to question. *Is it God's will?* they ask in doubt. Meanwhile the consciousness, which I normally have of my identification with Jesus, and of my perfected union with the very Trinity itself, is much weakened. Though at the centre of my soul I am tranquil, at its periphery (if I may express it so) I feel forlorn indeed.

'At the moment evidence accumulates and witnesses multiply against me. I need more than ever a confidant, to whom I can open all my heart. Now that, as insidious doubt suggests, even my physical suffering may not be God's will, that suffering, to which normally I give no thought, has become painfully hard to bear : if indeed it were not his will, it would become intolerable.

' Despite all this I have not lost my profound inner peace : indeed I have known a strange happiness, crowning that peace.

' For this thought has come to me : if, loving truth with passion, I yet were living in illusion, recognition of the latter would be an immense sacrifice. I told myself that even for that sacrifice I would be prepared, certain that such a humiliation would but add to the beauty of my life in him.

' Where once I saw merely suffering in my isolation, I see now definite danger. Because of this I think that it would perhaps be good for me to speak out without reserve, that all things may be *checked and based upon obedience and humility*.

' My feeling is that, lest I betray the secret of the King, I have suppressed this, half-suppressed that, and allowed the other to be falsely believed, rather than justify myself. The result is a somewhat ambiguous position, that may have left a false impression upon the minds of others. To have acted so may have been the cause of talk and even of scandal : the thought is exceedingly painful to me, whose wish was to have had my sojourn on earth marked only by a shining trail of truth and by a great fire of love.

' I long to be fast fixed in truth, and to know God's work in me verified. However, I am not impatient ; while I leave it to you to decide whether this suggested complete frankness on my part will be for the best.

' M. A.'

Aug. 16, 1916.

' You are in retreat. I am quite alone in my room, where my crucifix faces the statue of the Blessed Virgin—and so I too am in a kind of retreat. It is a sweet and lovely thing, this life perfected in unity with the Blessed Trinity—this life, whose unbroken music is " *Per ipsum, et cum ipso, et in ipso est tibi Deo Patri Omnipotenti, in unitate Spiritus Sancti, omnis honor et gloria.*"

' How good to live so, by love transformed into Christ, and consummated into the divine unity ! How impossible to set down in words our soul's unique need, our all, or the incredible rapture, come of contemplation of the unity of the Father, of the Son, and of the Holy Ghost ; come (I had almost said) of incorporation with them !

' It is when the soul's power to praise God becomes palpably inadequate, that it turns towards its fellow-men. What would one not give to exalt others above this temporal present into that one great and living reality, where they may walk in the light of wisdom, and know the blessed touch of the hands of truth !

' What would one not give to make them sharers of this beatitude, that by their love and gratitude the glory of the Most High might be added to abundantly ! Living still in him, a soul may give God to other souls, publishing truth to them and spreading love. This apostolate is simplicity itself : one needs but to dwell in him. For in him is the stronghold of every soul alive. Each soul, that lives in him, performs its every action in the name of all men. At one both with Jesus and with the world of men I seek to make my adoration universal ; in my unity with Jesus I make it infinite in each living soul.

' Further : one would give much from time to time to sing the mercies of the Lord. Yet that poor lyre, which is my soul, becomes then too vibrant for its case of solid flesh, and to such use can be put too seldom.

' Till now, I have not been able to go on with this letter, begun several days ago. For when praise of

x

him starts to make music in my soul, the first note
has such strength, that a second would snap my
lyre's taut strings. My body is too small for my soul,
and my heart cannot hold the love, with which I
love him. . . . It is not often that I can write to
you, as I have written this evening. I have been
able to do so now, only because I have denied my
eyes their desire to behold his face.

'MARIE DE LA TRINITÉ.'

The measure of an apostolate's perfection is dependent
upon its informing grace.[1]

The needs of men's souls are subtle and delicate :
who would impart to them the light of life, must himself
possess in full measure that same ' *lumen vitae.*'

Apostleship demands the depth and universality of
perfection itself.

An apostolate is the outward sign of a soul's inward
holiness. . . . The former is the latter's temporal fruit,
and its eternal seed.

Given a holiness come to ripeness and knowing exaltation, an apostolate is like a bell pealing through all
eternity.

If it have its springs in God, action can be as sweet
and as lovely as contemplation.

In works is exceeding beatitude.

At their highest and best contemplation and action
are one in God's unity.

Works are life lived in the light of his wisdom.

The soul, which is in tune with God, makes music
richly powerful and subtly sweet.

---

[1] From early April 1914 onwards, Marie de la Trinité notes
her supernatural illuminations at increasingly long intervals.
Her notes are often dateless ; while a single thought is frequently pursued by her for several days or even weeks. Her
life was becoming more and more single, and her soul making
a more complete escape into unity and simplicity.

The soul is the harmonious music of every virtue, made one in truth, made vital in love.

The soul makes one vast music of perfect praise.

An apostle needs but to yield himself to God, dwelling within him in such plenitude and perfection, in order to give himself to souls.

CHAPTER THE SIXTH

'IN UNUM'

January 1917 *to the end*

Jan. 1, 1917.

'MY dear Uncle,
'The difference between the way of Sister Elizabeth of the Trinity and my own is, as I perceive from her book, roughly this : for, as she herself says, the fascination of that greatest of mysteries lies in converse with " her Three Persons." For me it is their Unity that has the great appeal. Her master is S. Paul, while I am a pupil of S. John. In S. Paul are great riches, and for him I have great love. Yet at present S. John's lucidity attracts me more. He is my sole teacher : for me his writing is rich in grace. To give effect to Jesus' last prayer to his Father is the whole of my vocation.

'Increasingly my life glides into that perfected unity : he in me, and I in him. In Christ I have God's plenitude, and I am glutted by it. . . . In the Son, whom my soul possesses, I see the Father, who dwells in the Son : " *Ego in eis, et tu in me.*" At rest in the Son I rest in the Father : " *Ego sum in Patre meo, et vos in me.*" No, that is badly put ; for it is more than that : it is that " *in unum* " in which they are—that " *in unum* " in which we are " by Jesus, with Jesus, in God."

'Rich treasure has been given to me. I must give it in my turn. . . . First, to the Father for the

312

glory of the Most Blessed Trinity. . . . "*Per ipsum,
et cum ipso, et in ipso est tibi Deo Patri Omnipotenti in
unitate Spiritus Sancti omnis honor et gloria per omnia
saecula saeculorum, Amen.*" This is my best loved
prayer : it is the breath of my soul ; it is the epitome
of my present life.

'Next, my desire is to give God to souls. His will
is that all shall be one with him in charity, as he is
one with his Father in essence. To do his will, the
best means is to sow unlimited seed in men's souls.

'Above all I long to make those about me aware of
this infinite tenderness of the divine love. I seek to
do this by loving them in him, and by demonstrating
his love to them by those small and trifling attentions,
that are the outward symbols of this vast love. I
seek to make fragrant the atmosphere in which I
move, and by love to bring all things into tune with
his unity.

'Would that I could tell you, Uncle, of my exceeding love for him, whom you have taught me to know.
. . . I would kindle all men's souls with the fire of
his love, that all may be perfected for his greater
glory's sake. My longing for holiness is indescribably
intense. I would come to that holiness not by my
own way solely, but by all ways. More especially
would I be a true apostle. . . . Each of these desires
God sends : each re-ascends to God. It is my faith
that they are not altogether vain. I like to think that
I am being resolved into the seed of blessed vocations,
and that in other souls my desires shall have fulfilment,
particularly in those of monks and of priests.

'MARIE DE LA TRINITÉ.'

May 6, 1917.

'His will serves unfalteringly his greatest glory :
in that truth is my soul's great peace. My desire is

to be an apostle even to the consummation of the world. My need is to give without stint. My soul is exuberant with life, but my body is a broken thing. Which shall have the victory? As he wills, so shall it be! What joy to be dedicated to God's good pleasure!

'M.A.'

June 1, 1917.

'It is good indeed to have Jesus of the Host, and ceaselessly to render him honour and glory in the highest!

'To remain one with Christ is my ever growing need: so only may I with entire faithfulness play my part as host of praise.

'It is my delight too, when I have the strength, by the recitation of the breviary to give prayer and praise to our thrice blessed God. I like to think that this divine office—which is the teaching of the Holy Ghost, enshrined by the Church of Christ, for the Most Blessed Trinity's greatest glory—makes one music with the " *canticum novum* " sung in heaven. It is my favourite prayer—my ideal canticle of praise. I delight to discover in it the perfect harmony of every chord of truth with every chord of charity. I delight above all to be conscious in it of the living presence of God's most adorable Trinity and his indivisible unity. It is joy to recite this divine canticle to God's glory, in the name of Jesus and in the fellowship of the Holy Ghost.

'How merciful is our great God of love! He gives us both host and canticle, that we may praise him for all his works.'

Jun. 2, 1917.

'I continue to live in the Blessed Trinity. All that I am is drawn to God and dwells in God. In my life are realised those words of Jesus : " *Unum sint, sicut tu Pater in me, et ego in te, ut et ipsi in nobis unum sint. . . . Ego in eis, et tu in me, ut sint consummati in unum. . . . Dilectio, qua dilexisti me, in ipsis sit, et ego in ipsis. . . . In illo die vos cognoscetis quia ego sum in Patre meo, et vos in me, et ego in vobis.*"[1]

' Despite the diversity of the personal contacts, which I make in this life in God, for me its core is consummation in unity. All else notwithstanding, I remain a little " *consummata* " in that " *unum*," which is the soul's unique need.

' In this unity I perceive not merely the union of the Three Persons in the One God, but also in the simplification effected by that unity, the identification of all the divine perfections, one with another. I feel myself plunged deep into the wisdom of God. That wisdom gives all my being poise, and in my soul makes perfect music. I am content to let this life pervade me, to the end that my contemplation may find its complete fulfilment in works of grace for God's glory. I am content to be changed into that which my eyes behold and to be made rich by these excelling gifts, that in all my being I may manifest the perfections of him, who has summoned me from the darkness into his admirable light.'

Jun. 3, 1917.

' Still consummated in the unity of the Trinity, still kindled by his love, still serene of soul, in his love's mounting flame I know the need to give that love again.

' Because I love God, I would bring all men's souls to him ; equally, because I love men's souls, I would lead them to God.

<hr>

[1] S. John xvii, 21-26.

' In my view contemplation is nearer to perfection than action, much as the root is more vital than the branch severed from it. Only the two together can make one whole. It seems to me that the true apostolate, in which the two become one, is the ultimate perfection, and that to this God has called me. . . .

' Though he has allowed me to glimpse this apostolate, I have not seen it whole. Some fragments of it, however, I have divined. It is often said that in heaven the Seraphim contemplate God's majesty, and magnify it ; while the concern of the angels is with the charge of mankind. Not so do I visualise my own apostolate : I am, I think, to give grace to the souls of men, the while I give glory to God. I am to live in him ; to make his praise my ceaseless concern ; to know such burning zeal, that my outpoured peace shall be a gift to souls for ever.

' To return to earth : by intensity of love I must set myself more vigorously than before to do his will : so shall I best equip myself for a glorious apostolic career, lasting from the day of my death even to the consummation of the world. In little everyday actions I must give myself without stint to others, since God gives me the grace of a life, in which contemplation and action are at one. For must not each " put to service for others the gift which he has received " ?

' To me all things have been freely given : by me all things must be as freely rendered. Somewhere I have read that the name " Mary " means " illuminated and illuminating." In that connection I like to think that my own name of " Marie de la Trinité " is the true sum of my own vocation ; that I too can be illuminated, penetrated, glutted by God ; that, cipher though I be, in God I too can become illuminative, impregnative and donative for his glory's sake, and for the sake of the welfare of souls.

' How strange in such unity to realise the measure of one's own worthlessness and the mightiness of God's work in one's soul !

' Help me to follow wheresoever he may wish, and to thank him for ever and for all things. For I so intensely long to realise the ideal, which he sets before me, for his greater glory's sake : namely, that I may love him to the limit of love.

' MARIE DE LA TRINITÉ.'

Aug. 23, 1917.

' Day by day my spiritual experiences add to my knowledge of, and love for, God. I am becoming at the one time more active and more passive, while my perception of the smallest demands of his will grows increasingly keen.

' For a long time in the past the practice of the minor active virtues was a burden to me : on each occasion I had to constrain myself to action, and to restrain my soul's irresistible urge towards contemplation. Now, I like to think that all my soul, in accord with truth and in touch with living love, is fast in an unbroken thanksgiving, and spontaneously in tune with the promptings of the spirit dwelling within it. For me action has become as sweet and as lovely a thing as contemplation ; while I am aware of both as equally of God. The two together are but the echoes of his life and work in his kingdom of grace.

' He makes plain not merely his own work in me, but his specific will in regard to those with whom I have to do.

' I perceive that in the edifice of his glory each of the souls, which " he has given to be my charge," has its own place. I have no precise knowledge of the work, which I must do to realise his desire " that all may be one." There are, of course, those little opportunities, which everyday life brings with it. Yet I think that the greater part of his work is to be performed interiorly, and that it will be completed only after my death.

' I regard such an apostolate as the perfect vocation, less for the sake of its exercise than for the preparation which it demands, and the end which it pursues.

' An apostolate is but an evidence that the soul is saturated with God's grace : if it reach excellence, it demands the depth and universality of that perfection to which it witnesses ; it is the soul's temporal fruit and its eternal seed.

' MARIE DE LA TRINITÉ.'

A soul, whose life is wholly God's life—whose action is wholly inspired of God—in tranquillity knows the discipline of order, and in action unfettered freedom, notwithstanding.

The will, dissolved in God's will, is consciously faithful in its obedience to the rule of an immutable wisdom, and yet at the same time as consciously exults in its complete emancipation.

When grace has vanquished nature, grace and nature, those former foes, turn friends ; while the soul, altogether submissive to the Holy Ghost reigning within it, lives only in him, moves only in him, and only in him has the whole of its being.

The soul, conscious that its every fibre is in tune with its divine Author, needs but to remain one with him to make one music with the canticle, which is chorused through all eternity.

In that kingdom of his grace God's life and work are like sweet-pealing bells. In the smallest of things his good pleasure is performed with no less unction than spontaneity.

Be shut, my eyes ! . . .

Let my soul be both militant and peaceful !

'And blessed art thou, Mary, that hast believed, because those things shall be accomplished, that were spoken to thee by the Lord.'

Sep. 4, 1917.

'My dear Uncle,

'I want once more to thank you for those days last week.

'I have grown increasingly aware of the profit which comes of a director's help. Equally, I am the more deeply convinced that this was denied to me previously by the will of God. In my life I have constantly striven to walk by the light of his wisdom, with good sense and the need of the moment as my sole guides. This striving has tested my soul, and so served it well. This life of spiritual reticence—a reticence broken only when others' needs demanded it—has served me well, no less. Now that you have come and gone, a great sense of security possesses me. My way is very clearly marked out before me, and with no mental reservations I follow it unfalteringly. Doubting his kindly light that leads me on, I am like a body that has no soul ; unfalteringly following it, I know indescribable peace. Like a captive eagle set free from its captivity, that soars to the heights which are its home : so, I like to think, is my own soul. Because he alone is GOD, I am increasingly conscious that he alone is my sole need. . . .

'There most surely lies my vocation . . . "consummata" . . . of myself to be less than a cipher . . . to allow him, unhindered and alone, to work for his glory, " that all may be one " in the bosom of the Blessed Trinity.

'——I am glad that you considered it unwise for a soul to seek supernatural consolation for itself. This

leaves me more free. My need is to think only of
him and his work—not to take, but to give. . . .

'To conclude : I had great need to be assured that
my way was in accord with God's will and for his
greater glory. By his grace I have been given this
assurance. I have heard ; I have seen ; I have felt,
that mine is the " better part."

' MARIE DE LA TRINITÉ.'

Sep. 29, 1917.

'Let me tell you more of the mercies of our great
God towards his poor little nobody.

'*Consummata* . . . to extend the kingdom of its
God : the soul has no preoccupation save that.
" *In his quae Patris mei sunt oportet me esse.*" . . . Since
your stay, what joy I have known in feeling free to
surrender myself unreservedly to his potent spell !
I like to think that he—even he—would have me
altogether " appropriated in the public service." I like
to think too that, thus engrossed in the apostolate to
which he calls me, I need no more concern myself
with my personal sanctification.

'Moreover, I conceive that our great God draws
from his little " *Consummata* " complete and perfect
praise. I conceive too that, while her sole thought is
to work for him, he is pleased to clothe her in re-
splendent purple. Most surely I have found my
vocation, now that I am I no longer—now that God
alone lives in me for his great glory's sake.

'Completely emancipated from the bond-slavery of
the self, I give and I take those favours of God at their
inexhaustible source, wholly convinced that they are
altogether of God. Just as in the life of Jesus all
roads led to the Redemption and the glory of God,
which it served : so all that is in me must converge
upon that apostolate, to which he calls me for his

glory's sake. In all things I must forget my personal predilections, that I may further the welfare of others.

'Accordingly I prefer to appear quite ordinary— " more imitable than admirable "—that I may open the ears of all about me to the sound of the voice of God. To me he gives surpassing blessedness. No words may describe it. Moreover, any words with which I might seek to describe it, might well have an extravagant ring.

'CONSUMMATA IN UNUM.'

Nov. 6, 1917.

'For some weeks the Father's will has been my soul's pleasant surfeit. With me it has been his will, his will, and again his will. It is become my impregnable stronghold : nothing can touch me, safe within its walls.

'How may I tell of it? God in his prescience has surely known every insurmountable obstacle that human free-will could oppose to his divine desire, and so for his greatest glory he has decreed his will to be ultimate. God's plan unfolds, and none may alter it. . . . In this fact is my soul's peace. Of the sorry ruins, in which he leaves man's will, God makes a noble edifice. In that edifice is my soul's joy.

'It is my belief that, in that part of his plan affecting my soul, God saw that man's will would deprive me of rich means of grace—the sacraments, for example —and that he set aside his grace for me in other means—in that same deprivation, it may well be. Accordingly, I seek to take advantage of each small mischance, and, by exercise of all my love, to have of it all the virtue, which it holds for my sanctification and for God's glory.

'——Thank you very much for your short note. You are right. As Jesus of the Mass, so I would be his little consecrated host, in whom the Father discovers his glory and the souls of men their grace. I would remain constant in my adoration of the Father, unfaltering in my praise of him ; and, in the service of men, unwearied in my apostolate. As with his divine Host, so I wish that only the poor semblance of me may remain, happy to think that this worthless simulacrum yet holds fast the secret of the King, shared with none but him. ' CONSUMMATA.'

Dec. 23, 1917.

' In your last brief note you seemed to take objection to the term, which I frequently use to express my vocation. This name is rich in grace for me. Let me then try to tell you something of its significance for me, that, aware of it, you may allow me to keep the name itself.

' For me " *Consummata* " is a cipher wholly lost in God, that has no life apart from his life, and that in his life has larger and larger part. That cipher, which is *Consummata*, sees all things in truth, and does all things in love ; loves and is conscious of loving ; both contemplates and acts with spontaneity and yet with unction. All *Consummata's* capacity for love is expressed in works, while thanksgiving is operative in every fibre of her being, with the result that her contemplative faculties convey to her in its entirety God's good pleasure, while her faculty for action enables her unhesitatingly to accord with it.

' Delivered from the obscurities which veiled the divine will from her—delivered equally from the rebellious impulses which once delayed its fulfilment —in this adorable will she is made free. She is made free, because in her the self lives no longer ; she is an apostle, because Christ lives in her. *To be one with God, and to be no more* than that, is the literal meaning of *Consummata.*

' Plainly all the implications of such an union cannot be set down. Let me passingly touch on one of them. The soul is aware that God loves us not for what we are, but for what he is—love itself ; not upon our account, but upon his—for he is truth itself. Again, the soul loves other souls not upon their enticement, but upon God's compulsion ; not for sake of them, but for sake of God. Thus the soul's love embraces all " without respect to persons," giving to each his share according to God's good pleasure. Such love searches out souls with but one end in view : to lead them into that unique and living reality, which is God. It may be seen from this that another distinguishing quality of *Consummata* is impersonal disinterestedness.

' It is beyond my power to explain how this phrase *Consummata in unum* represents for me the double ideal of apostolate and praise, or how no other phrase so incorporates my soul's twin needs. My vocation's apostolate is born of my vocation of praise, much as fruit ripens on a tree that has reached the bearing stage, and, bearing fruit, yet continues to grow. These two vocations have now resolved themselves into a single vocation : this I follow in a life that is increasingly consummated in unity for the ever greater glory of God.

' Admit then that it was not a premature resting upon my soul's oars, nor a condition of static spirituality, that I discovered to you the other day. Admit that it was ripeness of praise, subsisting in apostolate, which is its crown. I am conscious that I have not seized his gift, as I might have seized it. Yet—as I strive, I grow ; as I grow, I strive. Zeal burns in me, and in my zeal is peace ; ardour consumes me, and in my ardour is serenity. In this union with him,

who is power, who is wisdom, who is love, is surely
the beginning of beatitude itself.

'MARIE DE LA TRINITÉ.'

'*Consummata.* . . .'
Apostolate. . . .
Let me be wholly ordinary ! . . .
. . . more imitable than admirable. . . .
Utter abnegation. . . .
Let me sacrifice every personal predilection for the
common good ! . . .
'Appropriated in the public service. . . .'
'*In his quae Patris mei sunt oportet me esse.* . . .'
In Jesus all roads lead to the Redemption for the
glory of the Father. . . .
'*Hidden with Christ in God.* . . .'
With Jesus, the Son of Man, who 'is in heaven,' let
me live in the bosom of the Father : be my life that life
of love, which God's own life is ! . . .
With Jesus, 'the Way, the Truth, and the Life,' let
me put this truth and this life within the reach of every
living soul, that all may be led to the Father ! . . .
'*Consummated in unity.* . . .'
In regard to heaven, let me remain *the Father's beloved
child !*
In regard to earth, let me be no more, and let me
seem no more, than may fill the measure of the needs
of others ! . . . to that extent let me give myself
without stint ! . . .
Good indeed is this life hidden in you, O my God !
And good is utter solitude, since none knows all the
truth to be found in me, your child ! . . .
'None knoweth the Son, save the Father.' O Jesus !
you have told me so much of him, that he has not one
feature that is not vivid and vital for me ! . . .
'And no man knoweth the Father, save the Son, and
he to whom the Son will reveal him.'

' Hidden with Christ in God.'

As Jesus of the Mass, so I would be his little consecrated *host*, in whom the Father discovers his glory, and the souls of men their grace. I would remain constant in my admiration of the Father, unfaltering in my praise of him ; and, *in the service of men*, unwearied in my apostolate. . . .

' *Consummated in unity.*'

Made perfect in love, the soul hears God's Only-Begotten Son speak to it ' *openly of the Father.*'

' *Hidden with Christ in God.*'

Let me live in the life of Christ—that life of love for the Father and of zeal for his glory ; that life, whose lot it is to sweep irresistibly on to the bosom of the Blessed Trinity, and whose part is in the great work which he has founded in his person by his Blood, and which he perfects in the Holy Ghost by his grace !

' *Consummated in unity.*'

For its God, be the soul complete and perfect praise ! It most magnifies him by striving that all may be ' consummated in unity.'

In proportion as it bears ripe fruit in an apostolate, so shall the root, which is praise, be a lovely thing. . . .

In proportion as I deny myself the joy of praising him, that I may spend myself wholly in making his the praise of others : so he makes close and still closer my union with him.

In God, in Christ and in the Church, the one stream of living truth flows on and on.

In its flow it makes for the peace of each according to the predestination of each ; it flows from triumph unto triumph towards that eventual glory of God, in which he ' shall be all in all.'

When by grace God has established his kingdom in our souls, we have no life apart from our life in his will, by which he lives and rules in unchallenged sovereignty.

Y

' *Consummata in unum.*'

Let me have no life apart from his will, in which he is and all his works.

The will of God !—the will of God !

God has sent me to do his will : its accomplishment is my soul's sustenance.

Practice makes perfect.

In Mary is all my trust.

Jan. 24, 1918.

' My dear Uncle,

' I write this from my sick-bed to beg the aid of your prayer, that I may be strong to do God's good pleasure for his glory's sake.

' His will is even now my retreat. Whether this retreat and its recollection end in heaven's triumphant life, or whether it end in a resumption of life militant on earth, may it be the beginning of an apostolic life as perfect as complete !

' My strength grows less. For some ten days I have not stirred from bed. Hence this retreat.

' Confronted with the alternatives of a long and painful illness that should end in certain recovery, and another short and less painful, that should end as certainly in death, my heart has spontaneously echoed the words of the little Théophane Vénard when he cried : " the longer the suffering, the richer the offering ! " I choose to have this refer to physical suffering, no less than to this life lived on earth. I do not know if God have granted me fulfilment of this desire, which he himself has surely inspired in me. Physical pain has intoxicated my spirit, and I have an irresistible longing that it may endure, and grow in strength. . . . Jesus, living in his poor little nobody, is her strength and her worth to God : it is joy in my own body to be acquainted with his sufferings, that thereby I may more mightily magnify God in his life, that is lived in me.

' Yet, as God knows well, though I say this or write that, I have no will but his will.

' In face of what may be impending death I know such happiness that I would ask for that death to be delayed. In this connection it hurts my heart that I should know such joy at a time when so many of my fellows know such suffering. Ah ! though it be folly to say it, so long as men fight and suffer on earth, so long would I remain upon it to love and succour them !

' These desires notwithstanding, my first wish and my last is for utter surrender to the will of God, whose might, whose wisdom and whose love alike lead on to his exceeding glory : surrender, as blind as complete, is the one word in which all other words are uttered. Let then these ardent desires ascend to the Father, who shall fulfil them, or who shall deny them fulfilment, according to his good pleasure and for his greater glory's sake !

' MARIE DE LA TRINITÉ.'

Feb. 22, 1918.

' I like to think that the one obligation left to me is to yield myself to the adorable will of our great God of love, that of his poor little nobody he may have his pleasure.

' It is my faith that love of God has for its crown love of our neighbour. Therefore I would spend the last of my strength in bringing gladness to others. With this in view I try to give them insight into the happiness, which I know in the divine will, and to keep hidden from them my body's suffering. Though only a few more weeks be left to me, I would have them preserve to the last the illusion that I am making progress, nor know that the progress which I am making is towards death.

' So I get up each day to take lunch with mother,

and during the meal contrive to be in great good spirits. When I have too little strength to go right to mother's bed to give her her kiss, I stop for a moment at the invalid-chair. So far (I think) they do not suspect how few are the steps which I am able to take. May God give me the strength to take these few poor steps, as long as it is possible at all !

'For my soul I ask, as I have long asked, for the consummation of our union. With this desire my soul is glutted, and I believe that God himself has inspired it. So only I be one with God, for me both life and death are of no account.

'I sometimes think that it is my heart and its too consuming flame, which is the cause of this complete exhaustion—that, in a word, it is love that is killing me. Whatever it be, it is his operative will. In that my soul stands fast in peace. Whether I die of congestion of the lungs, or whether I die of love, it matters not at all—so only I die in accordance with his will. His will ! more than ever it fills all my heart ; more than ever I perceive its excelling worth and its exceeding loveliness. . . . Joyously I seek to anticipate what it would have me do ; with brimming heart I set out to do it.

'When I stand before him, I feel myself a dwarf. His transcendency overshadows me : I become aware that I am a sharer in his nature only by virtue of grace—a sharer in his nature's similitude rather, in his nature's stuff. Of this awareness I have more joy than even of that which the intimate aspect of our union affords me. . . . The vast love, with which he loves me and with which he wraps me round, is sweet indeed. It is sweeter yet to feel that through all eternity he will be my GOD, ineffable in his Godhead, even in the eyes of the child whom he blesses with his tenderness.

'MARIE DE LA TRINITÉ.'

Apl. 26, 1918.

'My sole wish is this : in my life may the suffering that I know be small compared with the praise which I give to God !

'The more his love afflicts me, the more would I thank him, recognising that there is no better gift than God's !

'MARIE DE LA TRINITÉ.'

Noon on Wednesday of Holy Week.

'I think that I am going to die. I do not know, but indeed I think so. As he wills, so be it !

'May his will be done ! may it be loved ! may it be adored—adored and exalted by all men *in aeternum !*

'Very strange things are happening to me. I think, though I do not know, that He is the author of them all.

'However this be, I know great peace and great happiness. For I have no attachment save HIS WILL.

'I have no eyes save for *his will.* . . .

'My way is as it was : now and for ever it is his will . . . now and for ever to be identified with his will . . . now and for ever.'

CONCLUSION

'MISERICORDIAS DOMINI'

'MISERICORDIAS DOMINI'[1]

April 24, 1889	*Baptism.* Consecration to the Blessed Virgin.
	'None but God.'
	'Jesus of the Agony.'
November 23, 1898	First Absolution.
June 14, 1900	First Communion.
November 13, 1900	Confirmation.
February 2-7, 1902	*Retreat.* 'Take up the Cross.' The will of God.
May 31, 1904	Received as Child of Mary.
April 1904	*Nunc dimittis.*
November 13, 1904	Christ's call.
April 19, 1906	Lourdes. Faith.
September 21, 1906	*Conversion.* 'Love's inrush.'
September 21, 1906	'Take up thy cross . . . follow me. . . . Come . . . follow me.'
October 9, 1906	Montmartre. Trust.
October 31, 1906	*Vocation.* Betrothed to Jesus.
Christmas, 1906	*Misericordias Domini in aeternum cantabo.*
April 21-27, 1907	Retreat.
January 1908	'Take up thy cross ; follow me.' This my preoccupying meditation.
	Recollection.'

[1] Table drawn up by Marie de la Trinité herself, and discovered among her papers. It stops short in 1912.

333

February 23, 1908	Welcome, martyrdom !
February 29, 1908	Welcome, ultimate suffering !
May 5, 1908	' I was there.'
June 1908	Sacred Heart. Reparation.
July 16, 1908	*Nisi granum frumenti.*
August 1908	Love's joys. Ecstatic consolation. Lights of revelation.
August 29—September 2, 1908	Retreat of ' utter love,' love of suffering.
	Contemplation and suffering, my soul's orientation.
September 30, 1908	*Juxta crucem tecum stare* *Et me tibi sociare* *In planctu desidero.*
September 30, 1908	Ardent longing to suffer.
October 1908	Directing light of revelation : preparation for surrender of self.
November 13-14, 1908	Call to my soul to be *a channel* for God's love.
November 21, 1908	*Utter love.* Stigmatised.[1]
	First union with God himself. '*Si vis perfectus esse, veni.*'
January 25-29, 1909	Retreat. Thabor.
	God is my sufficiency.
February 2, 1909	*Vow of Chastity and Virginity.* *Ecce venio ut faciam voluntatem tuam.*
	Surrender.
February 19, 1909	Call to be *host ;* holocaust promised.
February 21, 1909	Promises.
May 5, 1909	Calvary in a tomb. Carmel.

[1] Nothing exteriorly visible. In regard to the nature of these hidden stigmatisations, see Poulain : *Grâces d'Oraison*, p. 256 ; and Mgr. Farges : *Les Phénomènes mystiques*, pp. 546-9.

May 14, 1909	Not of this world. Holiness.
May 19, 1909	Pray, suffer, act, to the limit of my capacity ; make life ' an uninterrupted canticle of praise, of thanksgiving and perfect love, a ceaseless martyrdom.'
June 20, 1909	God the inaccessible.
July 16, 1909	*Vow of ' the most perfect.'*
September 29, 1909	Suffering's price ; a means to union.
October 28, 1909	A glimpse of God himself. In him let me seek love's seed.
November 1909	*Qui manet in me, fert fructum multum.* Let me dwell in love ! Love's rayed light. Let love engross me ! This light of revelation as to my way : *In caritate perpetua dilexi te ; ideo attraxi te miserans.*
February 19, 1910	*Sacrificabo hostiam laudis.*
March 30, 1910	*Union* with the *Most Holy Trinity.*
March 30, 1910	' If any one love me, my Father will love him : and we will come to him and will make our abode with him.'
April 1, 1910	*Incarnation* of *Christ* in me, that in me he may continue his work. *Vivit in me Christus. Tabernaculum Dei cum hominibus.*
April 9, 1910	Life : *Splendor gloriae.*
September 8, 1910	*Vow of surrender ; vow to be host.*

January 20, 1911	Transformed into the Trinity itself.
March 1, 1911	The *Spirit of Love's habitation* in me. Union with him, and, through him, with God.
April 12, 1911	God in Himself.
May 19, 1911	Marie de la Trinité.
June 13, 1911	*Cum Isaac immolatur.*
October 4, 1911	God's light-in-darkness.
November 21, 1911	*Vow of Poverty and Obedience.*
July 17, 1912	Transformation made permanent.
	Introduced by Mary into the circle of my Royal Family : the Father, the Son, the Holy Ghost.
	Nostra conversatio in coelis est.
	My God and my All.[1]

Marie de la Trinité, alluding to her habitual life *in coelis,* said : ' My mission in heaven, is to pour upon earth the seed of love, which I draw in infinite abundance from God.'

Now that she is in the heaven of glory, how much more potent still must be her intervention ! Dying, she declared : ' Until this world shall end, I shall continue my apostolic work.' And again : ' In heaven I shall understand you better than on earth. In heaven I shall not know death, but only life. Though you be unaware of it, I shall be with you ; I shall help you.'

From her place in heaven may she sow abundantly in the soul of each who now finishes his reading of the

---

[1] The Life and the Letters, which this book comprises, give plain indication of the graces of God subsequently received by Marie de la Trinité.

noble work which God performed in her ; in the soul of the humble collator of these pages ; in every soul alive— ' the seed of love which she has in infinite abundance from God ! '

The Mayflower Press, Plymouth.   William Brendon & Son, Ltd.